IN THE SHADOW OF HER LEGACY

J.C. Flynn

Copyright © 2017 J.C. Flynn
All rights reserved.

ISBN: 154032513X
ISBN 13: 9781540325136
Library of Congress Control Number: 2016919636
CreateSpace Independent Publishing Platform
North Charleston, South Carolina

CHAPTER ONE

Mia was amazed as she looked at the panoramic view from her kitchen window. A blaze of color had transformed the landscape overnight, painting it with the vibrant, warm colors of autumn against the contrasting coolness of the blue sky. Her eyes swept across the clouds lazily drifting overhead. On the horizon, the shimmering water of the bay was fringed by the delicate sweep of mauve hills. She cherished the peacefulness of the afternoon as she awaited Jeff's arrival. Jeff. She was comforted by the thought of having him and his support gently guiding her through troubled times.

The shrill ring of the phone interrupted the splendor of the moment. She picked up the receiver. "Hello?"

"Mia, are you there?"

She paused for a moment, not immediately recognizing the voice on the other end of the line, though soon realizing that the caller was someone with whom she was familiar.

"Mia," the voice repeated. There was a brief hesitation. "This is Sarah."

"Sarah?" She seldom heard from Sarah. Why would she be calling now?

"Mia," her eldest sister continued, "are you there? This is Sarah. Mia...Nadia is dead."

Mia clung to the phone silently. She had known that one day this call would come, but she had hoped it would be after the family problems were solved and healing had begun.

Of course it would be Sarah who would notify her of their mother's death. Sarah lived in another country several thousand miles away. Some of Mia's surviving siblings still lived in the area, some only a few miles down the road. Others were scattered across the border. Yet Sarah was the one who informed Mia of their mother's death.

"Aren't you going to say anything, Mia?"

Mia continued to hang on to the phone. What could she say? What could she tell her eldest sister? She hoped Nadia would find the peace in death that she did not find in life. Despite the pain and devastation that this woman had brought upon her and her family, could she tell Sarah that she did not hate their mother? The hate was for what this woman—her own mother—had done to her.

She felt no warmth toward this woman. She only felt the pain of being her daughter and pity for a soul that knew no peace. The closeness a child should have with a mother had never developed because the mother did not give the child that chance.

Could she tell Sarah that the only reason this woman gave birth to her and bore other children was so that she could pass on her legacy? The legacy Nadia left behind haunted Mia and others in her family. How many other lives had been devastated by this hateful woman?

The only bond she felt between herself and the woman who gave her life was the power of the commandment "Honor thy mother." Could she tell her sister that? Fear was the only childhood memory she had of Nadia—fear of her own mother and fear of the demons she had threatened upon her. This fear was fueled by her eldest brother, Koss, and her other older siblings, who had fought each other for control and for their mother's insane, immoral gratitude.

Mia was angry. She was angry because that woman had never said she was sorry for what she had done. Mia could not forgive her because she did not ask to be forgiven. Mia could never forgive her. *Let that woman ask God for mercy.* Mia had to let it go. Maybe God would absolve Nadia of one of man's most immoral acts, one she inflicted on her own children.

Yes, Mia was angry. *Why did she die?* This disillusioned woman who lived to be a centenarian should have lived another lifetime. Then she might have come to terms with the horror she inflicted on her children. At one time, Mia felt that only the death of this woman would free her from the burden she carried. Free? Yes, now Mia felt free.

What is freedom but an illusion? A person's living presence can be replaced by his or her memory—that person's legacy. What legacy did Nadia leave behind? The skeletons in her closet.

I do not hate, Mia thought, *yet why do I still have these feelings of pity and anger? Are they the feelings one has in the aftermath of death?* Her thoughts dwelled not on her mother's death but on the deaths of her own childhood and other childhoods. Mia had repressed the memories of her childhood for more than five decades. They had only begun to surface a few years ago.

Silently putting the phone back on its cradle, Mia knew she could not speak to Sarah. She would bear her pain alone. If she spoke, Sarah and their other siblings would twist her words to confuse and control her as they had before. Mia was once again a child lost in a world beyond her control. Those things Nadia had not been able to deal with in life were left for Mia to deal with now. She reminded herself that her fear of Nadia and her control was in the past—that she had broken away from that control. She was in control of her own life now; she was free.

Ten years had passed since she last saw the woman who bore her. When Mia walked away, her only regret was that she had not done so years earlier. Mia was angry with herself for not being able to recall the horrors of her own childhood before others became victims of this woman.

Still, she was free now, free to choose whether to disregard or to acknowledge her family. She wanted a safe environment for her children. She had renounced her siblings for the sake of her children and grandchildren. When would her siblings realize and admit that they were all victims of their mother's diabolical legacy? It angered her that they buried their heads in the sand and did not seek help for the sake of society and the family generations that were still to come. No more would she allow her own children to be victims and inherit the hell that she had grown up in. Her siblings would have to take responsibility for their own mistakes.

Mia felt only anger toward her mother, and that anger would always be there. She realized her mother was a victim, too, but she had had a choice—whether to pass on the legacy she inherited or break the cycle. She chose to pass it on, making victims and perpetrators of her own children. Why was Nadia afraid to allow a healthy sibling relationship? Would it be a threat to her? Could she even do it? Was she afraid that her children might conspire against her and reveal the family secret?

Mia knew that time was a factor. Her siblings were getting on in age. Some of them had already passed on, taking the family secret to their graves. In their stubbornness, those who remained would not admit what happened behind the tightly closed doors of their childhoods. They fiercely guarded the family secret, and it angered them when Mia's memory revealed their painful past. Now time might not permit the remaining family members to reconcile.

Years ago, Mia had learned that most victims of incest pass on the abuse. It possibly was one of the reasons it horrified her siblings when Mia's memories stirred the skeletons in the family closet. It would explain their outrage.

The crimes carried out by Nadia against her children concerned her neighbors who knew; however, those neighbors who knew were helpless. They couldn't stop the dysfunctional acts in Nadia's house. What could be done about such a shocking crime taking place in this remote little settlement? It was the Depression years of the 1930s. There was no protection for the young and the innocent.

Parents conceived, gave birth, and were left to raise their children as they chose. As long as the child was registered at birth and attended school until the age of fifteen, and the parents were not deceased, they remain under the care of their parents.

Deeds of the Demon
Deeds of the demon in family untold,
Not to be spoken, not to unfold,
Deeds of the demon embroiled in cult,
Demoting the hallowed with infernal insult,
Exalting the evil, dejected with gloom,
Lusting in power, ravaged to doom.
Wallowed in pity, basking in greed,
Innocent children fulfilling her need.
Suppressed memories in armor concealed,
Not to be spoken, not be revealed.

Deeds of the demon in family unfold.
Deeds of the past now will be told.
Deeds, demon no more be concealed.
Now will be spoken, now be revealed.

CHAPTER TWO

Mia had not known her grandparents. Her mother never spoke about her own childhood. However, she would sometimes lash out at her children in anger, saying that in her father's house, things were done this way or that way. She vehemently instilled the fourth commandment, "Honor thy father and mother," in her own children, making it clear that this commandment had ruled in her father's house along with another rule: whatever happened in their house was not to be carried beyond the door.

Mia learned from whispers between neighbors that her mother had lived a hellish life under the diabolical rule of her father's hand. The neighbors feared her grandfather. If anyone angered him or stood in his way, he would work himself into an uncontrollable state of rage. He would attack them with what he had on hand. His anger left him frothing at the mouth.

Nadia had borne a large family, and she was determined to run things in her house as her father had in his. Mia remembered her mother's words to the circle of ladies from her church—words that she heard often as a teenager: "What I had for breakfast no one saw. What I had for dinner no one knows. And what happens in my house no one has to know."

"Yes." The ladies would laugh at Nadia's words; they agreed that no one should know what happened in the privacy of one's own home. Nadia ensured that her secret was well hidden.

Mia remembered the dreaded threat her mother spat out at her older siblings when they came home from school: "You must not speak to anyone about things that happen in this house; if you do, I will cut the tongues out of your mouths." At that time, Mia was not yet of school age. It horrified her to think that anyone might have his or her tongue cut out.

"Would Mother cut out my tongue too?" she would fearfully ask Hilda and Kassie.

"Yes," her older sisters responded sharply to her innocent question.

"But why would she cut my tongue out?"

"So you can't speak to anyone. You have to remember that if you tell anyone about things you are not supposed to, she will cut out your tongue. Those would be the last words that come out of your mouth."

"But it would hurt if she cut my tongue out." The child's reply to her sister's was hesitant and fearful.

"Yes, it would."

"But wouldn't people know if she cut my tongue out?"

"No, they would not because you would not be able to tell anybody. You would not be able to speak if she cut your tongue out."

"Would there be lots of blood if she cut my tongue out?"

"Yes."

"Then if there was blood all over, when Uncle Nikola and Aunt Rachel come to visit, they would see it. They would know she cut my tongue out."

"No, they wouldn't because we would clean the blood up before anyone came."

The threat of having her tongue cut out severely horrified the child. She looked up at her sisters. "Are there any children in school who don't have tongues?" Her question was a guarded whisper.

"No, there are no children without tongues in school now—there was one girl, but her family moved away."

"What was her name?"

Mia watched her sisters stir awkwardly before Kassie answered. "It was Ruthie...Ruthie Pulshe."

Mia knew that Kassie did not like Ruthie. She had fought in school with her. Mia had heard Hilda and Kassie discussing the problems that Kassie had with Ruthie.

"I hate her. I hate her. I wish she was dead!" Kassie had exploded in outrage one day.

"You know you are not to say that. You are not to wish death on anyone." Hilda looked at Kassie cynically and then added, "Well, what did she do this time?"

"The same thing she always does," Kassie replied. "She likes the same boys I do, and she takes my boyfriends away from me. I hate her!"

"Well, what happened?" Hilda probed. She busied herself with the housework, waiting for her sister to unload her problems. Mia had watched Kassie lower her head before she spoke.

"Yesterday, Willis asked me if I'd be his girlfriend for the day; he asked me before he asked Ruthie because I got to school before she did. But at recess I saw him walking out of the bushes with her. She took him away from me. I hate her," Kassie seethed.

"Tramp," Hilda hissed. "Is that why you were in such a hurry to get to school today?"

"I am not. Ruthie is the tramp," Kassie flared at Hilda in resentment.

Mia listened to her older sisters as they hassled and flailed at each other.

"What is a tramp?" she had questioned when the squabble between her sisters simmered down.

"Tramp?" Hilda looked at the child in astonishment. "Where did you pick up that word?"

"You just said it, and Kassie got very angry when you did. Why did she get so angry? What is a tramp?" Hilda looked at Kassie for a moment before she turned to the child.

"Well, didn't you see Kassie stamp her foot when I said it? 'Stamp' and 'tramp' mean the same thing."

Mia looked up at Hilda. "But you said it before she stamped her foot."

"It doesn't matter," Hilda snarled. "I said it because I knew she was going to stamp her foot. Why are you always bothering us? You ask so many questions. Get out of our way and go outside."

Later on the same day, Mia had asked Hilda, "How does Kassie know when a boy is her boyfriend?"

"If a boy kisses a girl, that means he is her boyfriend," her older sister replied.

Mia shuddered at the thought of Kassie going into the bushes to be kissed by a boy. The ways of the grownups were so foreign to the child's innocence. She thought of her sister's hateful declaration toward the other girl and wondered why her older siblings looked down on the Pulshe children.

"Keep away from them when you see them coming down the road. If they talk to you, you are not to answer them," they warned her. Being a lonely child, she wanted more than anything to talk to the Pulshes, but she obeyed her sisters. She would only smile shyly at them as they walked past their gate.

Mia sat silently for a moment. Hilda and Kassie said that the Pulshes had moved away. However, it dawned on her that the Pulshe children still walked past their gate on the way to school. She had watched them just the day before. They hadn't moved away. Why had her sisters said they'd moved?

"No." Mia looked at her sister as she spoke. "The Pulshes did not move away. I saw them walk past our gate, and Ruthie was with them. Can I talk to them? I will only ask Ruthie to open her mouth so I can see where her mother cut her tongue out."

Hilda and Kassie looked at each other; they realized that they were trapped in their own lies.

"No, wait…it wasn't Ruthie. It was a girl from another school," Hilda abruptly corrected Kassie's fib.

"But why can't I talk to her?"

"Her brothers do bad things to little girls, and she helps them," Kassie lied.

"There was one little girl who died after her mother cut her tongue out," Hilda added.

Mia listened to her sisters as they strayed from the subject of Ruthie while continuing their fabrication. It horrified Mia to hear that a little girl died because her mother cut her tongue out.

"What was the name of the girl who died?" She was overwhelmed by the thought.

"We don't know. It happened in another school," Hilda replied sharply, not wanting to get trapped in another lie.

Uncle Nikola and Aunt Rachel were not Mia's real aunt and uncle. They were distant relatives, a kindly couple who loved children and visited Mia's family regularly. They had no children of their own, but they appealed to children because of the love and kindness they showed them. But on Nikola and Rachel's next visit, Mia stood back and kept her distance from them.

"Come and talk to us," Nikola coaxed the child with a smile. Mia shyly looked at them from across the room and shook her head.

"Then come and stand beside us so we can talk to you."

Mia shook her head again, her tiny facial features sullen. Hilda had told her she talked too much, so she cupped her hand over her mouth, not wanting a breath or a word to escape her lips lest her mother cut out her tongue.

Nikola watched the child from across the room.

"The last time we were here, she opened up to us and spoke so nicely. What has happened to Mia since our last visit? Why is she afraid to talk to us now?" Perplexed, Uncle Nikola and Aunt Rachel exchanged glances, questioning the child's odd behavior.

Mia, already a shy child, withdrew further, afraid to speak to anyone. Her mother instilled fear in her at a very young age. She was afraid to disobey, say anything that her mother would disapprove of, or cause her anger.

The first memories Mia had of her mother were ones of fear. Memories of her mother bathing her, memories of being fresh and clean, which made her feel good, memories of looking up at her mother and seeing pale, vacant eyes looking down at her. The vacant look in Nadia's eyes filled Mia with an unsettling fear. Mia remembered whimpering, not knowing why her mother looked down at her and yet did not seem to see her. Nadia appeared to be shrouded in evil as she stood over the bewildered child.

Mia could not be certain what age she was at the time. In her memory, she felt young and defenseless as fear radiated through her small body. She knew her mother would hurt her again as she had hurt her before. Mia's whimpers would turn to screams of pain. It was during one of those times, as she screamed from the pain of being molested, that a face appeared behind her mother. Mia's father had responded to the child's screams and his wife's cantankerous voice.

"What are you doing to her?"

Like a whip, his shocked voice cut through the air, lashing out at Nadia. His wife's body stiffened as she froze from the shock of being caught. For a moment, only the child's wails of terror drifted through the room. Nadia faced her husband in shocked silence. Mia watched her father strike out in a fit of rage.

"You told me you would not do that to the children again!"

Nadia fumbled for words. When she found them, they lashed out at each other, and when Nadia could no longer hold her reign over her husband, she burst into tears.

"What is wrong with you? Why do you do this to the children? You are their mother! How can I leave you with them? You promised me you would not hurt them like that again." His questions were angry, but his eyes pleaded for some explanation, watching for some change to come over Nadia—an apology, anything.

Mia's cries ceased as she watched her parents. Frightened, the naked child sat and shivered. She no longer cried. As Nadia began to wail, the child was shaken with fear and confusion.

"Put her clothes on. If I ever catch you doing that to her or to any of the other children again, there is no telling what I will do to you." Her father words lashed angrily at Nadia.

When her mother's hand reached for her, Mia shrank back in fear.

"Look what you have done to her. She is afraid of you." Her father was enraged.

Angered at being caught, Nadia dressed the child roughly and put her down for her nap. Mia felt safe under the warmth of the bed covers; she thought that her mother could not harm her there.

Surely the bed covers will protect me, she thought as her father left the room.

As time passed, the molestation by her mother did not stop. It was as if Nadia were possessed. Mia hoped her father would appear again to stop her mother from hurting her. *He said he would come. Where is he?* She waited for his face to appear again, but he did not come into the house as he did that time he caught Nadia molesting her.

Sometimes she could hear his voice as he spoke to her older siblings outside before he left the yard. She heard his voice, but he did not come. *He cares about what happens to them because they are older. Why doesn't he care about what she does to me anymore? Why doesn't he come into the house and make her stop hurting me like he did that time?* The distraught child could only wonder. Eventually, in despair, she gave up hope. She thought her father did not come because he did not care. It was as if she did not matter. He appeared to no longer care that she was at the mercy of a mentally ill woman. He only cared about the older ones.

Mia blocked out her abuse. It was only many years later that she had occasional memories trickle in—memories of being hurt by Nadia. The flashbacks kept reoccurring and then faded into oblivion without answers. They were memories that left her feeling as if her soul had been ripped out as a child. Mia originally wondered why she was having such strange, disturbing memories—ones that appeared only to vanish again, still not ready to be revealed.

After Mia married she sat with her husband, Jeff, watching an emotionally stirring movie. The scene in the movie was of angry parents lashing out at each other over the parental rights of a child. The child in the movie lay crying in agony. That scene sent Mia back to her own childhood, triggering an avalanche of memories from her past. She relived each devastating event as it appeared, feeling crushed under the weight. The helplessness, the fear, and the cries for help returned. Mia's body writhed as the scene flowed before her eyes. Suddenly the screams she heard were not the child's screams in the movie; they were her own. The angered voices were those of her parents, spanning the distance from the past. They plunged her back through decades of time, back to her own childhood. The memory of her father catching Nadia came flooding back. She saw her parents verbally lashing out at one another. Her mind was filled with scenes of horror as she sat in her living room, stunned.

For a few moments, Mia was silent. The memory shattered inside her. She looked at Jeff sitting across the room, absorbed in the movie. When she could finally speak, the words came rushing forth uncontrolled.

"My mother sexually abused me when I was a child." Her words were hardly more than a stunned whisper.

Jeff turned from the TV and looked at her, alarmed.

"I just had a horrible memory. My mother abused me when I was a child." The words sounded hollow, echoing in her own ears as if someone else in the room were talking. But it was her voice. It rose in anger to a scream.

Jeff tried to calm her down.

"Why? Why did she do it?" The memory of the terror returned. She was shrieking now, overwhelmed by anger and fear. The emotions she bottled up for so many years surfaced and began to spill over. "My own mother! Why did she do that to me?"

Jeff reached over to her in an effort to calm her.

"No!" She pushed away from him. She had to get away from everything. She had to be alone, where she could no longer hurt Jeff. Nadia, her family...what kind of people were they? What kind of creature gave birth to her? What kind of sick monster was Nadia?

"What kind of a sick whore was she?" She flung the words as she passed her husband and ran out of the house and into the dark night.

She just wanted to keep running. It was as if she had to get away from those terrible memories unleashing themselves in her mind. As she ran, she felt that nothing could stand in her way—nothing. If a mountain stood before her, she would go through it. If a pit of burning embers or vipers lay at her feet, she would pass over them. Decades of pent-up anger and frustration came tumbling out. The scene of a crying, terrified child had triggered the memory. The terror felt in that child's cry was her own, spanning the years.

Mia ran until she realized that her feet were bleeding from the sharp pebbles cutting into them. The numbness throughout her body started to recede, which gave way to pain. Reality hit, and she became aware of her surroundings. She stopped. She realized she was not wearing her shoes. She stood in the dark but was not afraid of the strange surroundings and the demons anymore as once she had been as a child.

"Nadia, what kind of a sick fiend were you?" She screamed the words into the darkness at the beast that bore her. She dared the demon to stand before her, the demon with the face of her mother.

Mia found strength in anger. Something powerful erupted in her. She did not see the face of her mother but that of a demon. The apparition she feared as a child, the horns and cloven hooves it painted in her mind, now transformed itself into the face of Nadia, the demon, and all the evil she embodied.

"Just try me now," she cried out. She would trample it to the ground or die trying. There was no fear left in her, only anger, resentment, and pain.

Mia could not go any farther. She had to turn back, but she wanted to be alone. She would not unleash her anger in front of Jeff. The keys were in the car. Yes, she would go back for the car. She had to get away.

The road stretched ahead of her, into the darkness of the night. She drove and stopped and then drove some more. She stopped again. Time seemed to stand still. How long did she sit there, entranced, not really realizing where she was? Not caring.

The sun rose in the horizon. The light of dawn was reflected in the glimmering waters of the lake. Mia sat and watched, mesmerized as the glistening waves splashed, broke, and shattered into droplets against the rocky shore. Shattered like her life had been shattered. Would she be able to take the shattered pieces of her life and piece them together?

Mia sat in silence, the shore of the mighty lake stretching out before her. The childhood memories flashed through her mind and cut into her soul—over and over and over again. One after the other, each memory felt like a new tear in her soul as she groped for answers. *Why, why?* she kept asking herself. She knew she could not run from it anymore. She would no longer be safe with the repressed memories; she would have to face them. She battled demons in her childhood and would have to face them again now. It was the family into which she was born.

For the sake of her children, and for Jeff, she would face the demons with her newfound strength. She could not fight them when she was a child, but with Jeff and her children beside her for support, she would fight them now. The door to her childhood was unlocked. She shrugged in defeat.

I cannot hide from the past; I have to find the answers. My family would not help me when I was a child, and they will not help me now. Mia knew that the answers she was looking for would come from within. Any repressed memories would not stay repressed for long. Mia gasped for a breath. She felt as if she was immersed in a dark pit of despair; she was sinking, drowning, and suffocating in the slime of her family's tainted secrets. Her memories released themselves like a flood. The image of a horrified child crying in a movie opened the door to the monstrosity of her own childhood. She could not escape the past, and ahead lay the inevitable pain of the future.

Rejected

I came from her womb, not from her heart,
Rejected, rejected, right from the start.
She gave me birth, so callous and vain,
Rejected, rejected, in hurt and in pain.
I reached out to strangers, some comfort to find,
Rejected, rejected, longing to bind.
In strangers I found warmth a child longs for.
Rejected, rejected, rejected no more.

CHAPTER THREE

Fear. Mia's childhood was lived in bleakness and fear. She longed to reach out to the peaceful, bright side of things. She remembered Nadia swaddling her and setting her outside. The calmness of the sky and the peaceful, floating clouds mesmerized her. The tranquility lulled her to sleep. That feeling of safety was restricted to moments like that, however.

Nadia continued to use the swaddling method to bind her like a mummy until Mia was past the toddling stage. The child felt fear when Nadia did this, but she was much too young to realize that her fear was a signal that danger lurked around her. The dark trees looming around at her sides reached out and touched the peaceful sky. She could not understand why she felt threatened by their movement. Lying there helplessly bound, Mia felt fear smother her. Sometimes she thought she saw a threatening figure in the trees. Her sudden screams sent the figure scurrying deeper into the trees. Her cries brought one of her sisters to her side.

"Somebody is in the trees. I saw someone moving there and watching me! I think he is waiting for me to fall asleep. I'm scared he will come back and hurt me when I'm sleeping. I'm scared. I'm scared," Mia repeated between sobs.

"There isn't anyone in the trees. It is only the wind."

"But I saw someone standing in the trees watching me."

"Who did you see?"

"It wasn't Jacob 'cause my brother Jacob is not fat. It looked like Koss 'cause he is fatter and bigger than Jacob."

"Koss is your brother; you shouldn't be afraid of him. Why are you afraid of him?"

"I don't know. He didn't answer when I talked to him. He just hid behind a tree and watched me. It scared me when he did that. He didn't say anything, and when I started to cry, he ran away."

"Well, there is no one in the trees now. Just close your eyes and everything will be OK," her sister assured her before leaving her alone to nap.

Mia shut her eyes, closing off the movements around her and trying to block out the fear. She was wrapped in a large flannel blanket, arms tightly bound to her sides. Mia could not sit up or protect herself from any danger that lurked around her. Helpless, she fell into an exhausted sleep.

If Nadia did not bind too tight, Mia could free her arms and bring them to the surface. She would close her eyes and dig her fists into them to block the movements around her. Mia felt safer and more comfortable when she brought her hands to the surface. She would fall asleep more calmly, but Nadia usually bound her tightly, almost to the point of cutting off the circulation in her arms. She was seldom able to pull them out of the binding.

After Mia's outdoor nap, she called out until one of her sisters heard her and came to free her from the wrap that imprisoned her.

"Why did you pull your arms out of the blanket?" Kassie asked her abruptly.

"'Cause I was scared that there was something moving in the trees."

"You know there was nothing in the trees. It's just the wind moving the branches. The wind cannot hurt you." Her sister scowled as she brought Mia into the house.

"When Mia woke up, did she still have her arms at her sides the way I had wrapped them?" Nadia asked.

"No. She pulled them to the surface."

The child felt Nadia's anger lash out at her because she had pulled her arms out of the tight, uncomfortable cocoon where she was bound. It was an act that Nadia felt defied her. The next time, after Mia awoke, she tried sticking her arms back in the swaddle before one of her sisters came to fetch her. She was glad when it was Sarah who came.

"Please don't tell Mother I pulled my hands out," she begged Sarah. "I tried to stick them back into the blanket, but I couldn't."

"Mother says you must fall asleep with your arms tight to your sides, and you have to keep them there until you are brought into the house. Why did you pull them out?"

"The blanket was too tight, and I can't sleep 'cause it's so hot when my hands are inside. I'm scared there is someone in the trees. I like to watch the clouds in the sky, but I don't like the trees. They are dark. If I cover my eyes with my hands, I can't see them."

"Why did you take your hands out today? Did you see anyone in the trees today?"

"No, but those little flies sit on my face. I had to take my hands out to chase them away, and then I covered my eyes and fell asleep."

Sarah was more understanding of the child's situation than Hilda or Kassie.

"Those little flies come and sit on my face. They keep biting me," she said, scratching the red welts on her face.

"Mosquitoes?"

"Mos—" She hesitated over the new word. "Yes," she answered.

"OK, I won't tell Mother." Sarah smiled.

It was as if Nadia had to use brute force on the child to train her to accept the limits she was setting for her. Nadia trained her children as some people trained animals to obedience. Nadia would force her children early in life to adopt the roles that she formed for them. She molded a life for her children as hers was molded in her father's house.

In her husband's absence, to punish Mia for freeing her arms the previous day, Nadia angrily slapped the child before forcefully imprisoning her again in the tight swaddle. Then instead of laying the sobbing child in the shade, she set her in the hot sun as punishment.

"If anyone tells Father that I am punishing her this way, I will deal with that person severely when Father is not around." With her face flushed and her eyes bulging, Nadia spat the threatening words at the rest of her children.

Mia could only scream and struggle to sheer exhaustion. With the heat of the sun beating down on her, she fought for a breath of air. She felt she was suffocating and fought her way out of the grip of the swaddle. In anger, Nadia whipped and rebound the tormented child before securing the blanket tightly with large pins.

"I wouldn't have to do this to you if you didn't disobey me," she shrieked at the sobbing child.

Again, Mia fought and struggled for a breath of air. Her face was wet with tears and perspiration from the heat of the sun. She tugged at the binding. The weakened cloth ripped where the pins held it. This infuriated Nadia even further. She took a large new blanket she had sewn and again tightly imprisoned the exhausted child. In the struggle to free herself, Mia also ripped the new cloth where it was held by the pins. Enraged, Nadia beat the child for ripping her baby brother's new blanket. She rebound her. Mia cried herself into complete exhaustion before they brought her into the house and removed the binding. Yuri, the baby, lay peacefully sleeping on the bed.

"Look at Yuri. Why can't you go to sleep the way he does when I tell you to? Why are you giving me so much trouble?" Nadia's face was flushed with anger as she hissed the words at Mia.

The coolness of the room soothed Mia. She wanted to lie down like Yuri. She wanted to feel the safety of the house and the coolness of the shade. She did not want to be imprisoned like a mummy and feel threatened by the heat and the fear that surrounded her outdoors.

Nadia was still wrapping her up and putting her outside to sleep in the heat when she was four years old. Was this Nadia's irrational way of teaching her child that she had no boundaries? Was it a neurotic mother's way of teaching her child that she was not in control of her own life?

There was a ritual held in Nadia's house. It was one she had participated in as a young child. The ritual took place on Saturdays when the older siblings were home from school and their father was not at home. At first they didn't allow Mia to participate because they said she was too young. She sat on the bed where Yuri lay and listened to her older siblings in the next room.

"Mother would make a good teacher," Koss boasted with pride. "She lines us up and asks us questions just like the teacher does in school."

Mia wanted to go to school, but she was not yet of school age. She was anxious to have playmates who were close to her own age and to develop academically with them.

"Can I stand in the room with you so I can learn how the teacher teaches you in school?" she asked.

"We don't know. We will have to ask Mother if you can."

Later, they told her, "Mother said you have to answer the questions like the rest of us if you want to stand in the room with us."

"What kind of questions does the teacher ask you in school?" Mia asked Jacob.

"She asks us to count, and she asks us to add numbers," he replied.

The thought of learning to count and add numbers excited Mia. She asked her older siblings to coach her so she could give her mother the right answers to her questions.

"Those are not the kind of questions Mother asks us," Hilda informed the child as she gave Kassie a challenging glance.

"What kind of questions does Mother ask?"

Hilda was annoyed. "I don't have time for you. Ask Kassie to tell you," she snapped, irritated with the young child's inquisition.

"Mother asks us all kinds of questions, and we answer her." Kassie looked disturbed when she answered.

"But how can I know what answers to give her if I don't know what she is going to ask?" Mia asked anxiously.

"Just tell her the truth." Kassie's advice was given with a callous shrug.

Nadia waited until the next Saturday when her husband was not at home. She lined up her offspring for the usual ritual. When Sarah was around, she was spared from participating in the ritual with her younger siblings. Mia realized later that Nadia gave Sarah special priorities because she was the eldest daughter; she was also her favorite.

Nadia lined up the children where she could observe each one's face. It was when Nadia started questioning them that Mia learned her mother didn't want them to answer her truthfully. She interrogated them with questions. She brainwashed them. She only wanted them to give her the answer she wanted to hear. If she didn't get the expected answer, she would single the child out.

It bewildered Mia to be singled out; seeing her mother's raw rage frightened her.

Not telling the truth was difficult as Mia did not know how to lie. It was very confusing. Her mother had already put the fear of the demons in her, so she was afraid to lie.

"Do you like me?" Nadia demanded. Her voice was hostile.

Mia could give a positive answer to that question. She mothered them, and she gave them life.

"Am I a good mother?"

She was the only mother they knew. To whom could they compare her? Mia, along with her siblings, gave her the positive answer she wanted to hear.

"Do you like what I am teaching you?"

This question was confusing to Mia. *I would like to go to school,* she thought. *If this is how the teacher teaches us, I will say yes. If I don't say yes, they may not allow me to go to school.* She went along with the positive answer her older siblings gave.

"Do you like the things I do to you?"

"Yes."

Some of her siblings seemed to hesitate, but they gave Nadia the positive answer she wanted to hear. Mia remembered her mother hurting her when her father was not around. She hated being hurt that way. She was the youngest.

Kassie told her to tell Nadia the truth when she was holding the ritual. Innocently, the child stood thinking. She heard her older sibling say the teacher sorted the students in school into different groups. *Is Mother sorting us into groups? If she is, she must not know she hurts me. She must not know that I don't like it. I must tell her that I don't like what she does to me. If I do, she will stop doing it to me.* The innocent child justified her truthful answer.

"No, I don't," Mia answered.

Like the fallout from the sudden drop of a bombshell, everything came to a hushed standstill. Her siblings turned their heads and scowled at her. The child didn't know why they were angry with her. Why were they so angry? She lowered her head. Why would speaking the truth be wrong?

"What is wrong with her?" Nadia huffed and glared at Mia with her icy, cold eyes. "Who was responsible for talking to her? Didn't you tell her I want her to give fit answers to my questions?" Nadia snapped angrily at her older children. She surveyed the faces before her until her chilly glare rested on Hilda.

"It wasn't me. I didn't have time to talk to her, and I asked Kassie to do it." Hilda's response was sputtered defensively.

"You are older, but I will speak with both of you girls about this." With her face burning crimson and nostrils flaring, Nadia ended the ritual for the day.

Later, Mia was approached by Kassie for the second time.

"What am I supposed to say?" Mia still didn't understand what the ritual was about.

"Well, give her the answers you want to," Kassie spoke irritably. "Then maybe she will realize we don't like what she is doing and she will stop."

The next time their mother lined them up for the ritual, Mia looked at her and gave her a truthful answer again. This made Nadia explode in a wailing, emotional rage. She lamented wildly as she beat her chest and stamped her feet.

"Where have I gone wrong to deserve such ungrateful children?" she lamented hysterically.

Not only was Mia punished for telling the truth, but she was also at the mercy of her siblings for causing Nadia's fury.

"Did you see how angry you made Mother? Do you want her heart to burst?" Koss confronted the child with fury. "Do you want her to die? Or do you want me to beat you for not answering her the right way?"

Mia didn't understand why telling the truth would cause such an angry reaction. She wondered if the teachers in school beat their chests and stamped their feet like Nadia did when they were not given the answers they wanted to hear. Mia wailed.

"You have to listen to the answers we give Mother, and then you have to say what we say," Hilda firmly advised the child.

"But when she asks something, how can I say yes when I am thinking no?" Mia muttered mournfully as she stifled her tears.

"Listen to the answers we give and give the same answer we do," Hilda cautioned her.

"By the time I hear what you say, I have already given the wrong answer, and she gets angry with me. I am afraid of her," Mia lamented.

"We will stand where you can see us. Watch our mouths. If you see that we are going to say yes, you say yes. If you see that we are going to say no, you say no," her sister volunteered.

"Can you shake your head yes or no so I can see what you are going to say?" Mia begged.

"No, we can't because Mother will see us, and she will get angry if we do that."

As Mia stood in the lineup, she tried to read her sisters' lips. By trying to follow their answers, she was trailing with hers. Nadia angrily appointed her confidant, Koss, to stand beside the child and listen to what she said. Things were rocky, and Nadia had her hands full with observing the rest of her offspring to make sure they were not conspiring against her. One disagreeable apple could upset Nadia's whole cart.

Mia tried to mouth the answers as she squirmed and watched her sisters. She opened her mouth and moved her jaw, imitating their facial movements. With Koss listening beside her, she was afraid to have the wrong sound escape her lips.

"Mia isn't saying anything; she only moves her lips," he smugly reported to Nadia.

His mother rewarded him for squealing on the child.

"I want you to answer out loud so Koss can hear what you say." Nadia's harsh voice whipped through the air at the child. Mia lowered her head in frustration. She felt stripped of her self-worth and dispirited by the rituals. The ways of the grownups were unfamiliar to her. If the teacher was as antagonizing as this, Mia was not sure that she would like to go to school after all.

Her Command
Mirror, mirror on the wall,
Who is the greatest mother of all?
Is it not I, is it not me?
The greatest stands before you to see.

Block off your hurt—you must not cry.
You must look straight into her eye.
Echo the answer she wants to hear.
Block off your hurt; show not your fear.

Her secret we must withhold,
A secret that must not be told.
On us she cast a spell of fear
To not speak the truth nor shed a tear.
Honor your mother, her stern command,
The secret kept was her demand.

And as we spoke her evil lie,
We had to look straight into her eye,
For if we shuffled or looked downcast,
Her punishment was swift and fast.
She held us under her evil spell
With threats of demons and fires of hell

> *She reigned in power, she reigned in lust,*
> *Her father's teachings on us she thrust.*
> *Block off your hurt—you must not cry.*
> *You must look straight into her eye...*

Mia feared her mother and Koss. In the beginning, only her mother molested her. But after these Saturday rituals, her mother allowed Koss to abuse Mia. Sarah and Koss were the only ones their mother protected. Koss was her eldest son, so under Nadia's rules, she gave him the power. She trained him to be as aggressive and manipulative as she was. She gave him the authority to control and rule the weaker members of the family. Mia was not even allowed to control her own needs or her own life. She was a girl and a younger member of the family. Her self-respect was ripped from her as she became Koss's main target of control.

They did not allow Mia to sit on a chair when she was a child. When they gathered around the table at meal time, they insisted that she stand at her place at the table. After a long day when she was very tired, her father asked her older siblings to make room for her on the benches lined around the side of the table. Nadia would angrily scowl at her husband for the disturbance around the table. However, when they made room for her, it amused them to have her sit on the place where the two benches joined. Koss and Kassie would squirm on the benches, knowing that Mia would be pinched on her bottom as she ate. This caused the child to slip under the table to hide her painful tears. Her father scolded them. They put on a pretense of ignorance and hid their snickers; they would laugh at their cruel wit later.

She was forbidden to sit on any chair. It was as if chairs were reserved for a higher class of humans. Once, when Mia was hardly more than a toddler, she walked into the kitchen and eyed an empty chair. Thinking she was alone, she wondered how it would feel to sit in it. She bravely crawled onto it, thinking only a princess could feel as graceful as she did.

Koss, as usual, lurked in the next room, watching her. When he saw her sitting in the chair, he barreled into the room, grabbed her by the ankles, and pulled her off of it. Mia lay on the floor, unable to move. The fall off the chair had momentarily paralyzed her.

"Get up, you brat," Koss angrily commanded with a violent kick.

Mia also seemed to have lost her voice; she could not utter a cry. Nadia came to see what the child had done to upset her brother. Mia lay on the floor next to a cast-iron heater. Filled with a mix of terror and pain, she feared her mother would punish her for sitting on the chair and angering Koss. It was then that Sarah and Hilda came to her rescue.

"Why isn't she moving?" Sarah asked with concern.

"She must have struck her head on the heater," Hilda suggested.

They picked her up and put her on a bed. They examined her and couldn't find any bumps on her head.

"Where do you hurt?"

When Mia was able to move, she pointed to her lower back.

"He hurt her spine," Hilda noted, seething with rage.

Mia winced. The length of her thigh throbbed in pain.

"Look at her thigh. Why is it bruised?"

"She could not have struck her thigh on anything. Did Koss kick you again?" Hilda asked.

Riddled with pain and unable to speak, Mia could only nod her head.

In silent anger, Hilda helped Sarah. nurse Mia until her back healed and she was able to sit without too much pain.

Koss was beyond punishment. He was Nadia's confidant. He held authority in the family, and Mia feared him as much as she feared Nadia.

One morning, as Mia toddled around the kitchen, hungrily chewing on a piece of bread one of her sisters had given her, Koss came into the house. It was before breakfast, and her parents and other siblings were still outdoors.

"You brat, how dare you have something to eat before me?" Koss angrily attacked her. "Can't you learn to respect your elders? Don't you understand that you are not supposed to eat until your elders have eaten? When are you going to learn to respect your elders?"

With these words, he angrily shoved the child against the kitchen table. When she hit the edge of the table, she broke her nose. From then on, Mia was self-conscious about the scar on her nose. Koss ridiculed her about it constantly.

"Look at yourself. Not only are you ugly, but you are also stupid; nobody is ever going to like you. You don't have any brains in your head; you will never be as smart as Kassie or me."

Mia looked at her discolored, bruised nose and decided her brother was right she felt as ugly as the circumstances in which she lived.

Nadia's plan was to make a man out of her eldest boy by building up his self-esteem and giving him control of the family. Koss took pride in his looks even though he was repulsive looking. Mia thought his weight made him look like a spongy marshmallow. He had colorless hair, pale eyes, and a ruddy face. When his mother and the siblings he dominated were not around, he would lower his gaze. He looked out of place, sullen, and alone when he was surrounded by adults. He never looked them in the eyes as if he was afraid that someone would read the truth there and learn what he was trying to conceal. His thick, ugly lips drooped at the corners, causing his customary pout.

Later, he preferred to hang around with a much younger crowd. There, he felt superior. He used his power and spoke obscenities to draw attention and make himself popular.

One day when Mia awoke from an afternoon nap, she made her way out of the house. She could not hear or see any of her siblings, so she wandered toward the trampled heap of sand she'd discovered earlier. It was overgrown and hidden in the weeds. At one time, when her older siblings were young, the heap of sand had probably been fresh and clean. Now it no longer resembled fresh sand, but Mia knew no difference. It was her father who told one of her siblings to show her where the old sand pile was. It was a place where she could play alone.

She sifted the dirty granules through her fingers, content with her newfound amusement.

As Mia sat playing, her six-year-old brother, Jacob, came to stand alongside her. He unpinned his pants and took his penis out. It was as if he were going to do the natural thing and relieve himself.

"Do you know what I want to do?"

The child looked up at her brother with a questioning look and shook her head. She hoped he would just go away.

"Do you know where I want to stick this?" he asked.

"No." She shook her head and kept on sifting the sand from one hand to another.

"Guess where?"

"My eye?" she asked with the innocence of a child. "It hurts if you stick anything in the eye," she added. She feared he would hurt her and hoped he would leave her alone to play in the sand.

"No, not your eye, stupid."

It relieved Mia to know that her brother would not hurt her eye.

"Guess again."

"My ear?" She continued filtering the dirty sand through her fingers.

"No. You are so stupid. What is wrong with you? Don't you know anything?"

Mia looked at her brother. She just wanted him to go away.

"I want to stick it between your legs."

Mia looked wide eyed at Jacob. In surprise, she asked, "Why do you want to do that?"

"Don't you know? Because that is what boys do to girls." Her brother scowled down at her. "Why are you such a baby? Don't you know anything?" he asked sharply.

Mia was silent for a moment. "No, that would hurt." She looked disturbed. "Mother hurts me there." Remembering being hurt by her mother made Mia want to cry.

"Why are you such a sissy? It doesn't hurt," her brother scoffed with certainty. "Mother does that to us. It doesn't hurt us, and it doesn't hurt her either."

Mia remembered being hurt by her mother and the fear. She remembered the baths she liked, but she detested what happened after Nadia bathed her. She remembered how she cried in fear. Mia kept sifting her fingers through the sand, hoping her brother would go away. She did not notice Koss lurking nearby until he was standing beside Jacob.

"What are you going to do to her?" he hissed to his younger brother.

"Mia is such a baby," Jacob said tauntingly. "She doesn't know anything. She says it hurts when Mother does those things to her. I told her it doesn't hurt Mother when she does those things, and it doesn't hurt us. Kassie says it doesn't hurt her when she does that to her either."

Koss gave his younger brother a shove. "Go away," he said aggressively.

Mia watched Koss undo his pants. He then attempted to push her down. She shrieked in terror, and her mother appeared to see why she was screaming.

"You shouldn't do that to your little sister yet. She isn't ready. She is still too young," Nadia warned him.

Frightened, Mia got up, hoping her mother would comfort her. Instead, she lashed out in contempt.

"Get into the house. Sarah and Hilda are there. They will take care of you."

Mia ran into the house, sobbing. Sarah and Hilda questioned her.

"Why are you crying? Tell us what happened."

Although she wasn't able to explain what happened, they seemed to know, and it didn't seem to surprise them.

"What did Mother tell Koss?" they questioned the bewildered child.

"She said, 'Don't do that to her yet.'"

"Did Mother say 'yet'?"

Mia nodded her head.

Her sisters reacted with silence. "It is all in Mother's hands," one said, and they both nodded.

Until then, Mia felt that Sarah and Hilda protected her. Her mother stepped in and protected her from Koss that day. Despite that, the child felt threatened by the unknown. Why did the word "yet" hold the key to her sisters' reaction? Mia was already intimidated by her mother and Koss, but she was too young to realize what her sisters meant when they said that it was all in their mother's hands.

Sometime later, as Mia played in the yard, her brothers approached her. Koss, the elder, was the spokesperson. The child detested being probed and pestered by her older siblings. Her brothers spoke in front of her as if they wanted her to learn something from their conversation.

"We will have to ask Kassie to talk to her. She will tell her. She will teach her." It was staged as if they had an unknown pact. Mia was content with her child's play, but the harassment by her brothers continued.

"Next time you see Kassie come out of the house, go up to her. She will tell you something." Koss looked down at the child with arrogant superiority.

Mia couldn't understand what her brother wanted his twin sister to tell her. She was a timid child. She didn't have playmates who shared her interests. She played alone and wanted her brothers to leave her alone. But the prodding continued.

"Look, there's Kassie now," Koss insisted. "Watch where she goes, and then just go stand beside her. She has something to tell you about our secrets. Go to her right now."

The yard looked vast to the small child, and it took her some time to cover the distance. Usually, by the time she toddled partway to where her sister was, Kassie would be finished with what she was doing and was already back inside the house. Her brother was not pleased at these times.

Once, coerced to follow Koss's orders, Mia toddled across the yard to Kassie. Her father detained her older sister with some questions. When Mia reached her destination, her father was still talking to Kassie, and in her innocence, Mia spoke to Kassie in front of her father.

"Koss said he wanted you to tell me about your secrets."

Kassie's face paled when Mia delivered Koss's message. She didn't answer. Her father noticed Kassie's reaction to the child's words.

"What dose Mia mean?" he asked Kassie.

Kassie was silent. She didn't answer her father.

"What does Koss want?" her father probed again.

Kassie tried to hide her annoyance with Mia. "I don't know what he wants," she responded tensely.

Both Kassie and Koss were upset with Mia, and she was no match for their cunning ways.

"You are so stupid," Koss ridiculed her later. "Father is not supposed to know about our secret. The dumb brat asked Kassie to tell her about our secret right in front of Father."

They expressed their anger and harassed her. Mia knew she had displeased her older siblings, but she didn't know why. Koss carried his concerns to Nadia.

"We should beat the brat for just about giving our secret away. Father isn't supposed to know about our secret." Koss's ruddy face blustered with anger.

The secrecy confused Mia. She was too young to understand why their family was so divided.

"Don't talk to Mia about those things yet. She is still too young to understand. We must wait until she is older," Nadia instructed.

Koss scoffed in annoyance. "Mia is too dumb to learn the simple things in life. The things we want to teach her are easier to learn than the alphabet in school."

He wanted Kassie to teach Mia the realities that should have remained forbidden to any youngsters. Perhaps he thought Kassie could get the child to absorb what Nadia had introduced to them. They seemed to believe the child lacked the intelligence to learn the lessons they had learned so well.

Kassie didn't do well in school, but she learned Nadia's lessons at home very well. Kassie earned her mother's approval by helping and being one of her main instruments in instructing her brothers. She also took Nadia's lessons to school and taught others.

"You dumb brat, you are too stupid to learn anything," Koss repeatedly ridiculed Mia. "How do you expect to go to school if you are so dumb?"

Mia lowered her head and blinked to hide her tears. She was so anxious to start school.

There were so many things that Mia couldn't understand. The child's fear of her mother grew, but to avoid punishment, she attempted to figure out what brought on Nadia's fierce rages.

Much of Mia's fear was fueled by the violence she witnessed against her brother Jacob. Why did Nadia beat Jacob so violently?

"If you don't speak the truth or do as I say, the demons will take you to hell and burn you there," Nadia told her children.

Yet her mother became enraged with Jacob for telling the truth when she wanted him to lie.

Mia knew that her mother lied; so did Koss and her sisters. Why weren't they afraid of the demons?

She remembered the day Nadia stood over Jacob, beating him with a stick while she screamed at him. A bed was only a few feet behind him. Soon, Jacob was on the bed, cowering. He held back his cries and tried to ward off the blows with his hands. Nadia continued clouting him. Mia knew that if the children screamed or cried while Nadia beat them, it fueled her anger even more. Suddenly, Jacob went limp as if he had fallen asleep. She stopped and left him alone. Mia watched Nadia turn to Hilda and Kassie, still irate.

"He fell asleep. Take care of him." Her outburst was irrational. She stalked out of the house.

"Sometimes Jacob does play possum," Hilda muttered to Kassie as if she was trying to reassure herself that he would regain consciousness shortly.

They spoke quietly as they kept going to where their brother lay. They anxiously touched him. By their reactions, Mia sensed that her brother did not fall asleep during the beating. Something was really wrong with him. He looked like he was dead. Her sisters spoke in riddles as if they didn't want to alarm Mia or unmask their own fear. Jacob lay unmoving, and Mia sensed her sisters' anxiety.

"Is Jacob dead?" Mia's lips quivered as she whispered and timidly looked at her sisters, waiting for their answer.

Agitated, they turned on her as if they feared her thoughts could become a reality.

"No! Now go to sleep."

Hilda looked at Kassie and said, "You were at home the last time she did this to him. Do you remember how long he was out that time?"

"About half an hour."

"What about the time before that?"

"About twenty minutes."

They continued to check on Jacob as he lay unmoving on the bed. Time passed, and her sisters found their fear harder to control. Mia sensed their alarm and could not contain her whimpers.

"Go lie down and have a nap," Hilda snapped at the child.

"But I can't sleep." Mia tried to control her frightened sobs. "What is wrong with Jacob? I want him to wake up."

Hilda looked at Mia and exploded in a fit of rage. Her rage was aimed at Mia but also at Nadia. "Mother always does this to us; she beats Jacob and then goes to work in the orchard and leaves the responsibility for him on us. Not only has she left one responsibility on us today, but she also left us to take care of the sniveling brat and the gardening."

Mia couldn't fall asleep. She was afraid. They said Jacob was not dead, but she knew something was very wrong with him. Her sisters were angry with her. She timidly attempted to muffle her sobs.

Hilda angrily turned to Kassie. "OK, she doesn't want to fall asleep. It is your turn to deal with her today. You know what you have to do. I beat her yesterday."

Mia tensed. She knew that if she was not able to fall asleep when they told her to, they would take turns beating her. She tried to close her eyes and pretend she was asleep. If she couldn't outwit them and they knew she was faking, they would beat her until she cried herself to sleep. It was the way they rid themselves of the responsibility of taking care of her.

"Well, it is your turn to beat her today. I beat her yesterday," Hilda persisted.

Mia cowered on the bed, trying to close her eyes while her sisters argued over who should punish her for not being able to fall asleep. It appeared that with Jacob lying unconscious on the bed from the beating his mother gave him, they were afraid to beat her.

"Well, if you would have given her the whipping I did yesterday, I wouldn't have had to beat her again," Hilda fumed with anger.

"How many times has Mother done this to Jacob this summer?" Hilda strayed off the subject of the pesky child to the still form lying unresponsive on the bed in front of them.

"This is the fourth time," Kassie replied.

Her sisters were worried about Jacob. They were also afraid their mother would punish them if they didn't do the gardening they were told they must do that afternoon.

"Close your eyes," they snapped irritably at Mia as she lay on the bed. "If Jacob wakes up while you are sleeping, we will wake you up too."

Mia closed her eyes and shut out the sight of her brother's limp form. She finally fell asleep.

When she awoke from her nap, the room was quiet. She thought she was left in the house alone and expected to hear the sound of Jacob's chatter as he scurried about outdoors. She lay still, listening as the silence surrounded her. Then she heard the sound of someone quietly sobbing. She turned her head toward the sound. Kassie was sitting on a chair beside the bed where Jacob still lay motionless. She was weeping.

Mia knew that Jacob hadn't awoken while she slept, but she didn't know how long she had been sleeping. Her eyelids were getting heavy again when Hilda walked into the house from working on the vegetable plot.

"How is he?" She looked at Kassie questioningly, but before Kassie could answer, Hilda lit into her angrily. "Why were you crying?" It agitated Hilda to find her sister sobbing. Her words came in one sharp breath.

"I told you that you are not supposed to cry. What if Jacob heard you? If he did, he would think you were crying because he is dying. It would scare him, and then he might die. If I knew you were going to cry, I would have sent you in the garden, and I would have stayed with him myself."

"I was not crying," Kassie said defensively.

"Yes, you were. You know I am like Mother, so don't lie to me. You can never fool me like you can never fool Mother, so don't even try. I am in charge here, and if you lie to me, I can beat you like Mother beat Jacob."

"Well, Jacob didn't hear me because I was crying quietly," Kassie admitted meekly.

Hilda looked at Jacob lying motionless on the bed. "I will stay with him now; you go and tell Father to come home."

"No." Kassie looked distressed. "I will not go. I will not go. You know that Mother is working in the same plot as Father. She will be angry with me if I tell him what she did to Jacob. I will not go!"

"If you don't get Father, Jacob is going to die, and you will be to blame for his death."

"No, Mother will be to blame; she is the one who beat him," Kassie protested through her tears.

"Still, you were crying when you were sitting beside the bed. He could die because he heard you crying."

Mia lay still. She listened to her sisters argue.

"If he survives this beating, she will beat him again and again. She will keep beating him. She won't stop until she beats him to death."

"If she kills Jacob, who will she go after next?"

"You can be sure it won't be Koss. She never beats him. He is her favorite son. Jacob's beatings are incited by Koss."

The afternoon frittered on. Mia noticed longer shadows merging throughout the room. She continued to watch and listen to her sisters as they discussed the brutal beating Nadia had inflicted upon their brother. Although they were afraid that he might not recover this time, neither of them volunteered to get help for their brother. Their utmost fear was displeasing Nadia. They knew she would punish them severely if they told their father that she had beaten Jacob into unconsciousness again.

Mia heard them gasp and look toward the bed Jacob lay on.

"He moved." Hilda breathed a sigh of relief. Then they glanced at the clock, and Mia heard her say, "Two and a half hours."

They were relieved that Jacob survived the beating. After he regained consciousness, he opened his eyes and then slipped into a long, deep sleep. If their father walked in on situations such as this and asked questions, everyone kept their silence. Their fear held them in check, knowing that the one who told their father would be Nadia's next victim. They knew their father could not protect them from their mother; he was away from home much of the time. Even if he were close by, Nadia was in control of her household. Their mother fabricated stories to cover for recovering children, her usual story being that the sun was too hot and made them sick. If bruises were evident, she would say they had slipped off a ladder or fell.

A short time later, Nadia gave Jacob another beating. This time it was because their father had punished Koss for some wrongful doing. It angered their mother that he would discipline her firstborn son. When Koss did something destructive, Nadia wanted Jacob to step in and take the blame. Since Nadia held Koss in such high esteem, she felt that he was beyond punishment.

When her husband left for Ridgewood shortly after he punished Koss, Nadia angrily approached Jacob. Although she was aware of Koss's guilt, it enraged her that Jacob didn't step forward to take the blame for the misdeed. Nadia advised Jacob that he should tell his father that he was to blame for the offense when he returned from town. Jacob stubbornly refused.

First, she used a heavy switch. When the switch didn't get the response she wanted, she picked up a stick to beat him. Mia wondered if his screams of pain and horror would ever end. He was only a few years older than she was. Was she going to kill him as Hilda and Kassie said she would?

One of her sisters tried to calm Mia's cries.

"If you don't stop crying, she will beat you too," she whispered. Nadia would take her anger out on anyone she felt defied her. Mia muffled her fearful cries.

Jacob was telling the truth. He did not want to tell his father a lie. Perhaps he feared the demons as much as Mia did.

Finally, Nadia broke her son's resistance. Jacob said he would say what she wanted him to say. His mother would only stop beating him when he said he would lie and take the blame.

When her husband returned from town, Nadia ranted and lectured him for punishing the wrong son.

Gloating, she demanded, "Ask Jacob; he will tell you. It was he who did what you disciplined Koss for. You should have penalized him, not Koss."

"Are you the one who is guilty of the misdeed?" He looked at Jacob unbelievingly.

Jacob, like a beaten animal, stood shaking uncontrollably. With his swollen, discolored welts exposed, he was afraid to speak the truth. He could only nod as he tried to stifle his fearful sobs.

"I was positive it was Koss. Why did he say he did it if he didn't do it?"

"Because Koss is afraid of you, and he is afraid to tell you the truth." Nadia flared at her husband. "I have a way of getting the truth out of the children. If anybody needs discipline, next time I want you to leave the punishment to me."

"Look what Mother has done to Jacob. It is all because of you." Her sisters accosted Koss angrily. "You have to be the one to tell Father what she did; she wouldn't beat you if you tell him. If we tell him, she will be very angry, and she will beat us like she beat Jacob."

"Well, Mother was right to beat Jacob," Koss supported her arrogantly. "Jacob doesn't do what she tells him to do. When Father punished me, Jacob didn't do his duty toward Mother and me. He has to learn to take the blame for me when Mother tells him to. I am older than he is, and Mother says I should not be punished."

This wasn't only a lesson for Jacob to learn from but also for the rest of the children, especially the younger ones. They were the unacknowledged underdogs who didn't rank high by Nadia's standards.

The following Saturday, when she lined up her children for the usual ritual, she looked directly at Jacob.

"Did you like the beating I gave you?" she questioned harshly.

Poor Jacob—he looked so pale; parts of his body were swollen and still showed discolored welts. He trembled uncontrollably as he tried to hold back his sobs. Mia couldn't help but sob with her brother.

"Shush up," one of her sisters muttered. "Don't you know if Jacob doesn't say what she wants him to say, she will give him another beating? If she hears you whimpering, she will beat you too."

"Yes," Jacob moaned in a low voice.

"Speak louder. I didn't hear what you said!" Nadia's shriek cut through the room; her icy eyes did not leave her son's face.

"Yes," Jacob muttered again.

"Did you deserve the beating I gave you?" She angrily whipped the question at the trembling child.

Jacob didn't want to lie. He was beaten viciously by his mother for defying her by telling her the truth.

"Yes," he whimpered for the third time. He tried to hold back his tears. Mia watched him swallow the lump in his throat and give Nadia the answer she wanted to hear.

In the future, when recalling the vivid, horrid memories, Mia knew she could only retrieve memories, not answers. Her heart felt heavy when she remembered the days of so long ago. *Why?* Mia would repeatedly ask. Why did these awful things happen in their mother's house? Was Nadia mentally ill? Why else would she have done what she did to her children?

When Jacob took the blame for Koss, he was targeted for lectures and punishments in place of his older brother. Jacob suppressed his feeling with tight lips. Koss basked in his mother's deranged glory. Mia remembered time after time when Nadia clouted Jacob and angrily demanded, "I want you to tell me you did it."

Jacob learned to take his beatings; however, he firmly refused to lie to his mother. Mia couldn't understand why her sisters didn't beg their mother to stop beating their brother instead of tearfully begging Jacob to give their mother the answer she wanted. She stopped beating him only if he lied. With his mouth set stubbornly, he refused to give in to her lies. Later, he didn't even flinch when she beat him; he sat through the beating as if he were made of stone.

It was after Hilda questioned Jacob that they realized something was wrong with his behavior. He would go into trances while he was beaten, and after Nadia stopped, he sat unmoving for long periods, not speaking, unaware of what was happening around him. When he snapped out of the trance, he didn't seem to be aware of what had happened. He was repressing the beatings as well as the events that led to the abuse.

When his father found out about the beatings and Jacob's vacant state, he was very upset. Mia's father was a big, strong person, but he was no match for the insidious woman he married.

For a time, the family feared that Jacob had brain damage. Jacob's unexplained state also worried Nadia. When someone told her that Igor's mother said her son also suffered from memory lapses after she beat him, Nadia questioned her about it. Nadia was worried that Jacob might be affected like Igor, who was known as the neighborhood dimwit. She spoke to the woman and was told that Igor was born with slow perception and strabismus eyes; however, he also went into trances after she beat him.

Once Mia saw her father cry as he held her for what might have been most of the night. Now she realized that her father must have cried often when no one was there to witness the tears of a broken man.

Jacob's beatings continued. So did the pandemonium in Nadia's house. Jacob hid his feelings. He was not able to truly express them or show emotion. It would upset him when he heard anyone speak critically of his mother. Even as a grown man, he wasn't able to free himself from the control Nadia held over him as a child. None of Mia's other siblings could either.

Mia remembered the time when Koss intentionally left a heavy five-gallon pail along the path. Their father had made it clear that the pails should be put in the right place after they were used. Koss told Mia that if questions were asked about why the pail had not been taken to its rightful place, she was to say she was responsible for leaving it there. Mia was afraid that Nadia would punish her like Jacob for something Koss did. She was no more than a toddler, and the pail was too heavy for her to carry to its proper place, so she decided she should approach Nadia before there was any punishment to be had and confess to something for which she was not responsible. It seemed the pail was left there as a setup; they wanted to see if Mia would take the blame for something she didn't do.

It pleased Nadia when she took the blame and lied for Koss. The manipulation she was implementing on her children was taking effect.

CHAPTER FOUR

It was summer vacation, and Mia was playing outdoors. She could hear the voices of her mother and older siblings drifting out of the house. Jacob came to where Mia played and happily smiled and chattered as he strutted around her. A weather-beaten rail fence stood nearby. Mia watched Jacob; he stood on the first rail of the fence and then, without another thought, crawled onto the second rail. She envied her brothers when she saw them stand on the rails of the fence. It was something she was forbidden to do.

But she had not seen Jacob stand on the second rail before; she thought her brother was so brave as he stood and supported himself with his knees against the upper rail.

"Can I stand on the fence too?" Mia squinted her eyes as she looked up at her brother, begging him.

"No, you can't. You are too small," Jacob replied. "You are not supposed to stand on fences 'cause you will fall off and hurt yourself."

"You are not supposed to stand that high either. If you are big enough to stand on the second rail, could I stand on the bottom one 'cause I am not as big as you are? I will be careful. I'll hang onto the fence."

"No, you can't," Jacob repeated. "Koss can stand on the top rail because he is bigger than I am. I can stand on the middle one, but you have to stay on the ground. You can't stand on the rails at all because you are a girl, and you are not big enough. You don't even go to school yet. Besides, I have a secret, and you don't."

"A secret?" Mia looked up at her brother, shielding her eyes from the bright sun. "Tell me your secret, Jacob."

"No, I have a secret, but I won't tell. I won't tell." He taunted and teased her. Then, flailing his arms, he imitated a rooster perched on the fence.

"I want to know your secret, Jacob. Tell me your secret," she begged.

"No, I must not tell. Mother told me I must not tell."

Mia was disappointed. Everyone had secrets in the family, especially Kassie and Koss. Now Jacob said he had a secret too. They seemed to act as if having a secret was something that was very special—as if they were all grown up. Mia was disappointed because Jacob would not tell her his secret, and he wouldn't allow her to stand on the lowest rail of the fence.

She didn't see Koss lurking nearby until he came up to the fence where his younger brother was perched.

He looked at Jacob and said, "I know what your secret is. I have the same secret you do."

Mia watched as Koss stood on the top rail, balancing himself. He had four fingers stuck in each of his front pockets, his thumbs to the outside. His sisters often ridiculed him when he did that; they teased him for trying to imitate the grownup boys in school.

Mia knew he was just showing off because he had a secret and he was the eldest boy.

He looked down at Mia. "Go away, brat. Jacob and I want to talk about our secrets. We are grown up, and you are only a brat," he commanded gruffly.

Summer came to an end, and vacation was over. Mia's older siblings went back to school, and she was playing alone in the yard. It was just after lunch. Her parents were in the house, having their usual afternoon rest. Her mother spent much time in the house resting lately.

Mia collected pebbles alongside the path and listened to the voices of the children in the nearby school yard. From beyond the bog, she heard the school bell calling the children back to their studies; the lunch period was over.

As Mia picked up pebbles, her father came out of the house. She looked up at him as he walked toward her.

"Mia," he spoke quietly. "Your mother is tired. She is sleeping, and I have to go check things in the orchard. Stay close to the house and don't wander away." He added the usual caution, "Listen to your mother."

Mia obeyed. With the hot sun beating down on her, she continued scratching the pebbles out of the dirt collecting them in her fists. Their colors and smoothness fascinated her. She was still absorbed with her collection when Nadia came outside.

"Mia, come into the house."

Mia held her precious gems tightly in her hands. She didn't want to drop or lose any of them. Bending down, she carefully began to pile them on the ground. The child's dawdling aggravated Nadia.

"Mia, I want you to come into the house now, this instant."

Mia looked up at her mother and wondered why she looked so big and clumsy. She'd heard her siblings talk as if there was something wrong with her. She remembered hearing Kassie snickering, "Mother sure is getting bloated. If she doesn't stop bloating, her stomach might just burst open."

"What does 'bloated' mean?" Mia asked with concern.

"It doesn't mean anything," Hilda snapped, irritated by the young child's question.

"Then why did Kassie say it?"

"Because Mother is getting fat."

It worried Mia when the problem of Nadia's condition was brought to her attention.

"Would Mother die if she keeps on bloating? When she bursts open, will there be blood all over just like there would be if her heart bursts if we don't do what she tells us to do?" Mia probed.

"See what you've started?" Hilda snapped at Kassie. "Don't talk about Mother like that. You are a girl, and one day you will be in the same condition. You will be punished for making fun of your own mother. Sarah says we should never dishonor our mother."

"Well, I didn't say it. That is what Koss said," Kassie answered in a hasty defense. "He always tells me nasty things about Mother. Then he tells me it's our secret and we are not to tell anyone."

Mia was too young to realize that her mother's bloated condition was due to pregnancy.

Mia took her time as she carefully piled her collection of pebbles. Nadia angrily seized her arm and wrenched her toward the house.

"Come with me. I have to measure something in the house." Her mother uttered the words abruptly to the child.

She must be sewing a dress for me, she thought. *She wants me to try it on to see if it fits.* "Are you sewing a dress for me?" She looked up at Nadia as she was forced to move along beside her bulky body.

"Yes," Nadia grunted. "Sewing two dresses."

Nadia often sewed dresses for her older daughters. Then she used odd leftover remnants to piece a dress together for Mia. However, there was never enough material left over for more than one skimpy dress for her. She was pleased when her mother told her she was sewing her two dresses.

They entered the house. Coming in from the bright outdoors, it took some time for Mia's eyes to adjust to the dimness of the room. She looked at the sewing machine, but it was closed. She couldn't see a remnant of a dress.

"Where are the dresses?" Mia looked up at Nadia. "Can I try them on and go back outside to finish gathering pebbles?" The child spoke anxiously, wanting to get out of the gloomy atmosphere.

"There are no dresses. Come with me." She dragged the resisting child toward the bedroom.

She lied to me. There aren't any dresses here. Panic set in within the bewildered child. She didn't want to go into the bedroom with her mother. *Why does Mother tell lies?*

"Lie on the bed," Nadia ordered the child.

Mia's fears mounted. "But I'm not tired; I don't want to go to sleep."

"I didn't say you had to go to sleep. I told you to lie down."

Mia was trembling with fear. She realized what Nadia intended to do.

She stood in the doorway of the room. The beds were scattered and spread throughout the bedroom. Before, three double beds were set up in three corners of the bedroom, and one could walk into the room between the beds. Now the room was overcrowded. Her parents slept on one bed. Mia slept on the other with two of her sisters. Koss and Jacob used to sleep on the third bed with one of their sisters, who had to take turns sleeping with the boys.

She remembered one night when it was Kassie's turn to sleep with her brothers. Mia didn't know why her father's angry voice woke the whole sleeping household during the night. It sounded like all hell had broken loose.

"You say you can't fall asleep at night," he bellowed at his wife. "If you weren't sleeping, didn't you hear what was going on here?"

"What is wrong with you?" Nadia shouted back at her husband. "You've woken all the children!"

"What is going on in this house? You were not sleeping; you heard what they were doing. I will not allow them to sleep together again," her father's voice shouted over Nadia's.

"Well, they are only children. When you heard them, you could have gone to the bed quietly and told them to go to sleep. You didn't have to start screaming at them."

After that night, her father wouldn't allow the boys to sleep with their sisters again. Benches were set in the middle of the room, equipped with bedding. The benches served as makeshift beds for Koss and Jacob. Some mornings, Mia had to step over them to get to the other side of the room. Koss angrily forbid her to step on his bed and threatened to beat her if she did so again. They angled the makeshift beds at the foot of their parents' bed and had to move them to the side during the day.

"Father says I must sleep close to their bed so he can keep an eye on me," Koss snickered as he spoke to his younger brother. "He doesn't know I can reach out and touch Mother's legs any time I want to. I know what Mother and Father do in bed at night. I can watch them even if it is dark."

And now Mia stood in the cramped room—her mother with her bloated belly and icy eyes glaring down at her.

"Lie down there," Nadia ordered as she pointed to the bench on which Koss slept.

"I don't want to. It's not my bed."

"I told you to lie down there." Her mother's voice was tense and explosive.

"If I lie there, Koss will be angry with me. It is his bed. He doesn't like when I step on his bed. He will be angry if I lie on it."

Mia was stalling, struggling to hold back her tears. She hoped her father would walk into the house. She hoped Nadia would realize how upset Koss would be if she lay on his bed. Maybe she could get Nadia to change her mind about hurting her, and then she could go outside to finish picking up pebbles.

"Koss won't know that you lay down on his bed. I won't tell him," Nadia snapped impatiently.

Mia knew she couldn't fight the battle. She was at Nadia's mercy. If her father were there, he wouldn't allow her to do this. If her siblings were there, they couldn't stop her. They wouldn't even try. This woman was their mother; she taught them to obey and honor thy mother, a woman who was not worthy of being a mother. Mia lay on the narrow makeshift bed.

"Now close your mouth tightly; you must not scream," she forewarned the child. "Not even a sound," she added with a threat. Nadia held her icy, vacant gaze on the child's face.

Mia fought her tears. Out of fear, she bit her lips tightly as she was told to. But she couldn't stop the tears; they spilled out from beneath her clenched eyelids and trickled down the sides of her face. She felt them soak into the pillow, dampening it on both sides of her face. *Why does she hurt me like this? Why does she do this to me?* The child asked herself the questions, not knowing any possible answers.

"Now you can go." Nadia snapped the words at the child.

Mia could no longer hold back the whimpers.

"No," Nadia hissed at her like a viper. "I told you that you are not supposed to cry."

The distressed child looked up at her mother.

"You are not supposed to tell anybody what I did to you." Nadia stood looking over her bloated belly at the small, helpless figure.

"Remember, you are not to tell anyone." She hammered the words out. "It is our secret."

Mia's body shook as she tried unsuccessfully to hold back her sobs.

"Remember that it's our secret," she repeated coldly. "Our secret."

Her face streaked with silent tears, Mia repeated the word. "Secret?"

Then she remembered: Jacob said he had a secret, and Koss said he had one too. Did Kassie and Hilda have a secret? She didn't hear Sarah say she had a secret. *Does Sarah have a secret?* she wondered. Her sobs subsided.

"Then can I tell Kassie, and Koss, and Jacob that I have a secret too?"

"No. We have to keep our secrets to ourselves."

"But they say they have secrets, and if I could tell them that I have a secret, the secret wouldn't make me feel so bad." She wondered why Koss and Jacob were so ecstatic because they had secrets. Why did this secret make her feel so bad?

"No!" Nadia's cold gaze raked over the frightened child's face. "You can't tell secrets to anyone."

⇌ ⇋

Secrets Not to Be Disclosed
Like a bright-eyed little rooster, he on the fence perched,
Crowing his heart out, an audience he searched.
"A secret! A secret!" he crowed for all to behold,
"A secret! A secret that must not be told!"
Little chick playing nearby was not yet four.
"A secret?" she chirped. "Tell me more, tell me more!"
"Momma said must not tell, must not tell,
'Cause if I do, demons will snatch me and burn me in hell."

Older cahoot standing nearby proudly boasted a secret too
I know—Momma and I have the same secret you do...
Little chick chirped, as before,
"A secret? Tell me more, tell me more."
"Cannot tell, cannot tell 'cause if we do
Demons will snatch us and burn us in hell!"

One day little rooster and cahoot were in school,
Mastering the three Rs and the Golden Rule.

"Come with me, little chick. I'll make this your day."
Led little chick to her private bower,
Imposed on chick her secret to gain a sick power.
"Must not cry—must not tell—this secret—must not cry, must not tell!
'Cause demons will snatch you and burn you in hell!"
Little chick tried not to cry.
Demons she saw—demons in her mother's eye.

Must not tell—must not cry—
I do not tell—I do not tell—
Why do the secrets make me cry out at night?
I do not tell—I do not tell—
'Cause demons will snatch me and burn me in hell!
The secrets the demons upon us imposed
Through our mother's being—
We were not to disclose.

A few days later, Mia didn't know where Nadia was, and the sleeping arrangements were changed. She was told to sleep in the shack with her sisters. Koss and Jacob slept in the granary. Her father spent the nights in the house with Nadia. What Mia didn't realize was that her mother was in labor.

Sarah and Hilda stayed home from school. They went about their duties quietly. Mia didn't know why everyone acted so grim. She liked the new arrangements. She especially liked having Sarah at home to take care of her instead of Nadia. She watched her father stop and somberly answer her sister's questions when he came out of the house. Sarah and Hilda went in and out of the house during the day as they attended to Nadia's needs. Happily, Mia played outside. She neither missed Nadia nor understood the gloomy atmosphere that surrounded the family. She was happy that her father spent so much time in the yard. Her sisters were charged with her care, not her mother. Nadia hurt her, and she did not miss her at all.

She felt happy and carefree as a child should be. Mia couldn't understand why they told her she should play quietly when she ran outside and cheerfully let her emotions loose. Mia found a new freedom, and it was blissful.

Kassie moped around, crying as if she were in mourning. "Do you think that Mother is going to die?" Her whispers repeatedly implored her sisters. Her brooding would not stop.

"Something is bothering that girl. She wants to see her mother. Maybe we should allow her to see her," her father said. "It might help her get over whatever is disturbing her. Let her go and spend a little time alone with her mother this afternoon."

After Kassie saw Nadia, her doleful state didn't seem to leave her.

"Do you feel better now that you saw Mother?" Sarah asked her.

"Mother was sleeping when I went in. I don't know if she even knew I was beside her bed. I did tell her I was sorry after she opened her eyes. Do you think she is going to die?" she asked her older sisters again.

"We don't know. What did you tell her you were sorry about?"

"I told her that I am sorry I said her stomach would burst open if she didn't quit bloating. Koss should also tell her he is sorry for saying things about her. If he doesn't, she might die."

"Does she know you said those things about her?"

"I only told her I was sorry for what I said about her. If I didn't say I was sorry, I knew she would die, but I didn't tell her what Koss said."

"Why did you say those things about her?"

"Koss was saying most of the bad things because he was angry with her. I thought it was funny when he said it, so I started saying things about her too. But he said worse things about her than I did."

"What did Koss say about her?"

"First he said she was a big, bloated cow."

"Well, that wasn't nice. What did you tell him?" Hilda pried.

"I agreed she's as big as the biggest cow we have."

"Well, you and Koss were very rude."

"It was Koss who kept saying bad things. He was angry at Mother, and he said many bad things about her."

"It wasn't nice of you or Koss to talk like that about Mother. What else did Koss say?" Sarah asked, shaking her head.

"He said Mother was bigger than the biggest cow we ever had; he said that she was as big as the bull."

Kassie stifled her voice as she spoke as if she was afraid the demons might hear her or her mother might die if she repeated Koss's words too loudly.

"Why was Koss angry with Mother?"

"I am not supposed to say because Mother says it is our secret. He was angry with her and said many things I am not supposed to repeat."

"Well, you can tell us. What did Koss say?"

Kassie's thin face was pale and drawn from crying. Like some cornered animal, she looked trapped, caught between the secret she was afraid to expose and her conscience.

"If you want me to, I will whisper it in your ear. I can't say it out loud."

Mia came up to her three elder sisters as they huddled together in a whisper.

"What did Kassie say?" She looked up at her sisters and waited for an answer.

"Nothing," Hilda spat out at the youngster.

"But I heard her; she whispered something to you."

"Go away. You are too young to know. You shouldn't be listening to us when we talk. Go sit down and leave us alone." Hilda pointed to the cot at the far end of the room. Mia obeyed.

"Don't say things like that to anybody," Hilda lashed out angrily at her younger sister. "Don't ever say that again—never, ever, to anyone. If you say it again, Mother will die."

"What did Kassie say?" Mia probed her sisters from across the room.

"Never mind what she said. I told you that you are too young to know."

"Well, I should have told Koss that if Mother was as big as a cow, he should crawl on top of a cow instead," Kassie vented.

"Don't talk about those things to anybody." Hilda's anger flared while Sarah stood back in shocked silence, her hand over her mouth. They stood as if in disbelief that Kassie would even whisper to them about their secrets—family secrets that were never to be spoken but were to stay hidden for eternity.

"Remember, if you repeat a word to anybody about what you told us now, Mother will die," Hilda warned her younger sister.

"I asked Father if Mother is sick because we said bad things about her. Father said that wasn't why."

"Did you tell Father what you and Koss said about Mother?"

"No, I didn't, but I am going to tell Koss he must also tell Mother he's sorry for what he said if he doesn't want her to die. He should tell her the bad things he told about her too." It was as if by clearing her conscience and getting Koss to apologize too, they would help Nadia through the agony of childbirth.

When Kassie left, Mia sat listening to Sarah and Hilda discussing the family problems.

"We can't do anything to stop Mother from doing things she wants to do. If she wants to do that with Koss, we can't stop her. But Kassie and Koss know they are not supposed to talk about Mother like that. It is something they shouldn't talk about at all," Sarah uttered softly.

"Do you think Father knows about Mother and Koss?"

Sarah was taken up in thought. She was silent as if she didn't hear her sister's question.

"Maybe we should tell Father what Kassie told us," Hilda continued.

"No, we can't do that," Sarah quickly replied.

"Well, if we told him, he could talk to Mother and Koss; maybe Father could stop them."

"No, Mother is sick now." Sarah brooded silently.

"Then maybe we can tell him after the baby is born, when she is well."

"No. Do you know how angry Father would be at her? We have to be quiet about it. We must never mention what Kassie said again. Never, ever. We will tell Kassie to do the same. Koss has to learn to hold his temper and his tongue."

"If we can't tell Father, we must talk to Koss ourselves. How could he think of such things at such a time?"

"Mother spoiled him rotten. He is the oldest boy, and she lets him do anything he wants to do."

"He should never do that with her again."

"Still, it is not only Koss; it is Mother too. She is his mother, and he has to listen to her. He has to do what she tells him to do."

"He could say no."

"We can't say no when she makes us do things we don't want to do."

"Nevertheless, Koss is a very disturbed person. He should never do that with her again."

"Still, with Koss, it is different; he is a boy."

"Mother is married to Father. Why would she do that with Koss?"

"I don't know, but we must not tell Father. We will talk to Koss about it ourselves."

Mia sat and listened to her two sisters talking, and although she understood that they were very distraught over a problem, she was too young to understand what it was. They vented their anger to one another and cast the family secret in stone. It would be left hidden in the closet for many decades.

Nadia's skeletons would not be disturbed as her legacy would affect many more lives. Another generation would be damaged by the family secrets.

Koss was not as remorseful as his sister Kassie was about venting their anger at Nadia. The authority he gained was not to be jeopardized. Their father knew there was a problem between his children. He didn't know what the problem was, and it was a crucial time. He could hardly take his mind off of his wife's health. After all, who would take care of his children if she died?

Mia's freedom was short lived. Her mother was in labor for three days before Yuri was born. Then Sarah went back to taking care of Hanna's children.

"Do you want to see Mother?" Hilda asked Mia shortly after Sarah left.

"No, I don't want to see her," Mia expressed in panic.

"You have a baby brother. Don't you want to see your baby brother?"

"No," she was quick to respond. "Mother is there, and she will hurt me."

"Well, you have to see Mother. She wants to see you. She is sick in bed."

Fear gripped Mia. She remembered the last time her mother tricked her and told her that she was sewing her dresses. Now they told her that her mother was in bed and wanted to see her. Mia started to sob; she thought she was being set up for abuse again.

"No, she will hurt me. Let Koss and Jacob go to see her. I don't want to see her."

"Koss and Jacob have seen her already; you are the only one who hasn't seen her."

Hilda looked at Kassie. "It is evident that Mia is afraid of Mother. Do you suppose she has been abusing her when we were at school?" she muttered to her sister.

"She is going to hurt me. I don't want to see her," the distraught child begged.

"Mother is sick; she shouldn't be aggravated. Kassie will take you to see her. Remember, if you do anything to upset her, we will give you the worst beating you've ever had," Hilda told the child. "Mother can't hurt you; she can't get out of bed."

"But I don't want to see her; she hurt me in bed." The child wailed uncontrollably and dabbed at her tears.

The child's response answered Hilda's speculations. But even though Mia feared her mother, Nadia's wishes needed to be met. Hilda helped Kassie drag the distraught child to the door. They shoved her into the room and shut the door behind her.

Mia fought to catch her balance.

The bed where her mother lay was at the far side of the room. The makeshift beds that Koss and Jacob slept on were gone. The room was dark, and the air smelled musty. Mia stared at the floor, afraid to go closer. Kassie walked into the room, pretending to come in unexpectedly, but Mia knew it was to ensure that she didn't cry or show the fear she felt.

The baby was wrapped in a blue-and-white blanket. He lay beside his mother. Mia hung back; she dared not go any closer. She noticed a box on a chair beside her mother's bed. The brightly colored box had a picture of a man on it. Mia was glad the box was there. She could focus her attention on it. She didn't have to look at the floor or at her mother; she wouldn't take her eyes off the box.

"Do you want to see the baby?"

Mia shook her head. The baby lay close to Nadia; if Mia went closer to the bed to see the baby her mother might grab her. She continued holding her gaze on the box.

Hilda walked into the room.

"Did Mia have her breakfast?" Nadia asked her.

"No, she didn't."

"Do you want some of the cereal that is in the box?"

Mia didn't answer. She didn't know what was in the box and was not hungry, but she nodded her head. She was forced into the room to see the baby and the mother she feared. She wanted to get out of there to go outside, where she felt safe from Nadia and free to be a child.

"Take the box and give her some cereal." Nadia looked at Hilda as she spoke.

Hilda picked up the box and took Mia by the hand. Mia was happy to leave the gloom and fear she felt in Nadia's presence. She feared that the chance to be happy and carefree might come to an end.

"Can I play outside?"

"No, you can't play outside until you have had some cereal. Sit and wait until it is ready."

Mia didn't want any cereal, but she knew she must sit and wait as she was told. A big stockpot sat steaming on the stove. When it was at a rolling boil, Hilda emptied the box into it and watched over it.

While Mia waited, Koss came in and set his pudgy body in his father's chair beside the table, waiting to be served. He already had his breakfast, yet he still felt he should be the first to taste the new batch of cereal. He didn't want to lose the status in the family given to him by Nadia.

"There is a lot for everyone," Hilda announced. "I put lots of water in the pot, but I'll give some to Mia first because she didn't have her breakfast." She boiled the flakes of cereal for a long time, waiting for it to puff up and fill the pot.

"Well, they say a watched pot never boils, you know," Kassie said, looking into the pot.

"It is boiling, but what happened to the cereal?" Hilda was bewildered.

Koss looked into the pot. His ruddy face burst into anger. "There is no cereal left in the pot for me. You ate all of it! I am going to tell Mother you ate the cereal and just left water and an empty box for me. You are insulting me and making a fool of me!" He screeched out his annoyance.

"Remember, Mother said you were not supposed to laugh at or make a fool of me because I am the eldest boy. Your punishment will be twice as severe because I am going to tell Mother to punish you for two things."

"Two things?" Hilda looked at him in annoyance.

"Yes. For not leaving any cereal for me and for making a fool of me by lying about it." Like an outraged monarch, he shrieked at his subjects as if he were ready to behead them for provoking him.

"But we didn't eat the cereal. It is all in the pot."

His sisters defended themselves. "Mother is sick. You are not supposed to upset her."

"You are lying, and you can't stop me. I am going to tell Mother what you did. I didn't even have a taste of it because you ate all of it!" He continued screeching as he slammed the door and walked out.

Father came into the house. "What is wrong with Koss? What is he raving about now? Why did he go screaming out of the house? Your mother is resting. She shouldn't be disturbed."

"He is angry because he thinks we ate the cereal. We didn't eat any of it. It is still boiling in the pot on the stove," Hilda explained. "But there is something very wrong with it; it doesn't take rolled oats to cook as long as it is taking this cereal."

It was then that they learned that Hilda had boiled the dry cereal. Corn Flakes were meant to be eaten as a cold cereal with milk. The catastrophic results of her mistake were evident in the big pot sitting on the stove.

Mia was lifted to take in the unappetizing view of the shriveled traces of flakes floating in the murky water.

"Are you hungry?" her father asked her.

Mia shook her head. She wasn't hungry; she only wanted to play outside.

CHAPTER FIVE

Mia was in the house with her mother and Yuri, taking a rest. Kassie came running into the house to tell her mother that Sarah was sick. Nadia was extremely protective of her eldest daughter, so she rushed out of the house to be at her side. Sarah was slouched beside a tree some distance from the house. Father had just left for the far orchard, so they sent someone to get him. Mia followed her mother outside.

"Get back into the house and have your nap. I don't need anyone under my feet," Nadia snapped at the little girl. Mia turned and walked back into the house. From her spot on the bed, she could hear shrill voices drifting into the room.

She heard her father's irritated voice as he was trying to calm her mother and siblings. Their voices were closer to the house now.

"I want everyone to be quiet; the neighbors will hear us, and they will wonder what is happening here." Although Mia could hear that her father sounded angry, he spoke in a muted voice.

"Nadia, I want you to come into the house this instant. We have to talk privately," Mia heard him repeat several times.

When they finally they came in, they left the older siblings, including Sarah, outside.

Why didn't they bring Sarah into the house if she is ill? The loud voices of her siblings could still be heard outside. Koss sounded as if he was the authority; he was trying to drown out everyone else with his loud, know-it-all voice.

"Why did you let him do it?" Koss kept repeating. "You should have asked me to do it, and Jacob could have done it too. We both could have done it."

Their father was immediately angered. "What is wrong with that boy? What is he talking about? I told them to be quiet outside. Go and tell him to quit his ranting before the neighbors hear him."

Nadia went outside, and things were soon quiet. Mia's eyes were heavy, but she still was not asleep. When her mother returned to the house, she went to where the child lay and looked at her.

"She is not sleeping." Nadia hissed her annoyance under her breath. "She should go outside so we can talk."

"Are you tired?" her father asked.

Mia was tired, and she didn't like the sound of irate voices coming from outside. It frightened her to hear her siblings squabble; she felt safe in bed, so she nodded her head.

"No," her father said as he looked at Mia. "Let her stay in bed. She will fall asleep soon. If we send her outside, she will hear them talking and wonder what is going on. It is best if she stays here."

"I will not talk to you about Sarah while there is someone else in the room with us." Nadia's sharp whisper cut through the room.

"You will talk to me, and you will tell me what I want to know." Her father turned irritably toward Nadia. "So tell me what is so special about your Sarah? Why can't you talk about her in front of two sleeping children? Do you think they will contaminate her if they are in the same room when you talk about her? It is more likely they will be contaminated by what she has done."

"I told you I will not talk to you if the brat is not sleeping," Nadia repeated stubbornly. "I never tell anyone, not even my sister Kathryn, if Sarah does anything wrong, and I will not talk to you in front of the children now."

"Do you want me to take the baby and put him outside on the doorstep too?" her husband spat at Nadia. His voice was low, but he could not control his anger as he lashed out at his wife. "Look what your special Sarah has done now. When did you find out she was pregnant, and why didn't you tell me?"

"I didn't know she's pregnant!" Nadia flung the words at her husband.

Mia could not sleep with her parents feuding. Lying on the bed, she kept her eyes shut, pretending to be asleep. Nadia would be angry with her if she knew she wasn't sleeping.

"Didn't you think of asking her why she was sick? You have always treated her as if she is superior to the other children. Couldn't you talk to your daughter? Where did you find her?"

"She was under one of the apple trees."

"What was she doing under the tree?"

"What do you think she was doing? She was sick," Nadia snapped at her husband.

"Sick? How was she sick?"

Nadia sputtered but didn't answer.

"Well, what was she doing when you saw her? Did you find her lying down under the tree? Tell me how she was sick." He was losing his patience.

"No, she was sick, and she was holding on to the tree trunk." Nadia was irritated by the questions.

"Well, whose baby is it?"

Nadia's need to protect Sarah made her lash out in denial. "It isn't anyone's baby!"

Mia heard her father's voice rise. "Someone is the father of that baby; she did not get pregnant by herself."

"I don't know who the father is."

"Didn't she tell you?" He was appalled by her answer. "Doesn't she know who the father is?" He sat in stunned silence for a few moments. "If she doesn't know who the father is, were there two boys?"

Nadia didn't answer.

"Were there five boys? Were there six boys? Tell me how many there were!" He was angered, and although he dreaded what it might be, he waited for his wife's answer.

Nadia exploded angrily. "How could you say a thing like that about Sarah?"

"Then if there was only one boy, why won't you tell me who it is?"

After a moment of silence, she replied, "It's the Stephensons' boy."

"Baily Stephenson?" her husband asked in disbelief. "He is only a child."

"He is just about as old as Sarah," Nadia muttered defensively.

"Where did it happen? They only see each other in school. Is that where it happened? Did it happen in school?" His voice increased in anger. "If it did, I'm going to talk to the teacher and have that boy expelled."

"No, you can't do that. I don't want anyone to know about the baby!" Nadia's voice was hysterical. "They could get married."

"Married? Married?" her husband repeated in disbelief. "They are children; Sarah is only fourteen years old!"

"She will be fifteen when the baby is born. I don't want anyone to know what Sarah did. I don't want anyone to know about the baby!"

"You don't want people to know?" her husband burst out furiously. "Don't you realize people will know she was pregnant before she got married when the baby is born? Did you lose your senses?

Do you think other people can't count months like you and your sisters do?"

"They could get married and move away where no one knows them." Nadia spoke rashly; her face flushed as she babbled uncontrollably.

"How could you ever survive without seeing your precious daughter every minute of the day?" He spat the words at his wife in rage.

"Then they could get married right away, and we can say the baby came prematurely."

"Lie, just like you did?" He paused and held his breath for an instant. It was as if he didn't intend to stray from the current subject. "Don't you think that alone will make people talk—thirteen- and fourteen-year-old children getting married so suddenly?" He paused again before adding, "Maybe we should talk to his parents first. Maybe it would be better if they wait a month before they marry. It will give the neighbors a chance to get used to the idea while we prepare things."

"We can't wait a month." Nadia's voice was agitated. "If they get married right now, the neighbors might believe the baby came three months prematurely. Babies survive at that stage, but if they wait another month, it will be harder to convince them. People will gossip; I don't want them to gossip about Sarah."

Mia peeked out from her spot on the bed. She could see her father as he sat in silent thought. When he spoke, he sounded drained.

"Before we discuss this further, I want you to ask Sarah where it happened. I want to know if it happened in school. If it did, I will talk to the teacher."

"No, you can't talk to their teacher. I will not let you humiliate the children! If you talk to their teacher and have Baily expelled, everyone in school will know about Sarah. How can she ever hold her head up around her friends and neighbors again?" Nadia muffled her sniffles as she spoke.

"If you don't ask her, I will walk out of here and go straight to the school," her husband threatened. "I will give you fifteen minutes. If you're not back here with an answer, I will walk out that front door, and there will be no turning back."

Mia could hear Sarah's and Hilda's voices as her mother opened the back door from the kitchen and went outside.

The baby, Yuri, lay sleeping on the bed beside her. Mia opened her eyes. Her father was sitting, unmoving, with his hands on his knees, his head bent forward in deep thought. Life stood silently still except for the ticking of the clock. Mia closed her eyes again and waited.

Why wasn't her mother coming back? She could hear her father moving restlessly in his chair. Opening her eyes, she peered at him again. He glanced nervously from the clock to the door. Mia could feel her father's anxiety. *Why doesn't she hurry? Why doesn't she come back before Father loses his patience?* Her head felt like an overinflated balloon. She wanted to cry. Instead, she sat up in bed, wanting him to know she was awake. She hoped her father would send her out to tell Mother he was waiting and her time was up. She didn't want her father to stand up because if he did, he might walk out the front door as he threatened to. He would go to the school and talk to the teacher.

Her face was burning up, and her head was throbbing; it felt like it would burst. She wanted everything to be all right.

As she watched her father, the expression on his face suddenly changed. She also heard footsteps coming toward the house. She lay down and closed her eyes again. The door opened, and he asked, "What took you so long?"

"We had other things to talk about." Nadia sounded more relaxed now.

"I told you to find out what I wanted to know. What other things are there to talk about?"

"Hilda and Sarah wanted to talk about who Sarah would pick for her bridesmaids and the color of the dresses they would wear."

Her husband looked at his wife in disbelief.

Nadia's tears began. "Well, you said they should get married in a month, so we have to prepare things. We thought we should start wedding plans as soon as possible."

"What? You spoke of bridesmaids and the color of their dresses?" Her husband gasped. "She is fourteen years old, she is pregnant, and you talked to her about bridesmaids and dresses?"

"No, we talked about…other things too." Nadia's words faltered.

"Did you ask her what I told you to ask?"

"Yes."

"What did she say?"

"She said it didn't happen in school. It happened at his brother's house."

"At his brother's house? When?"

"When she went to babysit Hanna's children."

Mia's father trusted Hanna; she was Baily's sister-in-law. He was well acquainted with her parents and knew Hanna since she was a child. After losing two children, one to what was possibly crib death, Hanna was a very cautious mother. Sarah was allowed to keep watch over her children while she was doing things about the house or to watch the children while Hanna was in the yard, working in her garden.

"Where was Hanna when this happened?" Mia could tell her father was irate.

"She was in the orchard helping her husband."

"But Sarah is only supposed to take care of the children while Hanna is in the house or near the house. Why didn't you tell me she was being left alone with the children while Hanna helped her husband? What if something happened to a child while Sarah was alone with them?"

Nadia was silent. She knew her husband set specific rules about his eldest daughter's babysitting, but she was not telling him everything she knew.

"Sarah knew we only allowed her to take care of the children when Hanna was close by. She didn't even ask permission. Tell her to come in. I am going to have a talk with her."

"No, I will not let you talk to her. You will only upset her more," Nadia insisted. "You can tell me what you have to say, and I will speak to Sarah about it."

"No, I want to talk to Sarah myself. I need her to tell me why she didn't ask for permission."

The statement made Nadia uncomfortable. "She did get permission," she finally admitted. She paused and nervously blinked her bulging eyes before she said, "She asked me."

"What?" The response was abrupt. He paused as if in disbelief. "She asked you, and you said yes?"

Nadia fidgeted as she tried to devise quick lies to support her position.

"Why didn't she ask me?"

"Because she knew that you wouldn't allow her to, and—"

"Did Sarah tell that boy that she would be babysitting alone and arrange with him to come and see her?" her husband interrupted.

"No, she didn't." Nadia's reply was instant, her voice filled with irritation. Mia could tell her mother was not telling the truth.

"Well, how did he know she would be babysitting that day?" her father asked.

"Maybe he saw her when she passed their house on her way to Hanna's."

"Did she tell you if she saw or spoke to him on the way to Hanna's house?"

"No, she didn't speak to him." Nadia's answer was abrupt.

"How do you know she didn't speak to him?"

"Because she would have told me if she did."

"Then how did he know she was there?"

"He might have seen her walk down the road when she passed their orchard in the morning; you know their orchard is right beside the road. Or maybe he saw her walk down the road as he looked out the window. Yes, you know Sarah is a very pretty girl; everybody notices her, especially the boys."

Her husband was annoyed. He, too, knew he wasn't getting the truth from his wife.

"What about Hanna's children? Where were they when those two were carrying on?"

"She said the children were sleeping." Nadia was tiring of her husband's questions. She didn't like getting caught in her own web.

Everyone knew that Mia's father set strict rules, and he didn't want Sarah being left alone with the children. He felt Hanna should have an adult taking care of the children in case a problem arose that Sarah could not handle.

Mia remembered the day Sarah came home and was excited about babysitting while Hanna was helping her husband. Hilda and Kassie were there too.

"But Father doesn't want her left alone with the children," they reminded each other.

"I won't be alone. Baily offered to help me with them," Sarah pleaded.

"It will be OK, Sarah." Nadia smiled. "But it must be kept secret. Nobody should tell Father that Baily will be with you when you are babysitting Hanna's children," she added.

Mia sat and listened as Hilda and Kassie shared Sarah's excitement.

"Sarah is having her first date with Baily," they chanted jubilantly.

Mia couldn't understand their excitement. "What is a date?" she asked.

"That is when two people who like each other are alone," Kassie replied.

Mia thought that a date sounded boring, and she felt sorry for her eldest sister. Sarah would be stuck alone with a boy on her date. Mia wondered if she could do anything to help. She remembered seeing Baily at a distance once at a school picnic. Mia was excited because she was allowed to attend the picnic with her sisters. Nadia told Hilda and Kassie to take her to the picnic while she spent some time alone with Sarah. Mia could not understand why her mother wouldn't let her eldest sister go to the picnic with them.

"Why does Mother want to spend time with Sarah? Why can't Sarah come to the picnic with us now? I want to wait for Sarah."

Hilda and Kassie whispered to each other; they soon became irate at Mia's questions. Mia learned not to ask questions. Sometimes asking questions only got her a backhanded slap.

When they arrived at the school yard, rows of benches were set up for the visitors. Mia was told to sit and wait on one of the benches. She looked at all the people with interest, but they were strangers.

A pretty little dark-haired girl walked into the school yard. Her mother gently held her hand. Mia smiled at her shyly and hoped they would sit on the benches, too, so she could talk to the pretty girl. Hilda and Kassie returned to the bench, giggling and whispering.

"Watch Baily," Hilda said. "He is waiting for Sarah. Baily likes Sarah."

Then they giggled again. Kassie gushed dreamily, "He spoke to me."

"Baily spoke to you?" Hilda sputtered at her. "Why didn't he speak to me? I am older than you are. He should have spoken to me. What did he say?"

"He asked me if Sarah was coming."

"Oh?" Hilda replied. "Is that all he asked?"

The boy, Baily, looked scrawny and gangly. His hair had many cowlicks, making it look unkempt. His overalls barely came to his ankles, and bony knees poked through the holes in his pants. *He doesn't even look nice,* Mia thought. She wondered why Sarah liked him and what made Hilda and Kassie giggle foolishly and act silly when they talked about him.

"Sarah is lucky," she heard them say. "Sarah is tall. Baily is younger than Sarah, but he is the tallest boy in school. His teeth stick out, and he looks funny because his chin is flat. Still, he looks better than his brother, Davis. Davis has no chin at all." Mia listened to her sisters as they spoke. Each poke in fun was punctuated with giggles.

"Baily's pants have holes in them."

"At least he wears shoes." They nodded in agreement.

Sarah was late in arriving. When she came, she didn't walk into the school yard off the road. She walked through the trees. Mia wondered why, but she did not say anything.

Mia watched as Baily waited for Sarah with four fingers stuck in his pockets, his thumbs sticking out, just like Koss did when he wanted to look impressive. Baily went to meet Sarah, and they disappeared in the crowd.

Later, Mia sat consumed in confusion. *Hilda and Kassie said Sarah was going to have a date with that drab boy, Baily. A date must be a party,* the child thought. *Why doesn't Sarah ask Laverne Wilson, the girl from the store, to go on her date? The last time Laverne came to see Sarah, she wore such a bright yellow dress with big red flowers. Laverne's dress would brighten up anyone's drab date. It would be more fun to spend the afternoon with Laverne. Why would Sarah want a date with a boy who wears ripped coveralls, has messy hair, and has practically no chin?*

Mia couldn't hold back her curiosity, she spent the afternoon asking questions of Hilda and Kassie.

"But it cannot be fun if there are only two people on her date. Can I go with Sarah too? Why can't more people go on her date when she is babysitting?" Hilda and Kassie were not pleased with Mia's input. Mia heard them talking to each other.

"How did the brat find out about Sarah's date?" Hilda asked Kassie.

Kassie did not admit to being the one who let Mia in on the secret.

"Who told the brat about Sarah's date?"

"Well, I guess it isn't safe to say anything in front of the brat anymore."

"She asks too many questions."

"Mother is going to be irritated with us when the brat spills the beans."

"When Father finds out that Mother would even think of allowing Sarah to babysit with Baily, he will be furious with her."

"I would like to have a date. When do you think Mother will allow us to have dates?" Kassie asked Hilda.

"Who would you like to have a date with?" Hilda asked Kassie. Then she giggled. "I bet it's Alden."

Kassie hung her head and didn't speak.

"Well, it isn't Igor, his dimwit brother, is it?"

Of the two brothers, Alden was more intelligent. Igor was much older than his brother; however, his IQ did not qualify him to take up space in school. He had strabismus eyes. His peers and the community ridiculed him. Igor fancied Kassie. Sometimes he gave her a hankering look. She became angry if anyone teased her about Igor giving her that look.

"Well, if the brat spills the beans and Father finds out about Sarah's date with Baily, he will not allow you to have a date with Alden. Mother would allow us to have dates, but Father won't."

"Maybe by the time Father gets home, the brat will forget about it."

"Are you kidding? We are going to have to do something to make her want to forget."

Mia stood listening to her sisters. Her eyes widened with fear. Why were they angry? She couldn't help asking questions.

"Aren't you anxious to have a date with Josh?" Kassie asked Hilda.

Although Josh was a widower and was much older than Hilda, he was her secret admirer. He was friends with Alden and Igor. Josh did not seem to be very intelligent either, but he had a more pleasant appearance than his two friends.

"I will tell you a secret, but first you have to get the brat out of here. I don't want to say anything in front of her."

"Scat," Kassie demanded, pointing to the door.

Mia went outside and stood beside the door. She could still hear her sisters talking. Although she couldn't understand the world of the grownups, their conversation and actions captivated her. It gave her thoughts to fill her lonely days. *Why do grownups have so many secrets? Grownups don't tell the truth. Don't they fear the demons?* She stood beside the house and listened to their conversation for a short time. Then she silently slithered her way back into the house and hid behind a box. There, she could sit unnoticed while she eavesdropped.

"What makes you think I don't have dates with Josh?" Hilda asked smugly.

"You've had dates with Josh? When?" Kassie was skeptical. "I didn't hear you ask Mother if you could have dates with him."

"Who said I have to ask Mother?" Hilda mocked. "Just because Sarah is older than I am doesn't mean she can have a date with her boyfriend before I have one with mine."

"When did you have a date with Josh?" Kassie insisted.

"Do you remember when I said I went to Belcourt to see Laverne, and Father was so angry because it was very late when I got home? Well, I didn't go to see Laverne. I went to meet Josh in the barn at the school yard. He said he wouldn't tell anyone. We fell asleep, and that is why I came home so late."

While her sisters were absorbed in their conversation, Mia made herself comfortable. *Why would Hilda fall asleep in the barn in the school yard?* she wondered.

"Josh is such a gentleman. He cleaned the straw off my clothes. He said he didn't want Father to catch me lying." Mia listened as Hilda rattled on. "Josh wanted Father to believe I was visiting Laverne."

The sisters' conversation went silent. Although the spice of it was over, it didn't make sense to the child. *Why don't grownups tell the truth?* She recalled her mother's words: "If you don't tell the truth, the demons will know you're lying, and they'll take you and burn you in hell." Still, her mother lied, and her older siblings lied too. Weren't they afraid of burning in hell? Mia decided she would never lie, even when she became grown up like her sisters.

Mia stretched her cramped legs and sat up. That's when her sisters noticed her.

"How long has the brat been sitting there? Did she hear what I said?" Hilda spewed to Kassie.

"No, she must have just sneaked in now. Don't worry. She's too young to understand the things we talk about anyway. She's so dumb. That's why she asks us so many questions."

Hilda called Mia over to where they stood. "Did you hear what I told Kassie?" She was furious.

Mia shook her head.

"Good. You're lucky you didn't. Remember, you aren't supposed to say anything about Sarah's date to anyone!" Hilda stood menacingly over the child. "Do you understand what I am saying?"

"Yes." Mia trembled as she nodded.

She knew when Hilda said something and added that extra "do you understand what I am saying?" to it that it meant she was going to give her some extra excruciating punishment. Just standing there looking up at Hilda put enough fear in the child to keep her from talking for a long time.

"If you ask another question, or if Father finds out that Sarah has a date, do you know what I will do to you?"

Mia shook her head and closed her eyes, awaiting the sting of the slap.

Hilda added to the threat as she grabbed the child. "Do you know what else I will do to you?"

Sticking her fingers into each side of her mouth, she pulled at the sides of Mia's mouth until she cried in pain.

"I will rip your mouth from ear to ear just like Mother does. And Kassie will do the same."

She called Kassie over and told her to give Mia the same treatment she just gave her.

"Now tell me who hurt your mouth harder, Kassie or me?" Hilda's eyes blazed as she derided the frightened child.

Mia's mouth felt swollen and sore.

"You," she assured Hilda. She couldn't bring herself to tell Hilda that Kassie's fingers stunk of urine and other indescribable body odors. The stench of Kassie's unclean hands made her gag, and she preferred to have Hilda's fingers in her mouth.

CHAPTER SIX

As Mia lay in bed reflecting on Sarah's date and on Hilda's and Kassie's past conversation, her father's voice brought her back to reality. "I want to talk to Sarah. Tell her to come in. I want to talk to her right now...privately!"

"No, you can't talk to her; she has probably gone by now," Nadia replied.

"Gone?" Her husband sounded surprised. "Where did she go?"

Nadia hesitated before she answered. "Hilda was going to help her. First they were going to decide the color of the bridesmaids dresses. Then they were going to go and talk to the girls she picked for her bridesmaids. You know Hilda is a very smart girl; she suggested that Sarah have pink, yellow, or blue dresses for the bridesmaids because green would not look good for a summer wedding. She said the bridesmaids should wear a contrasting color."

Mia listened to Nadia. Her mother never had anything positive to say about Hilda. Why now? Was it because Hilda was her husband's favorite daughter, and she wanted to say something nice about her to win him over?

"What?" Her husband's face turned red with rage. "What is wrong with you, woman? Sarah is only fourteen years old, and she is pregnant! How old is that boy? He is much younger. We don't even know if there is going to be a marriage, and you are telling them to pick bridesmaids and dresses already?"

"Well, you told me they should get married as soon as possible," Nadia shrieked at her husband.

Mia could not pretend to be asleep any longer. Her parents were raging and screaming at each other, not caring if the whole neighborhood heard them. How could she possibly sleep? She sat up and cringed in fear as she listened to Nadia shrieking at her father. During her murderous rage, Nadia noticed her observing them. She turned her anger on the child.

"Look at her. She isn't sleeping!" The wild voice vibrated throughout the room. She lunged at the child. With one maniacal strike, she cuffed Mia off the bed and knocked her to the floor.

"She heard us. I'll have none of this. She heard us talking about Sarah. Get me a knife. I will kill her!"

The child shrank in fear as Nadia's hands reached for her. Her paralyzing scream reverberated throughout the room. Nadia's hands closed around Mia's throat and cut off her scream. Mia got a glimpse of her father rushing toward them. He wrestled his wife's hands from the child's neck.

"What is wrong with you? You are insane," he screamed. "Leave Mia alone! She is a child. She hasn't done anything to harm you."

"She heard us talking about Sarah."

Mia teetered on the edge of darkness. She felt herself shrink until she was no more than a speck on the floor as she gave in to the nothingness. When she resurfaced, she found herself lying on the floor groggily, unable to remember how she got there. She stirred and reached out, needing someone to comfort her. Images were swaying at her from across the room.

Nadia was thrashing around like a mad woman, trying to escape her husband's grip. Nadia's maniacal shriek continued; it reeled and circled throughout the room. Mia wanted to disappear again. Her throat hurt; she sputtered, choked, and closed her eyes.

Her husband bellowed, "You are insane! What did Mia do to you? What is wrong with you?"

"She heard us talking about Sarah. She heard us!"

Mia opened her eyes again. Across the room, her father held Nadia down. The woman's face was bathed in sweat, and her eyes blazed in madness. As Mia struggled to sit up, she whimpered. She wanted to reach out to someone, but there was no one there to help her.

When Nadia saw the child sit up, she thrashed wildly to break away from her husband's grasp. Recalling the horrific attack, Mia shrank back.

"Look at her; she is sitting up. She's watching us. Let me go. I want to get a knife. I want to kill her!"

Shaking uncontrollably, Mia knew that if Nadia had a knife, she would not only sever her tongue as she had often threatened, but she would stick the knife in her and slice her in half like her father did when he strung up an animal after he slaughtered it.

She sat shakily, still reeling from the attack. She wanted to disappear. She wanted to get up and run out the door. She would have to go past her parents, and she knew her mother would just reach out and grab her before she got to the door. She looked for a place to hide. The wood box. No, her mother would see her there. She would just reach into it and pull her out. The cupboard. It was close; if she could bring herself to move, she might try to hide there.

Mia watched her father as he continue to wrestle her mother, holding her down until she turned her anger at him. Mia sat on the floor shaking uncontrollably; she was too frightened to cry.

Nadia struck wildly at her husband and angrily accused him of not caring what happened to Sarah or the bridesmaids or the dresses they would be wearing.

When Nadia finally stopped thrashing her arms and screaming, her husband released his hold on her. She lay on the floor, sputtering and crying, her face crimson as if she was choking. She bellowed in rage and put on a wild, kicking, wailing tantrum. Her husband watched her, clenching and unclenching his fists. When the tantrum was over, Nadia froze into silence and refused to talk or answer any of his questions.

"Tell me where Sarah and Hilda went," he appealed to her cautiously. Nadia did not reply.

"Then tell me which girls she picked for her bridesmaids." Her father's voice had eased. He pleaded with his wife as he would have pleaded with a child. "Is that where they went? Tell me. We have to stop them before they talk to anyone. You said you didn't want anyone to know about Sarah's condition. You know what Hilda and Kassie are like. If anyone asks them why Sarah wants to get married when she is so young, they will blurt the truth for everybody to know." He continued to plead as he tried to coax his wife to talk.

Nadia lay on the floor, unresponsive to her husband's questions.

"Well, then, tell me what color the bridesmaids dresses will be," he urged her.

The subject of the bridesmaids dresses jolted Nadia back to reality. She finally muttered, "She wants her bridesmaids to wear pink or yellow or blue dresses." Her voice was distant and held no emotion.

Mia was tense, fearing her mother might spring up and lunge at her again. Nadia continued to lie on the floor, unmoving. Her face was slimy with perspiration, and her unblinking eyes were cold and vacant.

"Where did they go? Who are the girls they are going to talk to?"

Nadia stirred as she spoke. "Sarah said she wanted three bridesmaids—Baily's sister, Laverne, and Hilda." Nadia's voice was more attentive now. Mia watched as her huge bulk stirred into a sitting position on the floor.

"Three? Isn't one enough for her?" The words seemed to slip out unintentionally, but he brought his temper under control. Mia watched her father as he turned toward the door.

Fearing another eruption of her mother's murderous rage, Mia raced to the door, reaching it as her father opened it. She felt safe at his side.

Sarah was sitting beside the house. She looked so unhappy. Her father was relieved to see her there.

"Where is Hilda?" He waited for an answer.

"She's gone to Belcourt."

"Belcourt? Why did she go there?"

"She said she would talk to Laverne first. She said she would go to the Stephensons' place with me when she got back."

Hilda was a decisive person. She liked taking the reins and handling things on her own. Her father ran toward the road. Mia stayed close to his heels. Hilda was two-thirds of the way to Belcourt.

"I can run fast," Mia volunteered. "I can get Hilda back."

"No, I am afraid you can't; she is too close to the store," her father said. "Hilda!" he summoned loudly.

Hilda turned to see her father's signal to return. She walked with their father toward the house, Mia trailing behind them. Nadia sat beside the house, calming Sarah, who cried quietly in her arms. Nadia's anger was directed at her husband.

"See what you've done?" she hissed, her eyes blazing. "Sarah heard everything you said. Now she does not know what she wants to do, and it is your fault."

"We will talk about this calmly before we decide what to do. We cannot jump into things without reasoning. In the meantime, I don't want anyone in this family talking about Sarah's condition or about weddings." Her father spoke quietly, but his voice was firm. He stood for a moment before he turned and walked toward the plot that he had been working on earlier in the day. He looked as if he wanted to be left alone.

Everything was quiet and somber for the rest of the day. Mia tried to stay out of her mother's range, fearing that the rage Nadia displayed toward her earlier might be rekindled.

As evening approached, Jacob was sent to call his father for dinner. Upon his return, he announced, "Father said we should not expect him before dark. He said he has to do something first."

When her father returned, Mia was sitting beside the house. He approached from the direction of the Stephensons' place, a short distance down the road. Kassie and Koss came running, each wanting to be the first to announce his return. When he walked into the yard, his tall, lean figure was recognizable in the dusk, but Mia could not see his face. He stood quietly under the trees as if a stranger waiting to be invited in. Her mother's voice broke the silence from somewhere nearby.

"Did you talk to them?"

"Yes," he answered. "Let's go into the house, where we can talk quietly."

Sarah and Hilda were in the bedroom, where Kassie joined them. Mia knew they didn't want her with them, so she stayed outside. She didn't know where Koss and Jacob were. She sat alone for a few minutes. The dark shadows were creeping in around her; she hated the dark. She feared it and tried to be brave as she sat alone. Finally, she crept into the house and sat on the floor, against the wall, where she would not be noticed. Nadia was sitting and listening to her husband.

"His father agreed they are much too young to get married, especially Baily. He will only be thirteen on his next birthday. If he were eighteen years old or at least seventeen—" He paused. "His parents said they don't have any objection if they want to get married when they are older." He spoke haltingly before he continued. "We decided it wouldn't be wise for them to see each other alone again. I will talk to Hanna. Sarah will no longer be allowed to help her with the children."

Standing up, her mother spoke quietly. "I will talk to Sarah."

Nadia walked into the bedroom, where Mia's older sisters were waiting.

For the child, time was a span that took place between one incident and another. Mia could not indicate time as a day passing or a week passing, but time passed. She did not hear any more talk of marriage or Sarah's condition. Sarah was sick a lot. She did not come out of the bedroom; she spent the mornings and most of the days in bed. Hilda took care of her. Nadia always pampered Sarah, who had been a premature baby; she kept bringing it to everyone's attention that her eldest daughter was to be treated delicately, although she was close to being six feet tall.

"She only survived her birth because of the special attention I gave her." The family grew up with Nadia's constant gnawing and nattering. "If it wasn't for the shoe box I kept her in and the oven of the cast-iron stove, she wouldn't have survived but a few short hours."

When her father overheard Nadia's nattering, Mia couldn't help but notice the look of disgust he gave his wife before he skulked out of the house.

"How big was Sarah when she got born?" Mia whispered to Hilda.

"Ask Mother how big she was," Hilda said.

Nadia heard the child's question and started to embellish on the well-rehearsed account of her eldest daughter's birth.

"She was not even the size of the palm of my hand," Nadia retorted.

Mia opened her hand and looked at the size of it.

"The size of a newborn kitten," Nadia added.

Later, Hilda unleashed her pent-up feelings. "Did you see the picture Mother keeps on the dresser in her bedroom?"

"The picture of the baby?"

"Yes. That is a picture of Sarah."

Mia often wondered who the huge butterball was sitting in the studio chair.

"How old was Sarah in that picture?" Mia asked.

"She was six months old," Hilda muttered.

"Oh." Mia mused over her eldest sister's baby picture. She opened her hand and studied it again. A kitten would overlap the palm of her hand. The baby in the picture was a far cry from being the size of a newborn kitten; at six months of age, she looked huge.

"Sarah sure grew big fast," the child muttered to herself.

Mia had never seen Sarah being sick before, but now her sister was very sick. Mia wasn't allowed to go into the bedroom. She could see her sister looking ghostly pale as she watched her through the doorway. A guarded atmosphere enveloped the house. Everybody was very quiet and somber. Her parents were silent. They didn't speak when the older children were around.

"I wonder what Mother and Father are going to do about Sarah?" Mia overheard Kassie and Hilda as they spoke.

"Do you think maybe it is not Baily's fault that Sarah is…you know?" Kassie's voice faltered as she spoke. "You know, there were those other two boys. Remember the time when Father was angry with Mother because she told Sarah to put on her new dress when she heard somebody in the school yard? She sent Sarah there to show off because she thought she looked pretty and wanted others to see her. Those two boys there, they did the same thing to Sarah."

"No, that was before; it is too long ago. You have to understand it couldn't have happened that long ago because Sarah is only… you know. It happened just…well, about three months ago."

"Well, if Sarah said it was those boys, maybe one of them would marry her. They are older than Baily."

"No, Mother couldn't fool anyone anymore. Now Father knows it was Baily," Hilda answered. "If Mother had thought of telling Father it was somebody older sooner…well, it is too late now. Father knows the truth. Sarah would have told Father the truth anyway."

"I wonder what Mother and Father are going to do?" Kassie muttered.

"I don't know. Sometimes when I hear their voices, I walk into the room to hear what they are saying. They stop talking when they see me."

"Yes, they do the same thing when I walk into the room."

One time when Hilda and Kassie saw their father coming toward the house, they devised a plan.

"Look, here comes Father now. Let's send Mia into the kitchen to eavesdrop on them."

Mia was a timid child. She feared her mother and didn't like the pressure her sisters put on her. The memory of Nadia attacking her and screaming for a knife was still fresh in the child's mind. It petrified her.

"I don't want to go into the kitchen to listen to them talk. Mother will be angry with me, and she will hurt me again." Mia trembled at the thought of her mother's uncontrolled fits of rage.

"She will not hurt you. Father will be there. Everyone has to do their share if they want Sarah to get well again." Hilda spoke with the authority of a person in charge. "I am the one who takes care of her during her bouts of morning sickness, and it is not pleasant."

Mia watched her sister scowl repulsively when she spoke.

"Why doesn't Mother take care of Sarah when she is sick?" Kassie wondered.

"She can't stand the sight of Sarah turning green with puke—that is why. She only wants to pamper and cuddle her."

"Well, it's my job to sit with Sarah and keep her company during the day," Kassie added defensively.

"Can I trade places with Kassie? I will sit and talk with Sarah," Mia volunteered. She missed her eldest sister. "Kassie can listen to what Mother and Father say."

"No, everybody has to help. If you want Sarah to get better, you have to listen in on Mother and Father. That will be your job. You have to tell us every gesture made and every word spoken between them. You have to remember everything, even if you don't understand what they are talking about."

"I want Kassie to listen to what Mother and Father say."

"No, Kassie is too big. Mother and Father will notice her when she goes into the room. You are small, so they won't even know that you are in the room with them."

Hilda and Kassie convinced Mia that she had a duty to fulfill in order for Sarah to get better.

Out of obligation to her eldest sister, Mia hesitantly did as she was told. She was too young to know that her parents were too preoccupied to notice her when she was in the room; she believed they didn't see her because she was somehow making herself invisible. This was a puzzle to the child, and she gathered the courage to talk to her sisters about it.

"Can I make myself invisible when I walk into a room?" she quietly asked Hilda.

"Why do you ask that?"

Mia didn't want Hilda to get angry at her asking too many questions. She watched the frown on her sister's face before continuing.

"'Cause I don't think Mother and Father can see me when I am in the room," she whispered.

"How do you think you are making yourself invisible?"

"By just wishing they can't see me and wishing I was invisible."

"Yes, it is possible," Hilda assured her little sister, her face belying her actual amusement. "Well, what did Mother and Father say?"

"I don't know. I don't think they said anything. Well, maybe they did, but I forgot."

"Well," Hilda warned her, "you have to be more mindful if you want Sarah to get better."

The next time they sent Mia to listen in on her parents, her sisters cross-examined her again.

"What did they say this time?" they coaxed the child.

"They don't talk much. I don't know what they are saying."

"Well, you have to tell us what they say even if you don't understand what they are talking about."

"Father only said, 'Well, when?'"

"What did Mother say?"

"She didn't say anything. She went like this." The child shrugged her shoulders, imitating Nadia's response.

Mia felt empowered. If her parents didn't see her when they spoke because she was invisible, she would try to use her new powers on her older siblings. She desperately wanted to see Sarah. She decided to quietly walk into the bedroom where Sarah lay. Her older siblings surrounded Sarah as she lay on her bed. Her new-found power emboldened the child. She liked being invisible. She moseyed into the room on the tips of her toes, avoiding the creaky floorboards. The creaks in the floorboards would give away her presence. Jacob sat on the bed with his arms crossed over his chest. She wondered why everyone stopped talking and looked at each other when she entered. Creeping up to the bed, she quietly sat beside Jacob. She crossed her arms over her chest in imitation of Jacob's pose. Maybe if she tried, she could even cross one leg over the other without losing her balance. It was as if she fit right into the family with her new power. Her older siblings didn't look unhappy as they appeared to be before she entered the room. They looked at each other and smiled.

She sat poised in security and looked around. Sarah didn't look sick. She was smiling broadly. Hilda and Kassie tried to hide their smiles. Jacob looked straight ahead and showed no emotion. It was Koss who lurched toward her as if to strike her and rudely burst her bubble.

"You damned brat. You are stupid. You think you are invisible; you are not invisible. Stupid, stupid…that's what you are!" He lashed out at the child's ignorance. "Get out of here. You don't belong here with us, brat," he bellowed. "Get out of this room now!"

"No, let her stay." Sarah lay on the bed, still smiling faintly.

"No, I will not allow her to sit with us. We are grownups, and she is just a brat. I am the oldest boy, and what I say goes. Get out!"

Mia left the room. At least she saw Sarah, if only for a moment. Now she had a job to do. She wanted Sarah to get better, so she must try to pick up as much of her parents' conversation and gestures as possible.

She watched Nadia as she burst into wild sobs.

"No, I can't do it. I can't do it!"

"You said you did it before," her father responded.

"But, I can't. I can't do it to Sarah." She paused. "Anyone else but not Sarah!"

"Time is running out. It has to be done soon," her husband firmly insisted.

"But I am afraid. It is getting late in her time. What if something goes wrong?"

"We can't put it off much longer. If you can't do it, talk to your sister Kathryn. We talked about this before. It has to be done, and it has to be done soon."

Mia tried her best to report on her parents' conversation to Hilda and Kassie even though she didn't understand the meaning of morning sickness and that her father wanted Sarah's pregnancy terminated.

Her mother acted very cheerful in front of Sarah. She didn't want to upset her. She also hid her anxiety from Hilda and Kassie lest they tell Sarah something to upset her.

Later, when Mia was sent to listen in on their parents' conversation, it appeared that Nadia had been crying. Her face was red, and her eyes were swollen. Mia watched Nadia muffle her sobs into a pillow as she spoke.

"I asked Kathryn, but she wouldn't do it; she told me to ask Elana."

Mia knew Kathryn and Elana were her mother's older sisters.

"I want Kathryn to do it," her mother continued. "I know she can do a safe job. I am not sure about Elana."

"Kathryn helped you when you needed help. Why doesn't she want to help with Sarah now?"

"Kathryn said that was different. She did what she had to because she wanted to help me. Do you know what else Kathryn told me?" Nadia lashed out at her absent sister. "She said our father was wrong. She said we had to realize that performing an abortion is taking a human life. How could she say things like that about our own father?" She sobbed. "I told Kathryn if she were such a strong believer in God, she wouldn't say such things against her own father. I told her she was committing the gravest sin by dishonoring our father and his teachings." Then, stifling her sobs, she added, "Kathryn said every mother should talk to her daughters about acting responsibly and set moral values for them. She said if Sarah had an abortion now, she would continue getting herself into the same situation over and over again."

Mia watched Nadia put the pillow over her face to muffle her sobs.

"Well, it doesn't seem that Kathryn talked to her own daughters," her father responded angrily.

"She said she did later." Nadia spoke between heavy bouts of crying. "How could she say what we learned in our father's house was wrong?"

Mia listened to her parents' conversation. She didn't understand what they were saying, but much later she realized that her Aunt Kathryn didn't have control over her life. The fourth commandment controlled her in her father's house. He controlled everyone by force. When Kathryn realized that her father's belief was wrong, she could not undo the past, but with a clear conscience, she would devote her future to her religious beliefs.

"When did Kathryn come to all these conclusions?" Her husband looked at Nadia questioningly. "It was OK with her a few months ago when she helped you."

"It is that demon in the church she goes to, Mr. Gabriel. He preaches all that nonsense to everyone. She said it was a hard decision to make, but she did it because I had other children to take care of and they needed me. She said she was afraid of what might have happened if she didn't help me, and she said the children needed me."

"Can you try to persuade her to do this for us just one more time? You are her sister; doing it just one more time shouldn't make that much of a difference to her."

"I tried," Nadia answered. "I begged her like I never begged anyone before. I cried, and she cried with me, but she said she made a vow to that demon who preaches in that hell church. She promised him she would not to take a human life again. Human life! What human life?" Nadia sputtered angrily. "Sarah may die. I am afraid to have Elana perform the abortion. Sarah may die!"

It frightened Mia when she heard Nadia say that Sarah might die. Mia left the room. She wanted to cry. When Hilda and Kassie asked her to tell them what she overheard, she couldn't hold back the flood of tears. She blurted out the words.

"Mother's face was all red. She put a pillow over her head and cried very hard because Sarah might die."

Her sisters tried to hide their fear as they questioned Mia to get the rest of the story. They tried to convince her that Sarah would be all right. Mia looked at their troubled faces and kept sobbing.

"I don't believe you. If Sarah isn't going to die, you wouldn't look so sad. You would look happy and you would smile."

Hilda looked at Kassie before she turned her face away. "Could you?"

Kassie nodded and forced a smile.

Mia looked at Hilda. "But you're not smiling."

Hilda looked at Mia and forced a stiff smile. "OK, now we want you to wipe your tears and smile before you go outside. You must not let anyone see that you've been crying. No one must know what Mother said," Hilda said, trying to make light of the situation.

Outside, the warm sun touched Mia's numb body. Even though she felt comforted by its warm caress, the heat could not touch the icy feeling in her heart. She tried not to think of what she overheard. With tears trickling silently down her cheeks, she wondered if she could ever smile and be happy again. With her head lowered, she didn't see Koss lurking close by until he stepped before her. Caught off guard, she swiped her telltale tears and tried to force a brave smile. Her mouth would only quiver; she could not stop trembling.

Koss's aggressive and manipulating ways terrorized the child; she had a persistent fear of her eldest brother.

"Why are you crying?" he hissed into her face like a viper.

Mia could not speak.

"I want you to tell me what Mother and Father talked about. What did they say? Why are you crying?" Her brother lurched toward her.

She flinched. He stood blocking her way to the house. She couldn't escape him.

"I am not crying," she said as a tremor of fear flowed through her body.

Koss was quick to show his anger. When he wanted to show his power, Mia was the main target of his viciousness. Now he had her cornered, and she could not hide her fright from him.

"Mia, I want you to come into the house right now." Their father's voice interrupted the situation.

Mia was glad to get away from Koss. She carefully made her way around him and dashed to the safety of the house. There, she found her mother in the bedroom, comforting Sarah.

Sarah was crying hysterically. "I told them I didn't want to hear anything anymore. I told them, but they kept coming into the room and talking. I told them to go away, but they wouldn't listen. They wouldn't go away."

Hilda and Kassie stood beside their father; his expression was one of anger. When Mia walked in, he turned to her.

"Did they send you to listen in on what your mother and I were talking about? Did they tell you to tell them what we said?"

Mia looked up at her father. He didn't seem to be angry with her.

"Yes." She nodded. "They told me I had to listen and then I had to tell them what you said. And if I didn't do what they said, they told me Sarah wouldn't get better."

"We didn't tell Sarah," Kassie interjected defensively. "She said she didn't want to hear anything, so we were just talking to each other. We can't help it if she heard us talking. It is not our fault that she was eavesdropping on us."

"You were the one who said she was going to die," Hilda fumed angrily at Kassie.

"You both talked in the room where Sarah was so she could hear you."

Hilda and Kassie looked at their father's infuriated face. "Yes, we did." With lowered eyes, they sheepishly admitted their crafty ploy.

Mia didn't hear her parents talk about Sarah or her condition again. They must have decided that discussing family problems in front of her was a mistake they would not repeat. As time passed, the atmosphere in the house was mysteriously quiet.

※ ※

Usually, in the mornings, Mia was allowed to sleep until she was no longer tired. One morning, she wondered why they woke her when it was still dark outside. They told her to dress and have her breakfast. She moped around the room, too tired to eat anything so early in the morning.

"You should have let Mia sleep; there was no need to wake her up so early," her father said as he prepared to leave.

"What if she woke up before we finished and walked through the room?" her mother responded, obviously irritated. "We can't be interrupted by her. The girls will take care of the brat."

The breakfast dishes were washed and put away. Hilda and Kassie straightened the kitchen and swept the floor.

"Who is coming to visit?"

Her sisters ignored her. Mia wondered why everybody was being so mysterious and secretive.

What are they hiding from me? The child was confused.

※ ※

She remembered another time when they had awakened her in the middle of night. It was very cold in the house at that time. She realized that it had happened shortly before Christmas of the previous year. At that time, the house had only a kitchen and one bedroom that the whole family shared, although extra rooms were added sometime later.

Mia recalled that Yuri was only a few months old then, and her mother was having terrible fits of rage. Kassie had whispered to Mia that there would be another baby in the family.

"Could we get a little girl this time?" Mia had asked excitedly.

Although Yuri was still young, he was a huge baby. He was close to thirteen pounds when he was born. Her parents wouldn't allow Mia to touch or hold him. They said she might try to pick him up and drop him. Mia wanted a tiny little sister she could touch. Maybe they would allow her to put her arms around her or even hold her gently. With the news of another baby joining the family, Mia overflowed with happiness. If there were two babies in the house, surely they would let her touch one of them. Later, Mia was disappointed.

"You shouldn't have told the brat about the new baby because there might not be one." Then Hilda warned Mia, "Don't say anything about the new baby because Mother might hear you and attack you like she attacked me."

Mia watched Hilda show Kassie the bruises and deep gouges that ran down the length of her arm.

"Look what she did to me."

"Where did she attack you?"

"She was behind the house. It looked like she was sick and had been crying."

"What did you say to make her so angry?"

"I only asked her if she was feeling OK. I told her she should not worry; we would help her take care of the new baby too. She turned on me and screamed, 'He told you?' Then she went into one of her vicious rages and attacked me."

"How are you going to explain your bruises and scratches to everyone in school?"

"I don't know. I could tell them I got the bruises from a fall, but I don't know about the scratches; they are so deep. I could bandage my arms for a while. It will take a long time before they heal and the scabs are off."

"You could say an animal attacked you."

"A cat? No, the gouges are too wide."

"Then maybe a dog? A dog's claw is wider than a cat's."

"No, the gouges are long and too wide to be made by a dog. They can't be passed off for an animal attack. You can definitely see a human made them."

"You could say an animal attacked you. You wouldn't be lying if you did. When Mother loses her temper, she is worse than an animal."

Mia feared Hilda and Kassie's actions. They were unbecoming to the child. Mia sat and listened to her two sisters talk, but she tried to avoid running into clashes with them.

She witnessed Nadia's savagery and harbored a deep fear of her mother. She was too young to know why Nadia was having such fits of rage.

Sometimes Mia heard Nadia as her father tried to calm her through bouts of rage.

"Do you want me to hold a baby in each arm? I don't want another one. It is too soon," she raved. "I have too many, and I don't like them all."

Mia watched her father try to calm Nadia and help her through bouts of morning sickness. Her mother's face was flushed with anger; her pale eyes glistened and bulged as she lashed out at her husband. Then something was wrong with Nadia. She would wander away and not return for many hours. When she did return, her husband didn't ask her where she had been, avoiding the trigger of another uncontrollable outburst.

Hilda took care of Yuri then. She bathed him, but he cried continuously. Hilda looked worried as she turned to Kassie.

"Father has gone to buy a bottle and nipple. I tried to feed him with bread soaked in milk. Father says he might choke on it, so I tried to give him milk with a teaspoon, but he keeps crying. He wants his mother, and she doesn't even come home to feed him."

When their father returned, he helped Hilda feed Yuri with the new baby bottle. Later, Mia overheard her father talking to Hilda and Kassie over some concern.

"I have work to do in the orchard. I won't be gone for long. If the baby wakes up, give him the bottle again. I want you to watch over him and keep a close watch on Mia," he instructed. "I do not know what state her mind will be in when she shows up again or from where she will be coming. Tell Mia not to wander close to the bushes in case she's lurking, waiting there."

Mia sensed the apprehension in her father's voice.

"Who is Father talking about?" she asked her sisters when he was getting ready to leave.

Hilda and Kassie looked at each other for a moment. Mia noticed they exchanged a knowing glance.

"Who is Father talking about?" Mia repeated.

"Somebody might want to hurt us, and he wants us to be careful."

"Who might hurt us?" she insisted, wide eyed.

"We can't tell you."

Mia didn't know where Nadia was, and Sarah was not at home; she spent much time at Hanna Stephenson's place.

"I wish Sarah was here," she whispered to Kassie.

"What about Sarah?" Kassie asked her father. "She is not even at home."

"Sarah will be OK. She will not harm her."

Before her father left, he went to his youngest daughter. "Stay close to your sisters and listen to them."

"Who might hurt us?" Mia asked again.

"Maybe we should tell her. We don't know what state she will be in when she comes back. We should all be prepared." Her sisters spoke quietly to one another.

"You are right," Kassie agreed. "We should tell her."

"If you see anyone in the bush, you shouldn't go to them, even if they call you," Hilda warned.

"Who is in the bush?" Mia asked.

Neither sister answered.

"Is it the man who wears a brown suit jacket and walks down the road asking people for money because he has only one arm?"

"No, it's not him," Kassie answered. "I guess we should tell her who it is." They were finding it difficult to explain the problem to the child.

"Do you remember how Mother gets so angry sometimes?"

"Yes." Mia nodded.

"Do you remember the time she beat and scratched Hilda?"

"Yes. I must not talk about the new baby because she could beat and scratch me too."

"Yes, that's right. And we have to be careful because Mother might do something worse than scratch us."

"What might she do?" Mia asked, trying to hide her anxiety.

"She might want to hurt us very badly. So we have to be very careful. Kassie and I are big, so we can fight or run away from her. However, Yuri is a baby, and you are small. Father told us to watch so she does not hurt either one of you."

"Why does she want to hurt us?"

"Because she is very angry and she is sick."

"I saw when she was sick and angry with Father. He was talking to her and trying to make her get better." Mia was silent for a moment. "I think I could run away from her, too, just like you and Kassie."

"Well, if she grabs us by the neck and starts choking us, we could get away, but you probably can't. That is why you have to stay close to us so we can watch you."

Mia looked at her sister, apprehension growing. "OK, I will stay close to you. I am bigger than Yuri, and I will help you watch him.

If he wakes up, I will tell you. If I see Mother put her hands around his neck, I will call you."

She spoke with courage even though what her sisters told her was disturbing. The child had witnessed Nadia's derangement, and it frightened her.

"Mother is angry with Father, but he is worried that she might harm the young children and herself." Mia listened to her sisters as they whispered to each other.

As time passed, Nadia's rants continued. There was no peace for anyone, especially her husband. Mia learned to keep out of her mother's sight.

Then came the cold, dark night.

Someone had woken Mia and told her to get out of bed and go into the kitchen. She was so tired. She did not want to get out of the warm bed. The house was so cold. Kneeling on the rough kitchen floor in her scant underclothes beside her brother Jacob, Mia couldn't keep from crying as she tried to keep warm.

"It's so cold. Can I go back to bed? I want to sleep." She couldn't hold back her sobs.

"No, you can't. You have to stay here with the rest of us."

"But I am tired, and I am so cold." She continued to shiver and sob.

"Father has gone to get more firewood. He will be back soon, and the house will be warm when we build up the fire."

Some of her older siblings put on their heavy winter coats. Koss smugly strutted around in their mother's heavy winter jacket. He obnoxiously put something under the coat, pretending he was a woman with breasts. Kassie argued with him. She took off her own coat and wanted Koss to give her the one he was wearing.

"I am older than you. Give it to me. I want to wear it," Kassie bickered with her brother.

Although Kassie and Koss were twins, she felt entitled because she was born a few minutes before him.

"But I am superior to you. I am the oldest boy in the family, and besides," he answered with the authority he claimed, "I had it first."

They were coming close to blows when their father returned with an armful of firewood. He stopped their argument.

"It's cold. Why didn't anyone put any warm clothes on Jacob and Mia?" he asked.

"Mother told me to boil some water; I am trying to get the fire going in the stove," Hilda replied.

"Where is Sarah?"

"Mother wants her in the bedroom with her."

Jacob got up and put his coat on.

"Could someone give Mia her coat?"

"She doesn't have one that fits her; her coat is too small. It only covers her shoulders."

"Well, what about the one Aunt Kathryn passed down for her?"

"Mother said it still is too big for her and she should not wear it until it fits her."

"Well, where is it? You can still put it on her to keep her warm."

"It's in the bedroom, and Mother told us we were not allowed to go back there. She said after we get out, we have to stay out. Only Sarah is allowed to stay with her for a while."

Even though Koss was wearing his mother's coat, he would not allow anyone to use his coat or put it on Mia to keep her warm.

"I will not allow that brat to wear my coat. I have to wear it to school," he blustered angrily. "She is crying. Her tears are going to fall on it. She might even leave snot on it."

Someone finally put the small coat Mia had outgrown over her shoulders. The rest of her body was turning numb in the frigid room. Her father stoked the fire in the rectangular cast-iron heater with a fireproof glass in the door.

"Go sit close to the heater and warm up." Their father turned to Jacob and Mia when he spoke.

"You can sit quietly and watch the flames in the heater," Hilda suggested.

"Yes, and if you sit very quietly, Santa might even come."

Mia knew that Santa Claus entered the house through the chimney. She looked over her shoulder to where the stove pipes led to the chimney.

"No, you must not look over your shoulder to the back of the room, or Santa will not come."

"But Santa comes through the chimney."

"No, he comes through the chimney when he comes to the schools during our Christmas concerts. When he comes to the houses, he comes through the flames in the heater," Koss mocked.

"You must look straight through the panel of glass into the red flames in the heater. If you don't take your eyes off the flames, Santa Claus will appear right before your eyes."

"But how could Santa Claus come through the flames without getting his clothes and whiskers burned?" Mia asked. She tried to contain her excitement, keeping her eyes on the flames without blinking, and asked questions upon questions. She heard whispers and footsteps behind her as her older siblings walked about the room. Then the door opened, and she heard somebody walk into the house.

"Is that Santa Claus?" she asked without turning around.

"No, it is not," one of her sisters answered lightly.

"He doesn't come through a door. He comes through the flames in the heater." Koss snickered again.

When she heard the door open and someone speak, she realized Aunt Kathryn had walked in. Her aunt didn't knock to announce her arrival; she spoke softly and laughed when she heard Mia ask if she was Santa Claus.

"Why doesn't Philip come in?" Mia heard her father ask her aunt.

"Philip said he'd wait outside until I am finished."

"But it's so cold outside," her father added with concern. "Philip should come in and warm up. I will ask him to come in."

"No, there is no need for that," Aunt Kathryn answered. "He is dressed warmly, and we brought comforters to wrap up in. If he comes into the house, he would have to put the horses in the barn or tie them up. He does not want to go through all that trouble. He will be OK."

After speaking, her aunt seemed to have vanished from the room. Her voice was heard coming from the bedroom.

Mia kept her vigil, sitting and wondering aloud, "How can Santa come through the burning flames?"

"If you watch long enough, you will see how. He just appears before your eyes like magic."

"How come he doesn't get his clothes and whiskers burned when he comes through the fire?"

"Because he's magic."

Jacob had long since lost his interest in Santa and left her side. Mia heard more conversation behind her, and then the door opened and closed. Aunt Kathryn was gone.

"Well, now we can go back to sleep," she heard her sisters say.

"But Santa Claus still has not come," Mia said, disappointed but still not turning away from the heater.

"No, he has not but come to bed now," Sarah coaxed. "Santa knows you were a good girl tonight, so he will come at Christmas time."

Satisfied that Santa Claus was pleased with her and would still come, Mia got up and crawled into bed with her sisters.

She heard Hilda say, "There now, Mother is going to be happy."

"Why is Mother going to be happy now?" Mia asked.

"You shouldn't have said that," Sarah warned Hilda.

"Let's go to sleep. She will forget it by morning," Hilda replied.

When Mia woke up in the morning, her sisters were in the kitchen, and her mother was in bed.

"You have to be quiet because Mother is sick," Sarah warned her.

"But why is Mother going to be happy now if she is sick?" She looked at Sarah and waited for an answer.

"Who told you Mother is going to be happy?" Sarah probed.

"I heard Hilda say, 'Mother is going to be happy now' before I fell asleep last night." She stood looking up at her sister, waiting for an answer.

"I did not say that," Hilda interjected sharply, trying to fend off the child.

"But I heard you say it just before I fell asleep." Mia fretted. She wondered why Hilda was so mean. Why wasn't her sister telling the truth?

"Then maybe you dreamed that I said it," Hilda snapped.

"No, I didn't dream it. I heard her say it after Aunt Kathryn left." She turned to Sarah in confusion.

"Who told you Aunt Kathryn was at our place last night? You didn't see her."

"No, I didn't see her because I was watching for Santa Claus. I heard her talking. And after she went, I heard Hilda say Mother was going to be happy. I heard her say it. I did!" Mia was close to tears. She did not know why Hilda was lying.

"Yes, Hilda, you did say it. I heard you say it too." Sarah looked at Hilda, putting her on the spot. "Why did you say it?"

Hilda hesitated for a moment. "I said Mother is going to be happy now because Aunt Kathryn came to see her." Hilda was satisfied with the flimsy answer she gave the child.

"But why did Aunt Kathryn come when it was so dark?" No one answered the child. "We were all sleeping when she came. Why is Mother sick now?" she continued. "Why was Mother happy to see Aunt Kathryn if she made her sick?"

She waited again for answers. Mia's questions were endless, but the answers she waited for did not come; her sisters brushed the questions aside as fast as she asked them. Aunt Kathryn and Uncle Philip always came to visit in the daytime or in the evening. Usually they came on Sundays. It was out of the ordinary that they would come in the dark of night. Why was this visit different?

Sarah picked up her coat and said, "I have to go now. Hanna Stephenson asked me to help her bake Christmas cookies today."

"I want you to stay home," Mia said and playfully grabbed her sister's leg. Sarah picked Mia up, and the child put her arms around her sister's neck and would not let go.

"OK," she bargained. "I will give you a kiss if you let me go."

It was a game Sarah used to play with her—it was a long time since they played it. Her eldest sister no sooner gave her a quick peck when Mia would grab her for another. Sibling affection was taboo in their house. It always displeased Nadia to see Sarah pay attention to Mia, but, at that time, Sarah was still free to give Mia a few hugs and pecks. Their mother was not there to dispute the child's play.

"What about Mother?" Hilda asked. "What if she needs something or asks for you?"

"Mother will be OK. If she wants anything, she will ask you for it."

Hilda gave Sarah a grimace. "Still, shouldn't you wait until she wakes up?"

"No, I'm late already. Hanna asked me to be at her place at eleven o'clock, but if I couldn't, I was to come when I could."

Mia playfully grabbed onto her sister's leg again. Sarah picked her up; the child put her arms around her neck and held on tightly.

"OK," Sarah said. "One more kiss if you let me go."

"Shouldn't you ask Mother if you can go?" Hilda looked resentful as she spoke.

"No, I asked her yesterday after I came home from school, and she said I could go."

"I don't want you to go," Mia whispered into her sister's ear as she clung to her. "Let Hilda go to make the cookies; I want you to stay home. Why don't you make cookies at home?"

Sarah spent so much time at Hanna's house, and Mia didn't see her eldest sister often. She missed the closeness. Her eldest sister was caring and patient; she didn't get angry like Hilda. She knew if she couldn't fall asleep for her afternoon nap, Sarah would suggest that she just lie down and rest, knowing Mia would eventually succumb to sleep. It was only noon now, and she was not tired, but she knew what awaited her after Sarah left.

Sarah quietly whispered to Hilda and Kassie as she prepared to leave.

"We know how to deal with her. After you go, we will deal with her our way." Kassie revealed their intent to Sarah.

"No, you must not spank her. She will cry, and Mother will wake up." Sarah left Mia to her fate.

"See? Mother lets her do anything she wants. She didn't even wait to ask Mother how she was feeling this morning. Sarah spends more time at Hanna's than she does at home."

Hilda sounded perturbed as she spoke. "You know why she spends so much time there. It is because of Baily. How many cookies do you think Hanna is going to bake? She can bake her own cookies. Baily is the one who tells Hanna to get Sarah to help her."

"When I am older, I will be just like Sarah. Then Mother will let me do anything I want to do." Kassie pouted enviously.

Mia sat and listened as Hilda and Kassie whispered to each other. Mia didn't like when the grownups had secrets or whispered.

"What did Hilda tell you?" she asked. Kassie didn't answer. "How far away does Hanna live, and what is her whole name?" Mia spoke in a whisper.

Again, Kassie didn't answer. She tugged at Kassie's skirt and motioned for her to bend down so she could whisper the question in her ear like grownups did.

"I can't hear what Mia said. Did you hear her, Hilda?"

Mia looked up at Hilda and repeated the question.

"No, I can't hear her either," Hilda replied.

Sarah told them not to spank her because their mother was sleeping, so by pretending they couldn't hear her questions, they set a conspiracy of silence against her. Mia knew it was pointless to ask questions. The silence was unbearable. She hoped she could go and find Sarah.

"Can I go outside?" she asked.

Hilda nodded to Kassie, and Kassie put a coat on Mia. It was big and went down to her ankles, but it was warm and so cozy. It was the coat Aunt Kathryn passed down for her. Mia never had a coat as warm as this one before. She stood in the room waiting. She couldn't go outside; her feet were bare. Finally, Kassie put a pair of shoes on her; they were also too big, but she didn't put any socks on her feet.

"Why didn't you put a pair of socks on her?" It was as though Hilda read the child's thoughts. Kassie whispered something to Hilda, who nodded. "OK, you can go outside."

"I want a pair of socks 'cause my feet will get cold."

"No. They will not get cold if you stand beside the house." They looked at each other and smiled at their foolish scheme.

The sun felt warm against the house, but the wind was brisk and cold. There was snow on the ground. Mia stood beside the house and wondered how far Sarah had gone. She knew Hanna lived past Belcourt, although she didn't know how much farther. She had tried looking for Sarah once but she couldn't go far because her coat was not warm. They found her crying at the side of the road. Her shoes were full of snow, and she was cold.

The child was lonely and missed her eldest sister. If she went looking for her now and found her, she could come home with her when she returned. Maybe Sarah would even give her a cookie.

Sarah wouldn't let Hilda or Kassie beat Mia for wanting to find her. Mother wouldn't beat her either because she was in bed. They said she was sick. Hilda and Kassie wouldn't care if she went to look for Sarah. They didn't want her in the house anyway. They didn't like that she asked them questions. They only liked to talk to each other about things she didn't understand. Still, she knew she shouldn't go down the road and look for Sarah. She didn't have socks on her feet, and her shoes would fill with snow again. So Mia went back into the house.

As she lay on the bed to await Sarah's return, she drifted off to sleep. It was Sarah's voice that woke her. She sat up in bed.

"Sarah is at home," she announced excitedly to Hilda. "I want to see her."

"No, you can't see her. Mother is awake. She wants Sarah to sit beside her bed and talk to her."

"Can I sit beside the bed with Sarah? I will be quiet," the child pleaded.

"No, Mother said she doesn't want anyone else in the room with her except Sarah."

The memory of that frigid winter night passed through Mia's mind. It was the night she waited for Santa Claus to appear through the flames in the heater. It was the time when her questions about Aunt Kathryn's mysterious visit went unanswered. It was when Nadia was ill and had to stay in bed.

Now, in the fall, Mia was once again awakened in the dark; she was told to dress and have her breakfast. She wondered why everybody was up so early that morning.

CHAPTER SEVEN

Sarah was still in bed. She had been spending a lot of time in bed as if she were ill. Koss and Jacob didn't sleep in the house anymore. Yuri, the baby, was still asleep.

Mia was not hungry. She watched Hilda and Kassie wash the breakfast dishes and put them away. Then they swept the floor.

"Are we having company?" she asked her sisters.

As usual, they ignored her question.

She remembered that frigid night when Aunt Kathryn made the mysterious visit. That was the night they told her Santa Claus would appear through the burning flames in the heater. Now, as she sat waiting with uncertainty, she tried to sort out those things she did not understand.

Santa came at Christmas time to give them treats; since last Christmas, an extension had been added to the house, including another chimney.

"Why, of course," she muttered to herself. "Santa won't know if he fits through the new chimney if he doesn't try it out before Christmas," she reasoned. "He must try new chimneys before

Christmas; otherwise, how could he know whose chimney he can fit through? Yes, that must be it." She waited with renewed excitement. "And they woke me up because they want to surprise me."

Mia continued to sit with her eyes fixed on the stove pipes, waiting for a squiggle or a bulge to indicate Santa's presence before he made his appearance.

"Why are you looking at the stove pipes?" Hilda frowned.

"I want to see how Santa is going to come through," she replied slyly, giving away that she was not being easily fooled.

"Santa Claus? Who told you Santa Claus is coming?" she asked the child. "Did Koss tell you that story again?"

"No. No one did, but I know someone is coming because you swept the floor and Santa is the only one who comes at night," she replied, trying to hide her delight. "Last time you woke me up at night, he was supposed to come but he didn't. Maybe he will come this time to see if he fits through our new chimney." Mia looked at Hilda expectantly.

"No, he isn't coming," Hilda replied, irritated with the child's explanation. "It isn't Christmas; it's too early for him to come."

"If he comes, he doesn't have to give anyone anything," the child bargained. "He can just come to see if he fits through the new stove pipes."

Nadia passed through the kitchen.

"Bring that out to the center of the room and put Mia on it." She indicated a bench that sat beside the west wall of the kitchen. Mia was set on the bench with her back toward the living room. Her older sisters sat on either side of her to prevent her from wandering about.

The living room had a spare bed in it. The bedroom that Mia shared with her sisters was on the other side of the living room. No doors separated the rooms. A drape that hung between the doorway of kitchen and living room was mysteriously drawn.

"Why is the drape to the room closed?" the child repeatedly asked, annoying her sisters by turning her head toward the drape.

Finally, Hilda admitted, "I don't like the drape drawn either. Let's open it a tiny bit to keep her quiet." She opened it a few inches.

A coal-oil lamp lit the room that they sat in, but the living room was dark. Mia felt odd not knowing why she was sitting on the bench between her two sisters so early in the morning.

It seemed that they were waiting for someone. Hilda and Kassie were getting impatient, and Mia was getting tired of sitting on the bench. Her parents' bedroom was off to the north of the kitchen. Nadia walked nervously from the living room to her bedroom. She would lie down for a few minutes then get up and walk back into the living room. Each time she walked through the draped doorway, she carelessly left it opened just a little bit more.

"Father said Mother didn't sleep last night, so she is tired this morning," Hilda whispered to Kassie. "I woke up when I heard her crying. Did you hear her crying?"

"No, but I heard her walking around a lot during the night," Kassie answered.

"Make sure Mia sits with her back to the living room and make sure to close the drape when the time comes." Nadia tossed the order to Hilda as she paced from one room to the other.

They sat on the bench and waited. Mia impatiently kept up a steady flow of questions. Hilda and Kassie were getting fidgety. Dawn broke, and it was no longer dark outside.

Suddenly, the stuck door to the living room opened with a sharp thud, and like with the other visitor who arrived in the dark of night, there was no knock. Except for the abrupt sound of the door opening, the visitor entered silently as if not wanting her presence to be known. After the tedious wait, her sisters forgot to draw the drape to the living room. Mia turned her head and saw the figure of Aunt Elana. She was dressed in black as if in mourning—or she did not want to be recognized by man or God for the sin she was about to commit.

Hilda stood up quickly and drew the drape shut.

"Did she see who came in?"

"No, she didn't. I covered her eyes," Kassie lied to cover their error.

Mia could hear her aunt in the next room.

"The boys didn't put the horses in the barn last night. We had trouble catching them this morning," she said, explaining her delay in a discreet whisper.

Nadia replied in a hushed murmur.

In her drowsiness that morning, Mia noticed a makeshift drape of bed sheets around the spare bed. Now she realized that Sarah was lying on the bed behind the drape. Aunt Elana and Nadia were there with her. They were speaking in muffled tones. She heard the sound of Nadia sobbing. When they got louder and she couldn't contain herself any longer, Nadia rushed through the kitchen into her bedroom and wailed in unrestrained hysteria.

Aunt Elana called out after her. "Nadia, take a few minutes to get yourself under control, but don't go far; I will need you here."

A while later, Elana's voice called from behind the drape. "Tell your mother to come back here when she calms down; I will need her very soon."

Hilda stood up and disappeared into her mother's bedroom.

"Auntie Elana needs you. Mother, Auntie Elana needs you."

There was silence for a few moments.

"Mother?"

Sounds of a deranged scuffle, muffled asphyxiation, and gasping noises erupted from the bedroom, followed by the fury of Nadia's inhuman shrieks. Spewing a string of vulgar names, she shrieked in blood-curdling madness.

"You slut! You whore! Why did you bring this disgrace on me?"

All the hate festering in Nadia for her second daughter suddenly erupted into a wrath of madness.

"Bring me a knife. Somebody bring me a knife so I can finish the slut off for disgracing herself and me!"

From behind the makeshift drape, Aunt Elana blared, "What is happening there? Nadia, what is happening? What are you doing, Nadia?"

"I want a knife so I can kill the slut for what she did. Bring me a knife right now!"

"Let go of me. Let go of me!" Hilda's voice sputtered and shrieked in terror. "Kassie, help me. I can't get away from her. Kassie, help me get away from her!"

"No. Get me a knife, Kassie!" Nadia's blood-curdling shriek erupted from her bedroom.

"No!" Elana's bellowing voice cut in. "Do not give her a knife. She doesn't know what she is doing."

A terrible crisis was at hand. Elana was not able to leave Sarah to help Hilda.

"Help me, Kassie. Help me! Call Father into the house. Please, Kassie, call him. Help me!"

"You whore! How dare you drag yourself around like a common bitch with all the trash in the neighborhood? How dare you disgrace me? Bring me a knife!" Nadia's shrieks were inhuman. Although Nadia's anger was at Sarah, she took it out at Hilda.

Hilda fought desperately. Her screams of terror echoed throughout the house.

Kassie huddled on the bench with the sobbing child. She was frozen in fear trying to calm Mia's terror and her own. She knew if she helped Hilda, Nadia would turn her fiery hate on her as she had on her sister.

From behind the makeshift drape, Aunt Elana kept hollering. "Nadia, leave Hilda alone; she didn't do anything wrong! Nadia, what is wrong with you? Have you gone insane? Let Hilda go. She is not to blame for Sarah's mistake."

Finally, Nadia eased her grip on Hilda, who lost no time in breaking away. Shaken, disoriented, and disheveled, she ran out of the bedroom weeping. She held her hands to her throat as she sputtered and retched. The buttons were ripped off her dress, her hair was in disarray, and the side of her face displayed a deep bruise.

"Why? Why did she do that to me? Why? She wanted to kill me; she really did. She is crazy! She was strangling me, and she wanted a knife. Why? Why?" In shock, Hilda repeated, "She just sprang and grabbed me when I leaned over to talk to her. Why?"

"Your mother is not angry with you, Hilda." Her aunt spoke to the distraught girl from the other room. "She is angry with Sarah for what she did. Don't be upset with your mother. She didn't know what she was doing."

"She is not angry with me? She is angry with Sarah?" Hilda repeated, still in a daze. The words Elana spoke were unthinkable. Nadia was never upset with her eldest daughter. She never displayed anger toward Sarah.

"She is not angry with me. She is angry with Sarah," Hilda repeated until she was able to get control of herself.

"What did you do to bring on the attack?" Kassie whispered. "What did you do to make her react that way?"

"I don't know. I didn't say anything. She looked like she was sleeping, but her eyes were open; they looked so weird." Hilda trembled uncontrollably, visibly shaken by her mother's psychotic attack.

"I don't know. I spoke to her. I told her Aunt Elana needed her, but she did not seem to hear me. So I leaned closer to her and that was when she sprang at me. She grabbed my neck and pulled me down on the bed. I tried to fight her off, but I couldn't get away. First, she was going to strangle me. Then she started screaming for a knife. That was when she loosened her hold on my neck and I was able to get out of her grasp. She looked like she was insane. I don't know why she did that to me." Hilda paused in confusion. "Why didn't you come to help me? Why didn't you call Father? She was going to kill me!"

"I was afraid; I couldn't move. I didn't have my shoes on, and Mia was shrieking in fright. I couldn't." Kassie revealed her own terror. "I was too scared to help."

Mia sat on the bench with her sisters and listened to them as they recounted their horror.

"Why do you think she did it? Do you think she found out about you and Josh having secret meetings?" Kassie whispered.

"No. She knows about Josh, but did not mention his name."

There was finally movement in Nadia's bedroom. Shrouded in fear, they watched Nadia as she walked zombielike to the room with the makeshift drape where Sarah lay.

Kassie somberly helped Hilda sew the buttons on her dress.

"We must not tell Father that she tried to kill me. He will ask too many questions. Then there will only be more problems to deal with, and he might find out about Josh."

"No, Father must not know," Kassie agreed. "He might find out things he must not know, and Mother would be infuriated."

"If I had a dress with a higher neckline, I would put it on. I don't want Father to see the red marks on my neck."

"What about the bruise on your face? You can't cover that."

"I can keep my head turned so he doesn't see it, and if he asks about it, I will tell him I tripped and hit the corner of the cupboard."

Although Nadia's anger was aimed at Sarah, the sisters assured each other that it was better that Nadia took her insane rage out on Hilda rather than Sarah, who was lying helpless and unconscious in the next room.

Nadia's self-control did not last. She spent only a few quiet moments behind the drape. Again, she shrieked hysterically and beat her chest as she ran back into her bedroom.

"Nadia," Elana called after her. "Calm down and come back here. I need you!"

Nadia was in the bedroom, sobbing hysterically and muffling her shrieks with her pillow. Her sister kept calling to her, telling her that she needed help.

Hilda looked at Kassie. "I am afraid of her," she uttered. "You go into the bedroom and tell her that Aunt Elana is calling her. But don't go close to her like I did or she might spring on you too. Just stand in the doorway when you talk to her."

Kassie did as Hilda cautioned her. It didn't take Nadia as long to get herself under control the second time. However, her rationality was short lived, and she shrieked through her third fit of hysteria. Again, she ran wildly into the bedroom, savagely beating her chest.

Elana was exasperated. "Nadia, I need help here. If you don't help me, something terrible is going to happen!"

Nadia continued wailing and crying hysterically in her bedroom. Hilda was hardly a teen, and Kassie was younger; they were caught in a crisis that terrified them.

"Nadia!" Elana's voice held a note of panic. "I have a life to save here, and I can't do it alone. Nadia, come quick!"

Hilda and Kassie glanced at one another. They were deathly pale. Kassie looked as if she were about to pass out.

"One of us has to help or Sarah will die," Hilda whispered, shaking from her earlier ordeal.

Kassie looked at Hilda uneasily. "You are older."

"But I don't know what to do."

"I need somebody here quick," her aunt insisted desperately. "If one of you girls will come, I will tell you what to do."

While Hilda tried to gather courage to be committed to what no child or adult should have to be committed to, there was a movement from their mother's bedroom. Nadia had gained enough sanity to help Aunt Elana. Hilda looked relieved as she sat on the bench with her younger sisters.

Mia listened to Aunt Elana's voice. She was heard, scolding—demanding—as if she were snapping Nadia with a whip to keep her from losing control again. Then things were quiet; Elana had the situation under control. When they came out from behind the drape, Elana was comforting her sister.

"Don't worry, Nadia; just let her rest. Sarah is strong, and she is young; she will be OK."

Nadia's head was bent. She looked ghastly pale. Her face looked drained.

"The blood...there was so much blood." She spoke as if in a trance.

Before her aunt left, Mia heard her mother ask a question but didn't hear what it was. She only heard the whispers among her sisters.

"A boy."

Then another question.

"I don't know. We will have to wait and see," Aunt Elana answered. She then left.

Later in life, Mia would remember that day so long ago. She had been a mere child, but she remembered. She'd wonder why the sex of the fetus would make any difference. It would not be given a name or a chance at life; it would never play or feel the comfort of the warm sun on its tiny body. It would never feel the kiss of someone healing its hurt. They took its life. They did not give it a chance because a cold, callous woman wanted to hold her head high among her neighbors and friends—a woman who would later go on to condemn other girls for doing what her daughter did. A woman who would ridicule others for not being as perfect as the daughter she held in such high esteem. She had no fear of sin, no fear of God, no conscience—she was a woman who sold her soul to the demons. Sin was something Nadia concealed from neighbors. God, forgive her; did she think she could conceal her sin from you?

Nadia allowed no one to go behind the drape where Sarah lay—no one except herself. A cloud of gloom enveloped the house, touching everyone within it. Nadia existed in a world that included only her eldest daughter and herself. She would take food to her and then bring it back untouched. Everyone kept their distance from Nadia, afraid that if they angered her by saying the wrong thing, she would lose control and harm them.

When the sun rose to brighten the sky and chase the shadows away, Mia felt more hopeful. At night she feared sleep, thinking that death would come under the cover of darkness at night and take Sarah away.

"Mother spends the nights with Sarah. She stays behind the drape and has the lamp turned on low beside her bed," Hilda muttered solemnly.

"How do you know she stays up with her?"

"I saw the light burning behind the drape, and I looked in to see what was wrong. I saw Mother sitting in the rocking chair beside the bed."

"Why does Mother sit beside Sarah's bed?" Mia asked.

"She does not want anything to happen to her during the night. She does not want her to die."

This gave the child some reassurance. She thought surely, with Father's help, her parents would not allow death to enter the house and take her sister during the night.

Mia had much fear instilled in her by her mother and older siblings. The fear of death and the fear of the demon were deeply rooted. The child was given a terrifying description of the demon and thought death somehow resembled it. Death was dressed in a black hooded garment and had vacant eyes. His grim task was done under the cover of night by knocking on doors and taking those he chose with him. The demon also walked among them; he looked scarier than death. He did bad things and punished people, and then he took them and burned them in hell.

"Sarah has not eaten for two days," she heard Hilda whisper to Kassie. "Today is the third day."

"Do you know how many days she can live without eating?" Kassie asked.

"Maybe she can live another day," Hilda responded hopefully.

The next day was cloudy and bleak. Mia felt uncomfortable, thinking death might have been waiting to appear on just such a day; she dreaded the coming of the night. Fear remained thick among them. The child didn't ask as many questions. She only listened to her sisters as they spoke and walked around like gloomy shadows.

"Could we all stay awake tonight and keep the lamps burning very bright?" Mia pleaded quietly. "If the lights are kept burning bright, death might not know it is nighttime," she speculated in innocence.

"Yes, he would know it's nighttime because it would be dark outside," they replied.

"Then if he comes to the door to take Sarah, could we beg him not to take her? Maybe he would listen to us if we tell him we like Sarah and want to keep her with us." Thinking they could negotiate with death, the child added, "Could we tell him to take Mrs. Wilmer instead?"

Mrs. Wilmer was a frail, bent woman who lived down the road. Mia often saw her walking down the road to Belcourt. When she walked she occasionally stopped to rest on her cane as if she was tired.

Hilda and Kassie didn't answer the child, so she continued. "Mrs. Wilmer lives alone. If he took her, nobody would even know she was gone. Maybe nobody cares for her. Could we ask death to knock on her door and take her? He could ask her if she would go with him instead of Sarah. Mrs. Wilmer is old; maybe she would be willing to go with him." Mia looked hopefully at Hilda and Kassie, waiting for an answer.

"Could we ask Father to go to Mrs. Wilmer's place before dark and ask her if she would want to die instead of Sarah? He could beg her. He could tell her that we don't want Sarah to die."

"No. If he comes for Sarah, he will not take anyone else in her place."

Mia was shattered.

"Do you think Sarah can live another day without eating?" Kassie asked again.

"I don't know. I'll ask Father how many days a person can live without eating," Hilda replied. "He will know, and he will tell me."

"Don't tell him it is Sarah we are worried about because that would make Mother angry."

"I'll ask him before dark, and I'll make sure Mother doesn't see me talking to him." Hilda shuddered as she spoke. "I don't want her to go off into one of her mad frenzies again."

"He'll be coming into the house soon. When you hear his footsteps, stand beside the water pail and pretend you are having a drink of water. Start talking to him before Mother knows he is in the house," Kassie advised her sister.

Mia watched Hilda speak to her father; she was the only sibling who had the courage to approach him. Even though their father was a quiet, soft-spoken person, it angered Nadia when she saw a bond developing between her husband and their children. Her father favored Hilda. Nadia developed a seething hatred for her second daughter and accused her husband of liking Hilda more than he liked her.

After Hilda confided in her father, she reported, "Father said a person could live many days without eating. However, he said

Sarah is not sick because she is not eating—she is sick because she lost lots of blood. She needs blood, but if she eats, she will get stronger and then get better."

"If Sarah needs blood, do you think if she ate some blood sausage it would help her get better?" Kassie asked anxiously.

Mia thought it was a brilliant idea and wondered why one of her parents didn't think of it.

"I will ask Father," Hilda volunteered again.

Later, Hilda reported back, "Father says Sarah can't eat blood; she would have to go to the hospital, and the doctor would put blood into her arm. But if he took her to the hospital, they would know somebody did something to her. The doctor would ask questions, and he would report it to the police. Aunt Elana would be in trouble. She would have to go to jail because of what she did to Sarah. Mother does not want Aunt Elana to go to jail because she is her sister and she has children to take care of too. We have to wait for Sarah to get better at home." Then Hilda added, "Father said we were not to worry about Sarah dying because he would take her to the hospital if she got worse."

Mia wondered how a doctor could put blood into someone's arm and make them well.

"We should tell the police what Aunt Elana did to Sarah," Koss angrily lashed out, using his authority of being the oldest son in the house. "It would serve her right if they put her in jail."

Koss did not like Elana. If Sarah died because of the abortion, somebody would have to take the blame. He wanted that person to be his aunt. He would not blame his mother.

The darkness of night was followed by the dawn of another bleak day. Mia was relieved there had been no knock on the door during the night; the dreaded visitor hadn't come to take Sarah. With the approach of another evening, darkness and silence again descended on the household. Mia watched her father in the bleakness of their surroundings. She watched Nadia as she came out from behind the drape. She spoke to her husband and put the bowl she was carrying on the cupboard. Her husband looked up at his wife and then down at the bowl.

"What do you mean she ate? It doesn't look like she even touched the broth."

"Well, she had a few tablespoons." Nadia looked more relaxed.

"Sarah ate some broth." The whispers flitted around the room. "Sarah is improving. She is going to recover."

Nadia turned to Hilda and Kassie. "I told Sarah when she is able to eat a whole bowl of broth, I will allow her to have company. You will be the first ones to see her."

The next day, with Nadia's coaxing, Sarah ate the whole bowl of broth. However, Nadia set more restrictions. "Hilda and Kassie are older, so I will allow them to see Sarah tomorrow. Koss is the eldest boy, so he and Jacob will be allowed to see her the day after. Mia is the youngest, so she will have to wait until the third day."

Mia missed Sarah. She was disheartened that she would have to wait such a long time to see her eldest sister. Her father sensed the child's disappointment.

"Why can't Mia see her with Hilda and Kassie?" he asked.

"Koss and Jacob are older than she is, and she has to wait her turn. Besides, they might want to talk about something she should not hear," Nadia stated shrewdly.

"Do you think Sarah would even want to see the boys?" Her father spoke sharply; he disapproved.

"Yes. Koss has to see her because he is the eldest son!" Her mother was insistent, but she was also determined to protect Sarah. "Jacob can see her when Koss is visiting with her. Koss must see her even if she does not want to see him or talk to him." Nadia firmly dictated the order of precedence in her family.

When Hilda and Kassie went to see Sarah the next day, there were giggles coming from behind the drape. Nadia snapped at the two girls.

"Sarah is sick. You should not be laughing."

"Leave them be," her husband spoke calmly. "There has been enough gloom in this house."

Sarah told Hilda and Kassie to take down the drape. She wanted to get out of bed. Nadia was horrified.

"Leave them alone," her father cautioned again.

They pulled the drape down to reveal Sarah sitting on the edge of the bed, looking pale but smiling. She asked Mia to come and stand beside her. Mia looked at Nadia, afraid to displease her. Nadia had made it clear she wouldn't be allowed to see Sarah until after Koss and Jacob. Her brothers were still not in the house. To Nadia's horror, Sarah stood up and slowly walked to where the child stood. She showed her mother she wasn't as fragile as she made her out to be.

A few days later, Nadia spoke to Hilda. "Sarah has been up for a few days. I am going to leave her with you and Kassie while she is asleep. I have to go to the Stephensons' to tell them it was a boy."

Mia could not grasp the reason her mother gave for going to the Stephensons' place. "Why did Mother go to Stephensons'?" she asked Kassie.

"Mother went there to tell them Sarah had a baby boy," Kassie told the child.

"Sarah has a baby boy?" Mia asked in surprise. Then, in disappointment, she added, "But we have a baby brother already. Why didn't Sarah get a girl?" With mixed feelings, she said, "I want to see Sarah and her baby."

Hilda entered the room, infuriated by what Kassie told the child.

"Why did you tell the brat about the baby?" Not wanting to awaken Sarah, she hissed the words at Kassie under her breath. "You know Mother didn't want Sarah to know it was a boy. Why did you tell the brat?"

Standing over Mia like a thunder cloud, she added, "Sarah does not have a baby. She doesn't. It died, and you are not to tell anyone about the baby. You are not to ask questions about Sarah's baby. If you do, Sarah will cry and get sick again."

Mia was confused by the events of the previous days. "I want to see Sarah," she muttered.

Her lips trembled as she fought her tears and her fear of Hilda. The child wanted to make sure they were telling the truth. So many confusing things had happened in the last few days. She knew the grownups didn't always tell the truth. She wanted to see if Sarah had a baby wrapped in a blue blanket sleeping beside her.

They let her see Sarah while she slept. Kassie held back the drape in the doorway. Hilda picked her up, and Mia looked down at Sarah. There was no baby lying beside her. She wouldn't ask questions because she didn't want the sister she loved more than anyone else to cry and get sick again.

When Nadia returned from the Stephensons' residence that evening, her husband came into the house.

"Where have you been?" he asked, studying her warily.

"I went to talk to Mrs. Stephenson," she replied.

"What did you have to talk to her about?"

"I had to talk to her about something," Nadia replied, irritated.

Mia noticed the troubled look on her father's face. "What was your reason for talking to her?"

"I wanted to talk to her about what happened here over the last few days."

"You wanted to talk to her about what happened in our house? What was your purpose for that? What did you expect to gain?"

Mia noticed her father spoke the words through clenched teeth; he also clenched his fist like he did when he was upset. He didn't wait for her answers; he turned and walked out of the house in resignation.

The second question that Nadia asked her sister Elana after she performed the abortion was not answered for many years. The abortion Elana performed on Sarah left her sterile. Sarah was the only sibling who showed Mia love when she was a child. Her sister, who had so much love to give to a child, would never give birth to a child of her own.

Sarah's pregnancy and abortion would be cast in stone, hidden in the family closet along with the skeletons of Nadia's other secrets.

CHAPTER EIGHT

Koss and Jacob no longer slept in the house; their father would not allow it. Mia shared the bedroom with her sisters. Occasionally, the voices of Hilda and Kassie would awaken her after she fell asleep. Sometimes they spoke of their intimate secrets. At other times, their enraged voices disturbed her sleep. One night it was Kassie's furious voice that interfered with Mia's slumber.

"Mother said if I did what she asked me to, she would stick up for me. She didn't say anything when Father scolded me. It was Koss's fault, not mine. She didn't even say anything when he slapped me. She saw Koss snickering and smirking behind Father's back. She knew it was Koss's fault, not mine. She made me take the blame. If Mother does not keep her promises to me, I am going to get a real boyfriend and get pregnant the first chance I get just like Sarah did. Then I will get married."

"But Sarah didn't get married, and she just about died when she had the abortion. You are younger than Sarah. Aren't you afraid of dying?"

"Sarah didn't die. Father said he would have taken her to the hospital if she didn't get better. Besides, I will get a boyfriend that is old enough to marry me. Look how Mother treats Sarah. She still lets her go anyplace she wants to, and she never scolds her. She treats her like a princess."

Hilda was silent, but she seemed to agree.

"If I just about died like Sarah, maybe Mother would treat me different." Kassie continued pouting, wallowing in self-pity. "She would feel sorry for me."

"Well, at least Mother treats you better than she treats me," Hilda said bleakly.

"You know Father will stick up for you; he always does," Kassie cut in bitterly. "Father never sticks up for me."

"When he is around, he does, but you know what she does to me when Father is not at home. We can't tell Father what she makes us do with Koss because she will get back at us the minute he leaves the yard. Shush, Mia is up. Let's talk quietly." Hilda's voice dropped to a whisper.

"Well, she says Koss and Jacob cannot get us in trouble because they are young. I heard that a brother can't get a sister pregnant because their blood is the same."

"Who told you that?"

"A girl at school told me." The blunt answer brought Kassie back to her previous objections. "And Mother promised me she would buy me a rubber dolly. Every time she goes to Ridgewood, I ask her if she bought me one. She always makes excuses."

"A rubber dolly? What do you need a rubber dolly for? You are too big to play with dolls."

"Mother said she will buy me one. It will be mine. She said it is not big, so I can keep it in my pocket all the time."

Mia dozed off to sleep to the sound of her sisters' whispers; they were waiting for Sarah to come home from visiting one of her friends. She heard Kassie speaking of wanting the rubber dolly, but she had no inkling of why she wanted it and why she said she would keep it in her pocket.

When Sarah was at home, Mother liked to keep her at her side. Nadia got angry with Mia if she tagged along after them. Sometimes after lunch, Mia watched them walk down a trail that led to the old storage shed at the far end of the yard.

"Can I go into the shed with you?" she asked Sarah one day.

"No, you can't, but if you want to, you can stand beside the path and wait for us."

"Remember, you are not to follow them when they go toward that shed," Hilda warned. "Do you understand? That building is off limits to you, and you are not to ask questions about it. If Mother gets angry, there is no telling what she will do to you."

Mia didn't know why Nadia and Sarah went into the shed. She watched them disappear around the building and waited beside the path for Sarah. Sometimes she would lie down beside the path and fall asleep before they returned.

"I don't want that ragamuffin waiting along the path for us when we go to the shed," Nadia angrily snapped at Hilda. "I want you to take her into the house and make her have a nap. What if a neighbor sees her sleeping beside the path? What if that meddling demon, Mr. Gabriel, passed by and saw her lying there? What if he came into the yard, and what if he asks to talk to me?" Nadia fumed.

"I won't fall asleep beside the path again," Mia promised Sarah. Her eldest sister picked her up and carried her back to the house; it was the highlight of her day.

"I like being as tall as you are. It's so much fun." The child spoke happily as she looked down at their mother walking beside them. Sometimes she made a gesture as if patting Nadia on the head, and Sarah would laugh at the child's wit. It would anger Nadia to hear Mia giggle with Sarah. Mia was a small child starved for the bits of affection that Sarah showed her.

"Leave the big cow alone," Nadia angrily snapped as she looked up at them.

"Why does Mother call you a big cow?" Mia fretted into Sarah's ear.

Nadia's insult didn't seem to bother Sarah, but it disturbed Mia that Nadia would degrade her eldest sister by calling her names.

"Why does Mother call Sarah names?" she later asked Hilda, disheartened.

"What does she call her?" Hilda probed.

"She calls Sarah a big cow," Mia muttered.

"Mother doesn't call Sarah names." Hilda's laugh was bitter. "It is you she is calling a big cow. Mother is angry with you because she doesn't like that Sarah pays attention to you. Keep away from Sarah, or Mother might get violent with you."

Mia noticed the deep frown on Hilda's brow when she spoke. Even though she was lonely, she was afraid to upset her mother. She silently hid her disappointment, feeling the loss of the only friend she had. Dispirited, she started to avoid Sarah.

Once when Sarah went to look for Mia, she found her in seclusion, crying.

"Why are you crying?"

"I don't have anyone to play with, and I am afraid to wait beside the path for you."

"Why are you afraid to wait beside the path for me?" Sarah asked.

"Because Mother gets angry with me if I do. I thought she called you a big cow; I don't want her to call you names. But it's me that she calls a big cow. I saw her hitting a cow with a stick once, and she was calling it names. If she calls me a big cow, I'm afraid she will hit me with a stick too. She might even beat me like she beats Jacob." The child wept uncontrollably as she gave voice to her fears.

"Who told you Mother calls you a big cow?"

"Hilda told me it's me that she calls a big cow, not you. Hilda said Mother is angry at me, and that is why she calls me a cow."

"You can still wait beside the path for me. I will talk to Mother," Sarah assured her.

Mia continued to avoid Sarah and Nadia. When she saw them walking hand in hand, she turned away and pretended she didn't see them. She didn't reply to Sarah when she heard her call out.

Nadia's attention to one child over another and her favoritism fueled dissension among the family members. Hilda was the only one who could speak openly to their father about things that were not proper about Nadia's conduct. Then he would get angry with his wife. The seething hatred Nadia held for her second daughter escalated.

"You like Hilda more than you like me," Nadia screamed at her husband.

Like a trapped animal, she fought and spat at her husband and accused him of inappropriately carrying on with the daughter he favored.

Mia shared the bedroom with her sisters. She took turns sleeping with them. She would be awakened late at night by their father's enraged voice. He would come into their bedroom to find that Hilda and Kassie were not in their beds. Infuriated to find his daughters missing, he angrily questioned Sarah regarding their whereabouts.

"I don't know where they are," Sarah answered sleepily. "I didn't hear anything. They must have slipped out while I was sleeping."

"Why are you waking everyone up?" Nadia's voice could be heard blaring throughout the house. "Leave Sarah alone; she needs her rest."

The angry voices of her parents carried on until her father went outside to find his missing daughters. When he brought them back into the house, he was outraged. It infuriated him that he could not control the chaos in his house.

One night when he retrieved Kassie, she was shrieking when he brought her into the house. Nadia's angry voice cut through the darkness.

"Well, where did you find her? Who was she with?"

"She was with those undesirable nitwits and her brother."

"Well, what is the harm of sitting around and visiting with Koss and her friends?" Nadia lashed at her husband in the darkness.

When her husband was absent, Nadia forced improper behavior between her offspring. She encouraged it, and it angered her if they didn't take to her teachings. However, the secret had to be kept hidden behind her closed door. Promiscuous behavior by her daughters was also acceptable if it was done secretly and without causing a scandal in the neighborhood. Nadia helped Kassie concoct excuses about why she was not in bed when her father checked on her at night. Much to Kassie's satisfaction, Nadia was there to defend her with the invented excuses.

One night, after one of Kassie's rendezvous, she was again brought into the house by her enraged father. "I will not stand for this any longer. I have had enough of this girl carrying on the way she does."

Mia cringed as she listened to her father's infuriated rage as he punished Kassie. Her sister's cries sounded inhuman and terrified the child. The next morning after Nadia spoke to Kassie, she approached her husband about the previous night's episode.

"You know, Kassie says doesn't know how she happened to be outside last night when you found her."

"What do you mean she didn't know how she happened to be outside?" His anger carried over from the previous night. "I found her with those dimwits."

"Well, she must be sleepwalking," Nadia responded peevishly. "I've heard that sometimes children are found wandering around in their sleep."

Her husband looked at Nadia, infuriated, and stomped out of the house.

Time passed, and much to the outrage of her father and the approval of her mother, Kassie continued to slip out of her bed during the night.

"Can't you understand? Kassie is a sleepwalker," Nadia raved at her husband. "That is why you are finding her outside at night."

"If she is sleepwalking, why am I finding her with those dimwits? I forbid her to go outside after the lights are out."

"What is wrong with you? What if she has to go to the privy at night? Is she going to have to wake you up to get permission? You are treating her as if she were a child. Are you going to take her by the hand to the privy like a two-year-old?" Nadia mocked.

Still, he kept a watchful eye on his daughter.

"Can't a girl have privacy around here anymore? Kassie can't even go to the privy at night without being harassed and interrogated. What is wrong with you?" Nadia continued to complain.

Her husband's reply was cold. "If I hear her go outside during the night, I will give her a few minutes to get back. If she doesn't come back within that time, I will go outside to see that she is not going farther than the privy."

Nadia argued vigorously as she defended Kassie. She caused much friction about the tight rein her husband kept on her. In return, her husband retaliated with severe punishment to keep Kassie under control.

"She does not go outside to carry on with anyone. Don't you realize children sleepwalk?" Nadia's argument continued vehemently with her husband.

"I forbid anyone to use the word 'sleepwalking' in this house," he snapped at his wife in exasperation. "I forbid Kassie to leave the house after everyone is in bed."

Though her husband had a stern appearance, he had a gentle personality and was no match for the belligerent, demonic woman he had married. He was infuriated when Nadia kept concocting lame excuses for Kassie. Nadia was determined to protect Kassie and have her legacy live on through a daughter who was readily accepting her ancestral legacy.

CHAPTER NINE

Mia played beside the lush growth that swept from the marsh to the proximity of the yard. The ground was not level there; grass grew in green clumps scattered like little islands among the stand of the trees. Dips scratched out by the few chickens running loose in the yard surrounded the mounds of grass. The child was hopping from one green mound to the other, trying not to step into a dip left by the chickens. It was something she saw her older siblings do; it was a game they played.

When she had asked if she could join them, they taunted her and told her to go away, saying it was their play area and she was too young to play with them. Koss made derogatory remarks she could not understand.

"You can't play with us, you brat, because you can't spread your legs the way Kassie can when you jump." He snickered obnoxiously.

Mia looked at her three siblings. Kassie's lean form made her look like she was the tallest of the three; Koss was fatter, and Jacob was the smallest.

"I can take big steps like Jacob does," she said, hoping that they would permit her to play with them. With this, she demonstrated a leaping stride.

Koss sneered. "That is not the way Kassie does it. You have to show us how far apart you can spread your legs the way Kassie can."

He stood and vulgarly spread his legs apart as far as he could to show the child what he meant. Mia was confused. How could Kassie run in such an awkward manner? She stood and watched her older siblings as they played. Kassie was not running sideways. Koss just scoffed at Mia and continued to make her believe she was not a perceptive child because she could not match his wit.

Now, playing there alone, Mia decided she would try to leap from one mound to another like she saw her siblings do earlier. At first, she did not notice Koss slyly lurking among the trees, watching her. When she did, she anticipated that he would scold her for playing in the area they forbid her to play in earlier.

She watched Koss for a moment, waiting for some sign of fury or any reaction to her being there. However, he stood and lurked as he continued to observe her.

"If I run fast like Jacob, I can jump from one clump of grass to another without missing them." She hoped that Koss would not scold her for being there.

"I bet you can't jump on that clump of grass over by that bush." He pointed to a large green mound some distance into the growth that surrounded them.

"No, I can't; it's too far away."

"But you can go and stand on it." He spoke to her as if he were giving her permission to do something special.

Mia was warned not to go into surrounding bog for fear of getting lost; she obeyed and played in view of the house.

"No, I don't want to because I might get lost." She looked toward the house, feeling comforted that it was close by and in sight.

"You won't get lost," her brother assured her. "I will be with you; you know you can't get lost if I am with you. I know my way through the bog," Koss boasted.

The child hesitated. Her older brother urged her on.

"Come on. Nobody stood on that big mound, not even Kassie. I will help you." His words were reassuring. "If you stand on it first, it will be your mound. Then not even Kassie can claim it. I will tell her it is your mound."

With his usual trickery, Koss took her out of view of the house. He took her toward the mound, where he knocked her to the ground and brutally attacked her. He then ran away, leaving the child unconscious.

Mia didn't know how long she lay there; her body was paralyzed with pain and shock. She couldn't move, or cry, or whimper. She didn't know why her brother hurt her. She descended further into darkness and fear.

Finally, she heard voices; they seemed to be so far away. They were calling. They were looking for something. It sounded like they were looking for an animal; maybe the dog had wandered away.

They are calling the dog, the child thought.

Then she recognized her father's voice. He sounded close; he was in the grove of bushes where she lay. She opened her eyes and saw the profile of someone's head. It seemed to tower over her.

In her dissociated state, Mia didn't recognize her father. She wondered why this tall man was there. Her father was more than six feet tall, but from where she lay, he looked like a giant. She was afraid. Was this giant going to hurt her, too, like Koss did? Fear radiated through her body. She wanted to scream. She must have made a sound—a whimper, a moan, or a sound of fear. He turned his head toward her. It was her father.

"She is here," he called out. "I found her!"

Why didn't Mia know they were looking for her? Why didn't she recognize her name when her father called? Was it because she was never called by her given name? They labeled her with a degrading name that stuck with her for many years. It wasn't until she began school that they revealed her real name.

"She is here," her father called out again. "I found her!"

It was then that Mia knew they were not looking for the dog—they were looking for her. Her mother appeared and looked angrily at the child. Her parents exchanged a few words, and then she heard other voices. Her siblings were coming.

Mia lay unable to move. She still lay as her brother had left her. Paralyzed with fear and in shock, she was not able to utter a cry or make a sound.

Nadia's anger turned on the child. "Shame on you. Put your knees together and cover yourself," she snapped. "The others are coming. They should not see her like that."

Mia lay in shock and pain, tears slowly trickling down her cheeks. She was not able to move; her body was paralyzed. Nadia roughly slapped her knees together and angrily pulled her dress down. There was no pity, no sympathy for the child—only anger. Most people would show a wounded animal more empathy than the woman showed the half-conscious child lying on the ground beside her feet.

"Who did this to you?" Her father's wrath erupted.

The child couldn't speak; she had no concept of what was done to her.

Her siblings were gathering around: Sarah and Hilda and then Jacob. Kassie carried Yuri. They all were there except Koss. Her father looked at the children.

"Where is Koss?" he asked bitterly, looking to Nadia for an answer.

Nadia rambled without giving her husband a reply.

Then he looked at Mia. "Was it Koss? Did he do this to you?"

Koss? At that, the child's tears flowed faster; she could not speak and nodded her head. No one came to hold her, to comfort her or soothe her with understanding or sympathy. No one showed her any act of kindness. She lay in shock with no concern given to her. It was as if they were blaming her for bringing upon herself a contagious illness.

Nadia stood glaring down at Mia, wanting to protect her elder son from the consequences. She didn't want her other children to see what he had done, nor did she want them to witness their father's rage at his son.

"Koss?" Nadia lashed at the child. "Tell me what Koss did to you."

Mia had no concept of what Koss had done to her. "He hurt me," she whispered, cowering fearfully.

"Where did he hurt you?" her father asked.

Mia was not able to answer her father's question; Nadia continued to interrupt, lashing out at the child.

"He hurt you? How did he hurt you? Did he hit you?"

Mia looked at Nadia's infuriated red face, glistening with perspiration. Traumatized and numbed with pain, she couldn't explain how he hurt her; she did not know what he had done to her.

"Did he hit you?" Nadia lashed out again.

The child could relate the hurt with being hit. "Yes," Mia could finally answer, her voice breaking. "Yes, he was hitting me; he was hurting me."

Nadia continued to confuse the child with interruptions. She wouldn't allow her to answer her father's questions.

Yes, Koss was hitting me, the child thought silently as her parents stood arguing. *He was not hitting me with his fists as he usually does, but he was hurting me. He was hurting me more than he ever hurt me with his fists.*

She couldn't get the words out to tell her father how Koss hurt her. Nadia wouldn't allow her to speak. Her father stood there, knowing it was Koss who did this to the child, but Nadia wouldn't allow him to question Mia. She wouldn't allow Mia to give her feeble explanations as best she could.

"Didn't you hear what she said? She said Koss only beat her up," Nadia shouted at her husband for all to hear.

"Where is Koss? Why isn't he here?" Her husband flared. "I want to talk to him!"

"He is not here because—" Nadia blinked her icy eyes to give her time to concoct an excuse. "He is not here because I sent him to do a man's work in the orchard, work you should be doing!" Nadia flung the words at her husband.

"What had to be done in the orchard? There is nothing to be done there. Where did you send him?" He knew she was not telling the truth.

Nadia hemmed and hawed, but she could not give her husband a prompt answer.

"There is no work to be done in the orchard. Wherever he is, I will find him, and I will deal with him for what he has done. I will deal with him in *my* way," her husband responded in anger.

"He is only a child, and he only hit her. Didn't you hear what she said? She said he only hit her. I won't let you talk to him alone. I will go with you. There is no telling what you will do to him in your state of mind. You heard her say Koss only hit her."

Like a possessed woman, Nadia charged after her husband, afraid he would find Koss and beat the truth out of him before she could intervene.

"Don't you think you should stay here and help Mia?" He clenched his fists in aggravation.

"No, they can help her." Turning toward Jacob, she called, "Help Mia into the house."

"Jacob? How can Jacob help her? He is a child himself."

"He is the smallest. She can support herself against someone who is close to her own size and walk along with them," Nadia spoke spitefully, sweat rolling down her face. She turned and continued to follow her husband.

Jacob held out his hand to Mia. She took it and tried to sit up. Crumbling into a heap, she started to sob. She wasn't able to walk.

Nadia glanced over her shoulder. "Carry the brat into the house," she commanded Sarah and Hilda. She proceeded to catch up to her husband, lest he find Koss before she did.

The dead weight of the half-conscious child prevented Sarah from carrying her alone. She took the child's arms, while Hilda took her by her legs, and they dragged her to the threshold of the house. They stopped. They couldn't lift her over the threshold, so they made her stand and take the painful step herself.

"Hilda, would you help me lay her on the bed?" Sarah asked.

"No, that is far enough," Hilda said coldly. "We have to get her to tell us the truth before we take her any farther."

Inheriting Nadia's insidious ways, Hilda made the child stand in the center of the room while she cross-examined her. Mia stood swaying; she was in tears, and she wasn't able to answer her sister's questions.

"I want to lie down," she begged her sister.

"Hilda, help me lay her on the bed," Sarah repeated.

"No, she can't lie down. Not until she answers my questions," Hilda said sharply.

"Let's put her to bed, Hilda. Can't you see she is in no condition to be questioned?"

"No," Hilda snapped at her eldest sister. "She can't lie down until she answers my questions. What did Koss do to you?"

"I don't know."

"Well, you will just have to keep standing there until you know," Hilda snapped.

"He was hurting me."

"Hurting you? How did he hurt you?"

"I don't know." The child teetered from the nausea and pain. "I don't know. He was hitting me."

"Hitting you? How was he hitting you? What was he hitting you with?"

"Leave her alone. Let's get her to bed," Sarah repeated.

"No, she has to answer me if she wants to lie down." Hilda's voice cut at her sharply.

"I don't know. He kept hitting me with himself," the child kept repeating.

"With what?"

"I don't know. I think he had a sharp knife because it felt like he was cutting me up with something. He was hurting me very hard."

"Did you see the knife he was cutting you up with?" Hilda asked as if what she said amused her.

Mia stood in shock, fighting pain and nausea; she felt a trickle down her leg.

"Blood," Hilda gasped. "He raped her!"

Mia lost control of her bladder before she crumpled to the floor in a heap.

Over the next few days, she vaguely felt she was lying under bed covers. In a state of unconsciousness, she heard voices or felt a touch while she drifted in and out of consciousness.

"She must stay in bed; it took three days before I could get up." Sarah knew what Koss did. Her big sister understood, but she was unable to help Mia.

As Mia lay unresponsively on the bed, she felt someone slap her on her stomach. Yuri was able to pull himself up and walk along the furniture. She screamed in pain.

"Keep the baby away from her. You are supposed to be watching him."

"He didn't mean to hurt her. He only wants her to get up and play with him."

Mia slipped back into dark, peaceful unconsciousness. She couldn't open her eyes.

Between lapses of consciousness, she was aware of voices drifting around her. Jacob or Kassie came to where she lay to make periodic announcements. They disturbed her peace by announcing what time of day it was and how much longer it would be before she could get out of bed. She didn't want to be interrupted from the deep sleep. It was where she felt no pain or fear.

When she was able to open her eyes, she was unaware of how much time had passed. Still weak but aware of her surroundings, Mia felt better.

"She is awake," she heard someone say.

"Do you know for how many days you slept?" Kassie grilled her.

Mia looked at her sister and shook her head; it felt like it was morning.

"This is the third day," she announced shrilly. "But you still have to stay in bed until after we have our lunch. Sarah said you have to stay in bed for three days."

Mia was astonished. "I don't believe you." Her voice was weak; she couldn't believe that so much time had passed. "You are fooling me. I don't believe I fell asleep for that many days."

"No, I am not, and Sarah said you have to stay in bed for three days before you get well. She said that was how long it took her to get better. That means you have stay in bed for two and a half more hours. Then three days will be over."

Mia lay back in bed. What happened to her? Why didn't she remember? Kassie said she was in bed for three days. Why was she in bed for that long? Amnesia played its part in her recovery and protected her from the horror of what happened. That memory was blocked out of her mind; only a deep, unknown terror of her brother remained.

She couldn't close her eyes and sleep another wink. She would just lie quietly in bed until they told her she could get up. Sarah came to the bed and tenderly touched her stomach.

"Does your stomach still hurt?"

"Yes." Her stomach felt very tender, but she couldn't recall why. She continued lying in bed while Kassie and Jacob ran in and out of the house.

"Mia does not want to stay in bed anymore," Kassie shrieked loudly as she ran outside.

Mia listened to Sarah and Hilda as they walked about the room and spoke quietly. Hilda sounded bitter as she spoke; Sarah sounded accepting of things.

"Mother knows what Koss did to Mia, but she would not allow Father to punish him."

"Well, she said Koss was crying when they found him hiding in the shed. She said he must have been sorry for what he did to Mia."

"Mother would not let Father punish him and said if he struck him, he would have to do it over her dead body."

"She said seeing Mia lay unconscious in bed was enough punishment for Koss."

Mia closed her eyes to make the time pass faster, but she could not sleep.

When Hilda went outside, Mia sat up and slowly moved to the edge of the bed. She carefully dangled her feet over the side. Three days in bed was such a long time. Supporting herself against the bed, she tried lowering herself until her feet touched the floor. If she passed out like she did when they brought her into the house and interrogated her, they would have to put her back into the bed. Then she would have to stay there until her three days were up. She didn't like staying in bed if she was not sleepy.

When Sarah saw Mia, she came to her. "You don't want to stay in bed anymore, do you?"

Mia shook her head.

Sarah put her hand on the child's lower abdomen and gently pressed it again.

"Does that hurt?" she asked her.

Mia nodded her head. "Yes, it hurts a little bit."

"Would you like to get out of bed and walk?"

Mia felt very weak and unsteady; she was afraid to walk, but she nodded.

"I know how you feel. Once I felt the same way you feel. However, I was much older than you are. I will help you just like Mother helped when it happened to me."

Patiently, Sarah took hold of her as if she were tenderly teaching her to take her first steps.

Mia took a few steps before Sarah put her back into bed. By the end of the day, she was cautiously slipping out of bed and taking a few steps on her own.

"Look, I can walk. I can walk," she kept repeating in a shaky voice on the verge of tears. She bravely touched her stomach, saying, "And my stomach doesn't hurt as much."

An indistinguishable memory of happiness after those days of convalescing—walking and touching her stomach—emerged every so often throughout Mia's life. She couldn't understand why those memories, those flashbacks, kept recurring, emerging, and then burying themselves in her subconscious again. When Mia had a flashback, she would ask herself why a young child, a toddler, would have memories of such a pain. She could only associate the pain with that of severe menstrual cramps. She couldn't remember the cause of the pain.

Deceived
A child once listened to soft winds blow,
　Watched clouds drift calmly by
And marveled at all of nature's glow
　Watched birds soar in the sky.
Nature was the love the child knew
　Cheeks kissed by sun and rain
Bare foot she'd race in morning dew,
　Survival was her aim.
She innocently touched the butterflies,
　And watched the flowers bloom,
Though her life was of deceit and lies
　And all that sordid gloom
The little child was unaware
　Of the secrets locked deep inside,
No mother's love, no one to care,
　With God her only guide.
As years passed, the soft wind grew
　To a forceful, wailing tide.
The door unlocked, and memories drew,
　Of never a safe place to hide.
She heard the torrents of wind and rain,
　Saw the clouds in the tormented sky,
Then in her heart she felt the pain
　Of her childhood days gone by.
Oh, Mother, why did you deceive
　Your child's innocent trust?
Oh, Mother, hear your children grieve
　Because of your own ungodly lust.
　A little girl so unaware
　Of the secrets locked deep inside—
Now the door is unlocked, and in despair,
　God is her only guide.

CHAPTER TEN

Her father had to make a business trip to the Mitchells' place. Mrs. Mitchell belonged to the ladies' group that Nadia also belonged to, so she decided she would accompany her husband.

"We will take Mia with us," her father said. "We will not leave her at home with that dimwit."

"She can stay at home. Koss is not a dimwit," Nadia blazed. "What will she do at the Mitchells'?"

"She can sit in the house with you and Mrs. Mitchell."

"She will only be in our way. How can we visit with the brat sitting in the same room listening?"

The set of her father's jaw and his clenched fists showed agitation as he faced conflict with his wife.

Mia was devitalized by lack of sleep. The scorching summer heat agonized her and added to her exhaustion. She was on the brink of being physically ill and wanted to curl up where she would not be noticed and sleep.

"Please, Hilda," she begged. "I am so tired; tell Father you will watch so Koss doesn't hurt me while I sleep."

"Don't be a brat," Hilda hissed. "I will not be responsible for you."

When they arrived at Mitchells', her father left with Mr. Mitchell, and Mia followed Nadia into the house. Mrs. Mitchell was a stout, gray-haired woman.

Upon their entrance, Mrs. Mitchell was sitting in her chair. She pushed her silver-rimmed glasses back on her nose and eyed the child coldly. Snorting a greeting to Nadia, she indicated a chair to the child. Mia sat on the chair and relaxed in the cool, refreshing room. Her eyes started to droop heavily; the clean, rough floor looked inviting. Perhaps Mrs. Mitchell wouldn't notice if she slumped quietly to the floor and rested.

Suddenly a voice cut through the room and startled the dozing child. "Why don't you go outside and look at the flowers I planted in front of the house?"

Mia realized the penetrating command was directed at her; she opened her eyes and looked at Mrs. Mitchell. She felt downcast and reluctant; leaving the comfort of the cool room would only add to her exhaustion. She knew she could not lie down outside; the heat of the scorching day would be unbearable. However, getting the impression she wasn't wanted in Mrs. Mitchell's house, Mia had no choice but comply with the demand. She faltered into a standing position.

"You must not walk through the front room," Mrs. Mitchell's voice crackled. "Go out through the door you entered. You will find a gate that will lead you out to my flower bed."

Mia nodded her head and left. The child didn't realize the gate she was told to go through was right beside the house. She walked into the yard and looked at the strange surroundings. The hot sun beat down and made her feel lightheaded; she yearned for sleep. Standing beside the car, she looked at it. If she could open the door, she might lie down inside it. Her father warned the children of the danger of falling asleep in a hot car. The heat was unbearable, so she decided she would look for Mrs. Mitchell's flowers.

A heavy, crude fence surrounded the front of the house. A thick growth of trees stood behind the fence. Imprisoned in the weather-beaten pickets was a gate; she opened it and mustered the courage to walk through it. The dark trees and shadows frightened her; a tall growth of untrimmed hedges stood on either side of the narrow path, arching over and blocking the view of the house. Mia did not realize the path was so overgrown because the Mitchells did not use that gate.

Timidly, she stepped onto the path and made her way down the eerie trail. The branches stuck out and touched her. Fear gripped her; like long bony fingers, the branches reached out as if they wanted to grab her. Trapped in fear, afraid to go any farther, she looked over her shoulder and saw the distance she had come along the path was greater than the distance she had to go. Ahead of her, at the side of the path, she saw an opening, a little clearing. It was as if danger lurked, waiting to spring on her there. The feeling of danger was prevalent. "Is one of the Mitchell boys there? Is he waiting for me?" she whispered to herself. "Is he going to grab me and hurt me like Koss did?"

So great was the sensation of someone being there, lurking and waiting for her, she froze, feeling faint with fear and fatigue. She listened for a sound, the snap of a twig or a footstep. She realized she was very quiet when she walked down the path. *Maybe he didn't hear me*, she thought to herself. *Maybe he still doesn't know I am here. If I turn and run back to the gate, he will hear me running. He will come after me; he will pounce on me and hurt me.*

With her heart beating uncontrollably, she stood motionless, listening but hearing nothing but the thumping in her chest. Slowly her fear started to subside. *Maybe he doesn't want to hurt me.*

With caution, she silently made her way down the path. When she reached the edge of the clearing, she looked into it; the predator she anticipated was not there. Relief swept over her, but the suspense and fear left her drained.

Like a constant shadow, the fear the child encountered in Mitchells' yard followed her or reared before her intensely throughout her childhood and every day of her young life.

⇌ ⇌

Mia harbored a deep-rooted fear of Koss. At times, the fear overpowered her. If her brother appeared unexpectedly, the child froze in terror and could not control her screams of sheer panic. She only felt secure when she knew Koss was out of the yard.

"Mother says Mia must go outside and get some fresh air. She says she has moped around the house long enough," Hilda said.

"You know she is afraid of Koss, and I can't say that I blame her," Sarah retorted.

"Well, Mother says she has to forget what happened. We can't have her underfoot all the time. She has to get out of the house."

Mia listened to Sarah and Hilda discussing a problem that involved her. Although she did not remember what happened, the fear she had of her eldest brother would not release its grip on her.

"Koss is working in the far orchard; he is not in the yard. Mother says you must go outside to get some fresh air today. We will call you into the house before he comes into the yard for lunch."

Mia courageously ventured out of doors, but when she heard her name called, she hurried back into the protection of the house. Sometimes her brothers came early for lunch or her sisters forgot to call her into the house before the boys entered the yard. She was overwhelmed with panic when she saw Koss. She tried to hide from him, but he would sneer at her as he passed to show he saw her. There was no place where she could feel safe from her brother.

Although Mia suppressed the memories of the brutal attack, she endured a constant fear of Koss. Nadia instilled the fear of the demons in her children. The fear did not bother her older siblings as much as it bothered Mia. She felt the fear was somehow connected to the demons. She was tired and drawn, but she was afraid to go to bed early. The child fought sleep, trying to stay awake until her eldest sister came home. She only felt safe when Sarah was home.

Mia's frequent screams woke the household. She was not able to understand what was happening to her. Why was she waking up in the night and finding herself in terrorizing, grotesque situations? It angered Nadia that Mia was interrupting their night with her piercing screams.

"Tell that brat to be quiet," Nadia's voice hissed in exasperation as Sarah and Hilda tried to calm Mia.

"No, there are no demons here," Sarah assured Mia as she tried to settle her back to sleep.

"She is having another nightmare," she heard Hilda whisper.

"Nightmare" was a new word to Mia. *What is a nightmare?* she wondered.

Kassie and Koss picked up on Mia's fear; she heard them snicker and jeer. "Mia is having nightmares! Mia is having nightmares!"

"What is a nightmare?" she asked timidly.

"A nightmare is a scary horse. It's black, and it comes in the night and takes bad little kids to scary places when they are sleeping. Very bad things happen to them when the horse takes them there." Kassie and Koss sneered as they passed a look between them.

Night after night, Mia lay fearful and sleepless in bed after more terrible nightmares.

"Please don't go to sleep, Sarah," the child begged. "I am so afraid. If you fall asleep before I do, the nightmare will come back and take me again. Where does the black horse come from?" the troubled child asked Kassie. "We don't have black horses. Whose horse is it? Could we tell Father to tell its owner to keep him closed in his barn for the night so he can't come and take me to those scary places when I am asleep?"

"No, we can't do that. The horse doesn't belong to anybody." Kassie embellished her story with gleeful malice. "It is a horse that goes around at night and terrorizes little children while they sleep."

"Is the nightmare as evil as the demon?"

"Yes, he is."

"Is he all black, or does he have a small white spot on his head?"

"He is all black...black as a scary, dark night."

Mia thought for a moment before she said, "I wish he had a white face or at least a little white spot on his forehead."

"Why do you wish he had a white spot on his forehead?" Kassie asked in amusement.

"Because if he had a spot on his forehead, I could wake up if I saw a white spot coming toward me in the night. I could wake up before he got to the bed and took me outside." Mia was dispirited and exhausted from lack of sleep. "If he is all black, I won't wake up because I won't see him coming in the night."

"Well, I will ask Koss. He knows more about horses than I do."

Mia didn't know that Kassie was conspiring with Koss, using her as a pawn in a sick game they were concocting.

Later, Kassie told Mia, "No, Koss says the nightmare is as black as night and no one ever sees him coming unless they are wide awake."

Mia lived in constant fear. Not only was she afraid of Nadia, Koss, and the demons, now there was a frightful black horse called a nightmare that plagued her.

"I want you to stay awake with me," Mia begged Sarah after she had a particularly bad night. "I don't want to fall asleep. If I do, the horse takes me to that scary place when I am sleeping." She sobbed fearfully.

Sarah and Hilda questioned Mia and learned what Kassie and Koss had told her.

"Why are they telling such horrible things to her?" Hilda questioned.

"Well, you know what Kassie and Koss are like."

"Koss is weird. He is insanely freakish. But what is wrong with Kassie? She should have more sense; she should know better than telling Mia such horrid stories."

"Well, they seem to do as they please. Mother never tells them anything, and she gets angry with Father when he tries to discipline them."

Hilda and Sarah tried to soothe Mia; they tried to convince her gently. "A nightmare is not a black horse. A nightmare means you are having a bad dream while you are sleeping."

"But I don't want to have those scary bad dreams." The child shuddered. "They say the black horse takes me to a scary place at night when I am sleeping. Please stay beside me. I don't want you to let the horse take me to that scary place again."

"No," Sarah tried to assure her. "You are safe in bed when you are having the nightmare."

"But Koss and Kassie say a nightmare is a black horse that comes at night and takes me to those scary places."

"No." Sarah tried to assure her. "They are not telling you the truth. A nightmare is just a bad dream. Now go to sleep. We will be right here for you. If we hear that you are having a bad dream, we will be right beside you. Nobody takes you anyplace when you are having a nightmare; remember that. You are safe in your bed, and I promise I will be here with you."

With Sarah's promise, Mia felt more secure. She was happier now that Sarah assured her the nightmares were not a reality. Her eldest sister would protect her and make sure that nobody took her to a scary place and do horrible things to her. She could go to bed early, and Sarah would be there to help and comfort her through the bad nights. Her fear of the black horse they called a nightmare receded. She was usually exhausted, and even if Sarah still wasn't at home, Mia started going to bed right after supper again.

However, the nightmares did not cease; they got worse. Now she was not only waking up to scary situations in bed, but she was finding herself out of bed, outside in a half-awakened state. Sarah was not there to comfort her. There were forms around her, whispering and snickering. The dim light from the kitchen window cast a light across the grass to where she lay whimpering. In a bewildered state, she looked at the forms around her until they seemed to vanish into the dark. Only one remained.

"Sarah...where is Sarah? Why am I not in bed?" the terrified child whimpered.

"Go back to sleep. You are only having another nightmare," a voice hissed at her in the dark.

It was Koss's form she saw, and it was his voice she recognized.

"But why am I outside?"

"You are not outside. You are in your bed and are only dreaming that you are outside." He snickered. "Close your eyes and go back to sleep; this is not real. When you wake up in the morning, you will be in your own bed, and you will know this was just a nightmare. It is the same kind of nightmare you have when you are in bed."

Koss's voice came between the snickers and titters surrounding her.

"There is someone in the trees! Who is in the trees?" Mia asked in a terrified whisper.

"It is the demons; that's why you have to be quiet. You are not supposed to scream. If you do, they will hear you and come out of the bushes. They will hurt you. Close your eyes and go back to sleep, and they will go away."

Terrified, Mia closed her eyes. It felt like she was outside, but she didn't know how she got outside after going to bed. Nor did she know how she got back into her bed. She thought she was consumed in another frightful nightmare.

After the horrible nightmares outside, Mia would wake up with severe, unexplained stomachaches and spend most of the day in bed. Her father was concerned about his youngest daughter.

"What is wrong with Mia this morning?" he questioned Nadia as they sat around the kitchen table.

"The girls say she is not feeling well," Nadia answered irritably. "She just has a stomachache."

"Why does she have a stomachache so early in the morning?"

"She must have eaten something that disagreed with her," Nadia snapped at her husband.

"But Mia hasn't had anything to eat yet," her father pointed out with concern.

"Well, it must be something she ate last night. You know what children are like—always eating things they shouldn't." Her husband's probing questions irritated Nadia.

"Why didn't you come to the table and have your breakfast? Aren't you feeling well this morning?" Her father went to the bed where Mia lay to question her.

"My stomach hurts very badly," she whimpered as she tried to contain her sobs.

"Why does your stomach hurt?"

"I don't know."

"Did you eat anything you shouldn't have eaten last night?"

Mia looked at her father, wondering why he was questioning her. Sometimes she was hungry before bedtime because she was not able to eat her supper. She was given a crust of bread and some milk but nothing more.

"Who gives you the bread and milk when you are hungry?"

"Hilda does."

"Did you have anything else to eat?"

"No." Mia shook her head.

"Did you go into the bushes with anybody and pick some wild berries and eat them?"

"No." Mia shook her head again.

"Could it be appendicitis?" her father asked Nadia.

"No, it isn't; she is too young to be bothered with appendicitis. It is enough to hear Hilda whine about appendicitis. I won't have Mia whine every time she gets a stomachache. Leave her alone. She will be OK."

Nadia planted the idea that the stress of the nightmares upset Mia and gave her the stomachaches. Her husband's denial of and presumptions about his youngest daughter's well-being satisfied Nadia. However, later, when the family was around the supper table, their father questioned Mia's older siblings.

"I want you to tell me if you know why Mia is having so many stomachaches."

When he spoke, Koss lowered his head, and Kassie snickered.

"Why are you snickering?" Her father glared at Kassie. "Did I ask something that sounded funny?"

"No," Kassie muttered as she sheepishly lowered her head. Her usually pale face turned as crimson as her twin brother's normally ruddy one.

"Well, why were you snickering? If you think this is a funny matter, I can get the strap out and make you realize it is not. I want you to tell me what is happening to Mia."

Kassie and Koss kept their heads lowered. Jacob followed suit. Mia started to cry.

"Why are you causing a disturbance at the supper table? Can't you let us eat in peace?" Nadia flared at her husband.

"No, I want to talk to them before they eat while everyone is still at the table."

"How should they know what is giving Mia stomachaches? They can't keep track of what she has been eating." Nadia advised the children that if their father scolded them when their meal was just about over, they should stand up and walk out of the house. She would not allow him to scold their offspring at the table.

After supper, Koss accosted Mia. "You sniveling brat! Why did you have to start crying again? Father was scolding us, you little fool; he wasn't scolding you."

"Yeah, he wasn't scolding you, you fool," his younger brother echoed.

"I don't know why Father was angry. When he scolds anybody, it makes me cry," Mia replied in confusion.

"He doesn't know anything yet," Kassie whispered to Koss. "However, if she keeps sniveling when he is scolding us, he will know he is on to something."

"If Father scolds us at the table again, we will put our heads down so he thinks he is making us feel bad. You have to look at him and smile; if you don't, we will beat you to a pulp, and Mother will be furious with you. I will tell her to beat you too," Koss lashed out at the child.

Although Sarah was not babysitting for Hanna anymore, she was still spending a lot of time away from home. Once, Sarah was comforting Mia after a bad night.

"Remember, it is only a nightmare. Those bad things in the nightmare are not really happening to you." She spoke softly as she soothed the child.

"But, Sarah," Mia sobbed. "You told me not to be afraid when I am having nightmares. You said you would be by me, but you are not."

"Yes, I am with you most of the time," her sister replied.

"You aren't with me when I am having the nightmares outside."

"I told you nightmares don't happen outside. They only happen when you are sleeping in your bed. It might feel like you are outside, but you aren't."

"No, I have nightmares outside."

"When you are outside? When you are playing outside?" Sarah asked.

"No, when I am sleeping outside."

"But you don't sleep outside. When do you sleep outside?"

"I don't fall asleep outside, but I wake up outside. I think the nightmare takes me outside when I am asleep. It's very dark, and I am so afraid."

"You sleep in the house. You don't sleep outside."

"I fall asleep inside, but when I wake up I am outside."

"Why are you outside?"

"I don't know."

"How do you get outside?"

"I don't know. I think the nightmare takes me outside."

Sarah studied the child before she spoke. "Tell me what happens when you are outside?"

"Koss is there, and the demons are there too."

"Can you see Koss when you are outside?"

"Yes, I see him, and he talks to me."

"What does he tell you?"

"He says I am having a nightmare and I should go back to sleep. He says I have to be quiet, and if I don't stop crying, the demons will hear me, and they will come and hurt me too."

"The demons? Have you ever seen them?"

"Yes," Mia answered cautiously.

"What do they look like?"

"I couldn't see them well because it was dark. They hide in the bush, and I see them moving there, and I hear them whisper and laugh."

"Then what happens?"

"Koss hurts me very hard. He says I should close my eyes. If I cry, the demons will hear me, and they will come out and hurt me too. I am very scared."

"How do you get back into your bed?"

"I don't know."

Sarah and Hilda listened to the child.

"Do you suppose that is why she wakes up in the morning with those stomachaches?" Sarah whispered to Hilda.

"Kassie is at home; she is supposed to be watching her." Hilda flung the words at her eldest sister, absolving herself of responsibility for the child.

"Where are you when this happens? Why aren't you at home?"

"Well, maybe I like to see my friends just like you go to see yours."

"You have been sneaking out to see Josh after I leave, haven't you?"

"Well, Mother allows you to see your friends. Why can't I see mine? I am not going to get pregnant like you did. If I did get pregnant, at least Josh would be man enough to marry me," Hilda spat at Sarah.

Sarah stood unmoving for a moment, a hurt look crossed her face. Then she whispered, "We have to tell Father what Mia told us."

"Yes, fine, you can talk. There will be questions to answer. Think of the trouble I would be in for sneaking out to see Josh. I won't tell Father. He would be very angry with me if he finds out about Josh."

Mia repressed the horror of finding herself outside, thinking if she closed her eyes, the tittering, the whispers, and the demons would not be there—the horrible things would not be happening to her; she would not be outside. But her terrors continued. She feared the dark and didn't know how she happened to find herself outside after she had gone to bed at night. Sometimes she would find herself back in bed, not knowing how she got there.

Later, when they learned she was missing from her bed, her father would send one of her sisters to look for her. They would find Mia wandering outside despondently or crying in a half-awakened state. Other times, she would find her way to the kitchen door. Disoriented and unable to open it, she would stand beside the door until someone heard her cries and let her in.

Her father sat in the kitchen reading the paper. He was surprised to find Mia crying at the door, dressed only in her underclothes. He questioned Nadia.

"Why is Mia wandering outside? I thought she had been sleeping for hours."

"How should I know why the brat is not in bed?" Nadia glared angrily at her husband.

"Why isn't she in bed? Where is Sarah?"

"You know she has friends. She has gone to see them and is not back yet."

"What about Hilda? Where is she tonight?"

"She went for a walk and isn't back yet either."

"Who is taking care of Mia when you let Sarah and Hilda gallivant during the night?"

"Sarah and Hilda put Mia to bed before they leave; Kassie is at home so she takes care of Mia."

"Why aren't you sleeping, and how did you get out of bed?" he asked the child.

In her current state, Mia could only sob hysterically. Her father continued his questions; this time he firmly questioned Kassie.

"You are supposed to be taking care of Mia. Why is she crying and wandering around outside after she has been put to bed?"

"Mia must be getting out of bed and sleepwalking." Nadia defended Kassie before she could answer.

Sleepwalking was a term Mia was not familiar with, but it scared her. She remembered the chaos it caused when Nadia defended Kassie by saying she was not in her bed because she was sleepwalking. She remembered her father's infuriated anger. Mia feared violence.

If Sarah was not at home, Mia turned to Hilda. The child wanted a better understanding of why she found herself outside in the nightmarish situations.

"Hilda, what does 'sleepwalking' mean?" she asked.

"It means that you get out of bed while you are sleeping at night and walk around."

"But why do I do that? I don't want to walk around when I am sleeping. I don't want to sleepwalk. I am afraid of the dark, and demons, and nightmares. Father will be angry with me like he was with Kassie when she was sleepwalking." The child sobbed as she fought her anxiety.

"No, Father won't be angry with you if you sleepwalk."

"But I don't want to sleepwalk. I am afraid. Father was so angry with Kassie when she walked in her sleep. I don't want him to be angry with me. I don't want him to punish me like he punished Kassie."

"No, Father won't punish you."

"Then why did he punish Kassie for sleepwalking? Why did he beat her?"

"To stop her from sleepwalking."

"I don't want him to beat me to make me stop sleepwalking."

"That was different. Kassie is big, and you are not."

"Why does a person sleepwalk? How can a person walk if they are sleeping?"

"I don't know."

"When I sleepwalk, why does my stomach hurt so much, and why does it hurt when I wake up in the morning?"

"Well, maybe because you trip over something and hurt your stomach when you fell."

"Why don't I hurt my arms or legs when I fall? Do people keep their eyes closed when they sleepwalk? I don't want to sleepwalk. I can't see when my eyes are closed, and I can't see when it's dark outside. I'm afraid of the dark."

"I don't know." Hilda was getting annoyed by the questions and the fear in the child she could not muffle. "You must ask Kassie. She was the one who was sleepwalking."

"I don't like to talk to Kassie. She tells me scary things. Sarah says the things Kassie says are not true."

"I will call Kassie, and I will ask her to tell you. I will listen to make sure she does not tell you scary things. Kassie, come here." Hilda motioned to her sister when she entered the room. "Tell us what happened to you when you were sleepwalking."

Kassie turned pale and looked about the room. It was as if Hilda was trying to set her up and get her into trouble. Her father had forbidden her or anyone to use the word "sleepwalking" in his house.

"There is no one else in the room." Hilda giggled at Kassie's reaction. "I won't tell Father anything. I just want you to answer Mia's questions."

Kassie looked about the room and guardedly answered Mia's questions.

Mia was tired; she wanted to go to bed early, but she was afraid to go to bed unless Sarah and Hilda were at her side.

"Please stay beside me," she begged her sisters wearily. "I want you to watch me while I am sleeping. I am afraid of the nightmare. Please don't let it take me outside. I am so afraid of the dark. Don't let me get out of bed and sleepwalk. I am afraid if I sleepwalk, I will fall or get lost, and you won't know where to find me." The child's voice wavered with fear and fatigue.

"When you go to bed, we will keep watch over you while you sleep," her sisters assured her.

With the knowledge of her sisters' presence, Mia was able to fall into a more secure sleep. However, her sisters were not always there for her. The horrors of the night continued. Soon she was not only seeing Koss in her nightmares, but she also recognized her half uncle, Ivan.

When she asked Sarah and Hilda why she saw him in her nightmares, they explained that anyone's image could appear in nightmares but it was only his image, not really him.

Ivan was the same age as Koss and Kassie. He lived a short distance down the road. Mia was afraid of him, for not only was he mean to her, but he had a frightening deformity of his face and body. He also wheezed with each breath he took. His peers accepted his company when he had money to buy them candy; their friendship only lasted until the candy was gone. Then they ridiculed him and his deformities again. The few pennies he had to spend attracted Kassie and Koss.

Mia was exhausted by the end of the day. She felt protected when she fell asleep with Sarah or Hilda watching over her. However, her sisters were not always there. Sometimes in a half-wakened state, she would hear Kassie and Koss. Mia was tired and would doze off again, knowing she was in her bed.

Titters in the room disturbed Mia's sleep, and on occasions she was found wandering into the house in a dazed state. However, she still didn't know how she happened to find herself sleeping outside until one night when Sarah tucked her into bed and left Kassie to watch over her. Her sleep was broken by the disturbing snickers, and she felt herself being carried across the room.

"Watch so you don't drop and wake her," she heard Koss whisper loudly as he passed her to someone through the opened bedroom window. In a drowsy haze, she saw the deformed image of Ivan.

"Go to sleep. Everything is OK. You just woke up for a moment with a little nightmare. I am here taking care of you." It was Kassie who spoke.

Mia obediently closed her eyes and drifted off to sleep again.

Mia's constant stomachaches were not exceptional anymore. Her father still questioned them, while Nadia hid her youngest daughter's strange complaint.

"Let Mia stay in bed this morning. We will allow her to sleep till noon." Mia lay in bed and listened to Nadia speak to her eldest daughters as if in secrecy. "However, she will have to be out of bed when Father comes in for lunch. If she is still in bed when he comes in then, he will ask questions again."

Nadia controlled the family with a demonic grip; not even God could transcend her and the demon within. Sarah and Hilda, caught in the web of Nadia's mental illness, were aware of what was happening to Mia, but ignoring the child bought them their freedom.

Mia wasn't getting a good night's rest. One day, it was early afternoon, and she was so tired, but she was crying because she feared sleep. Terrible things happened to her while she slept. When her father heard the child's cry and Nadia's anger, he came into the house to take matters into his own hands.

"She is overtired and needs her sleep," he agreed with Nadia. "However, things have been happening in this family that shouldn't be happening. If she is afraid to go to sleep, I will ask Hilda to sit with her while she is napping to make sure nothing happens to her."

Mia was soothed and put down for her nap. She felt safe with Hilda sitting in the next room.

"Hilda is wasting her time sitting in the house with the sniveling brat. Nothing is going to happen to her. You are turning Mia into a spoiled brat." Nadia resentfully hissed the words at her husband. "There is work to be done in the garden plot, and I need Hilda to help me with it."

"No. You let Sarah run all around the countryside. If Sarah is not wasting her time, Hilda will not be wasting hers by watching over Mia."

"Well, if someone has to sit in the house with her, why can't it be Kassie or Koss?"

"No," he lashed at his wife. "They can help you with the gardening; I won't allow them to sit with her while she sleeps."

"Then what about Jacob? He can sit in the house while the brat sleeps."

"No, not even Jacob."

"Hilda!" Nadia spat the girl's name like a viper, her hatred and venom projected at her husband. "You spoiled your Hilda as much as you are going to spoil this brat if you let her get away with her quibbles."

Her father spoke to Hilda as Mia lay resting on the bed. "I want you to sit in the house; if you have any homework, take your books out and study. This time I don't want you to fall asleep. Mia is afraid. She is having the nightmares, but I think there is something more that is frightening her. If you need me, I will be in the yard for a while."

Mia was completely exhausted. Feeling secure with Hilda in the next room, she fell into a sound sleep.

What could have happened? As if in a nightmare, she found herself outside, lying in the trees. She was awaked by an assailant who was smothering and hurting her. When she could, she let out a terrified scream, and her assailant ran. She opened her eyes and saw a chubby figure run deeper into the trees and disappear. Trees surrounded her. The terror of being ravaged and not knowing where she was consumed the child. She had been asleep in her bed…why was she now outside? How did she get there? Where was Hilda?

Too young to know what direction would lead her out of the trees, she shrieked in terror until she heard angry voices. She got up and walked toward them. It was her father's furious voice she heard next.

"What do you mean you don't know where she is? You were supposed to be in the next room. I left her in your care. You were supposed to be watching her! How could she have disappeared from under your nose?"

"I couldn't help it. I left her sleeping. I left her for only a few minutes. I had to go to the privy, and I wasn't gone for long!" Mia heard Hilda screaming the words and weep hysterically.

Mia stumbled toward the voices until she got to the edge of a clearing. She saw Hilda and her father. They were standing beside the house. Her father slapped Hilda as he scolded her; seeing this, Mia was terrified. He rarely struck anyone. Hilda continued to cry. Mia shrieked hysterically along with her sister. As her father came toward her, she sank into the grass. Her memory mercifully abandoned her.

Later, she was awakened by her parents' angry voices. She lay in bed as their argument carried on into the evening.

"If she sleepwalks, why didn't she get out of bed and walk out of the house while Hilda was in the room?" Her father exploded at Nadia. "Somebody was watching the house. When they saw Hilda leave, they came in and carried her out while she slept. I want to know where Koss was when this happened to Mia."

"It was not Koss!" Nadia's anger matched her husband's. "He was with me the whole time. Ask Kassie and Jacob."

Kassie and Jacob lowered their heads and haltingly agreed with Nadia.

Waking up outside in the dark, disoriented and crying, was now a common occurrence for Mia. She would feel the terror of the demons and hear their whispers around her. One night as she lay crying in the dark, she became aware that she could hear someone else crying out there. The demons had hurt her, and she was crying, but who else was crying? Then, fully awake, she recognized the voices.

"Tell him to shut up before Father hears him and comes to see what is wrong," Koss hissed into the dark.

"Ivan is crying because he is afraid to go home. He says he is afraid of the dark, and he wants me to take him home." It was Jacob's voice, and it came from the same direction of the sobbing.

"Well, take him home, dammit. Take him home before Father comes out and finds out what we are doing. Where is Kassie? She can go with you."

"Kassie went back into the house when Ivan started to cry. She said she didn't want to be caught with us in case Father came out to see what was wrong. She said she would be in real trouble if she was found with us."

"Don't talk so loud, dammit. Take him back alone then. Get the sniveling bastard out of here quick."

Mia was fully awake now. What did Koss and Kassie and Jacob have to do with the demons, she wondered, and why was Ivan there? It was as if the demons quit tittering when he started to cry. She wondered why her brothers were angry with Ivan.

It was sometime later when Koss and Jacob came home from school that Mia overheard conversations between them.

"Ivan says he can't pay the money he owes us, but he gave me his eraser. He said it is just about new. He hardly used it; it costs three cents. He said he would pay us the rest of the money when he gets it." Jacob made his report to his older brother.

"You damn fool! Why didn't you tell him we don't want his pencils or erasers? We want the money!" Koss looked at the eraser and hissed at his younger brother again. "You fool. It has his initials on it. If the teacher sees you with his eraser, she will make you give it back to him. Ivan might even get you in trouble by telling the teacher you stole it, and then she will strap you."

"Zachary told me to rub his initials off like this, and I did. See? You can hardly see Ivan's initials. I will rub them some more. I'll put my initials on top of his. That is what Zachary says he does."

"That is a good idea, but where did he learn to do that? Does he steal erasers in school and put his initials on them? You know the teacher says many erasers are missing in school. She said if she found anyone with an eraser that did not belong to them she would use the strap. I want you to tell me if it is Zachary who steals the erasers."

"No. Zachary doesn't steal erasers in school." Jacob faithfully defended his friend.

"Are you sure?"

"Yes, I am sure. Zachary is my best friend, and I know he doesn't steal."

"Then who steals the erasers in school?"

"I don't know. Maybe it is one of the Abraham boys. They are always getting into trouble."

"Well, why does Zachary rub initials off erasers and put his over the top?"

"He said when he needs an eraser, one of his older brothers gives him a used one and buys a new one for himself. His brother showed him how to rub the first initial off and put a Z over it."

"Are you sure? I will tell Mother about this first, and then when I go to school I will tell the teacher 'cause you know Zachary could be lying about the erasers."

"No, Zachary doesn't lie. He is my best friend. You can ask his older brothers about the eraser." Jacob was annoyed with Koss; his face flushed as he defended his friend.

"OK, OK, I won't ask his brothers. They are bigger than we are. I don't want to get involved with them. I just thought we could use the stolen erasers as a hold over Zachary."

Mia stood at a distance and watched Koss and Jacob examining the eraser.

"Well, remember, if you keep his eraser, we will take it out of your share of the money he owes us. When he gives you the money he owes, you have to give it all to Kassie and me. We will split it between us."

"I will hide the eraser. I won't take it to school until I get Ivan's initials rubbed right off it. How much money does he still owe us?"

His older brother shrewdly calculated the figures.

"Well, you tell him you will allow two cents for the eraser because it is used, and then he still will owe us nine cents. Remember, when Ivan pays you, Kassie and I will still give you a candy to even off your share of the money."

As Mia listened to her brothers, she wondered why they were angry with Ivan and why he owed them money.

Later, she heard Koss again talking about money owed. "You have the easy job. All you have to do is collect the money from him; Kassie and I have to do the hard part. We have to do the planning, and we have to set things up. If anything goes wrong and we get caught, it would be Kassie and me who would be in trouble."

"But how can I get money from Ivan if he says he doesn't have any?"

"If he doesn't come up with the money soon, we will corner him and rough him up again. This time we will not stop when he starts blubbering and crying like he did last time."

Nadia's lifelong hatred of her stepmother, Margareta, and her half brother, Ivan, meant she forbid any of her offspring to associate with them. However, when Ivan knew their parents were away from home, he would stop in on his way to Belcourt. Koss, Kassie, and Jacob accompanied him to the store to buy candy. They told Mia and Yuri if they didn't leave the house while they were gone, they would bring them a treat. Mia's older siblings had money to squander on candy, but Nadia didn't seem to care where the money they spent came from.

One time when Hilda was at home, she accompanied them to Belcourt.

"Where do you get the money to buy so much candy?" Hilda quizzed her younger sister. Kassie ignored the question. "You get money from Alden and Igor, don't you?" Hilda accused Kassie. "They pay you for sleeping with them, don't they? I will tell Mother on you. You are nothing but a tramp."

"What about you and Josh?" Kassie lashed back.

"Josh is different. He says he will marry me when I am older."

"Why doesn't he marry you now?"

"He would have to ask Father. He says he's afraid to ask him yet and will ask him when I am older."

"When you are older? How much older?"

"He said he'll wait till I am fifteen."

"That is two more years."
"No, it is not; it's only a year and a half."

Kassie and Koss developed a greed..They were addicted to sweets. Selling Mia to Ivan and their friends and splitting the pennies they were given was not sufficient for their habit. Kassie also seemed to have her own spending money. Was Koss acting as her procurer, or was Kassie selling herself? Was their addiction to candy, greed, and Nadia's madness overpowering the children? Money enticed Koss, and Mr. Wilson's cash register at Belcourt caught his attention.

Koss's anger at Ivan escalated. Ivan owed him money and was not paying him. Mia heard Koss speak to Jacob again. This time he spoke of threats and violence against his half uncle.

"I want you to talk to Zachary." Koss gave Jacob an inflamed look as he spoke. "Tell him after school is dismissed for the day, we will lure Ivan into the bushes. Then tell Zachary to help you beat Ivan to a pulp."

"But Zachary wouldn't want to do that. Besides, he lives on the other side of the school, and everyone will ask him why he isn't going home. Ivan is bigger than Zachary and me; I think he would be afraid to fight with Ivan."

"Well, Ivan is a big blob, but he is a sissy. He cries like a baby. I bet you and Zachary can beat him up all by yourselves and make him cry."

"No, I don't want to fight, and I don't think Zachary would want to fight either. We will get in trouble if we do."

"If Zachary is your friend, he should do what you ask him to do." Koss pouted. "I will figure something out," he added. "If he is your friend, then just get him to promise he will help you if Ivan gets nasty with you." Koss paused before he continued. "You know if a friend makes a promise, he can't break it. Maybe if you started an argument with Ivan, you can pretend he hit you; you can fake it. Hold your stomach and pretend you are crying; call Zachary and tell him to help you. You don't have to worry. I can happen to come along, and I'll get Zachary's big brothers to jump in too."

"I don't think that would work," Jacob said reluctantly. "What if he really hit me in the stomach and ran away before I called Zachary?"

"Then ask Zachary to tell his brothers to hide in the bush with you and Zachary. You can wait, and when Ivan comes down the road, you can ambush him."

"But Zachary and his brothers don't fight. They would ask why we want to beat Ivan."

"We don't have to tell them the real reason. Nobody likes him in school anyway; that would be enough reason to beat him. If you get the boys to beat Ivan, I will even jump in and help. Then everyone will treat us as if we were heroes. The boys in school would want to be our friends. After we lay a beating on him, I will tell him that everybody is angry with him because he owes us money."

"But Zachary doesn't fight; he doesn't like to." Jacob continued to reject the idea.

"Well, he doesn't really have to fight; he can just start it, and he can let Ivan hit him once. I will tell his older brothers that Ivan is beating Zachary. His brothers will go to help him."

"I really don't think it is a good idea. He said his brothers told him he is not supposed to fight. If he hit Ivan, his brothers would scold him. They wouldn't fight with Ivan if Zachary started the fight. They would scold Zachary. Besides, they are older than Ivan. His brothers don't like when anyone fights."

Koss's attempt to instigate a fight with Ivan was futile.

It was after Koss and Jacob went to the store at Belcourt one day that Mia heard Koss commenting to his younger brother, "Did you see all the money in Mr. Wilson's cash register? He has lots of pennies, nickels, and dimes. I even saw a quarter."

"Yes, I did." Jacob nodded. "Nigel says sometimes his father even has more than one quarter in the cash register."

"Mr. Wilson is rich." Koss paused for a moment before he added, "I wonder who brings the quarters to his store?"

"Nigel said sometimes his father brings a bag of flour from Ridgewood for somebody. When they pay him for the flour, he has quarters and lots of money in the cash register."

"A quarter is a lot of money," Koss said wistfully and then continued. "You know Ivan won't pay us the money he owes us."

"He told me he doesn't have the money now. He said his mother gave him a few pennies for school supplies, but he doesn't have any money left."

"Well, you got the eraser from him, and I didn't get anything." Koss sulked.

"Ivan said when his stepsister comes to visit, she gives him lots of money. Sometimes she even gives him a whole dime."

"But his stepsister only comes to visit once a year. By the time she comes again, Ivan will have forgotten. We will just have to take turns reminding him he owes us money."

"He did say that when he got the money, he would buy us some candy at Belcourt."

"When is he going to get any money?"

"He said he didn't know, but he said he wouldn't buy candy for any of the other kids; he would only buy candy for us."

"Mr. Wilson has lots of money. Why don't you talk to Nigel? I bet if Nigel took money out of his father's cash register, he wouldn't miss it."

"Nigel says his father doesn't allow him to go behind the counter. He only allows Laverne or Mitch to go there when he is busy."

"Well, Nigel is lying. I saw him go behind the counter, and I even saw him take a candy. I bet he could go behind the counter and take money." Koss brooded for a moment after he spoke. "I have an idea. Talk to Nigel tomorrow. Tell him his father has so much money in the cash register that if he took some, his father wouldn't even know it was missing."

"You mean he should steal some money?" Jacob looked at his brother in astonishment.

The next day, as Mia played outside, she heard Koss and Jacob discussing the events of their day when they got home from school.

"Did you talk to Nigel like I asked you to?" Koss grilled his younger brother.

"Yes, I did."

"Did you tell him what I told you to say?"

"Yes."

"Well, did he agree to take money out of his father's cash register?"

"No, he said he didn't want to do that. If he did, he said he wouldn't have anyplace to spend it. His father owns the store, and he can't buy anything from his father."

"Well, you should have told him he could give us the money, and we would buy things in his father's store. We could buy candy, and we could give some to him too."

"He said he didn't have to. His father treats him with a candy when he is pleased with him. Mr. Wilson even gave me a candy once."

"He did?" Koss asked in surprise. "What did you do to make him give you a candy?"

"I didn't do anything; I was only playing with Nigel."

"Well, Mr. Wilson doesn't give me any candies." The news upset Koss. "It would serve him right if someone took money from his cash register. Tell Nigel we wouldn't only give him one candy. We will buy candies and share them with him if he does what we tell him to do."

"Nigel told me his father would know if there was any money missing."

"Well, his father has a lot of money. How would he know if there was some missing?"

"Nigel said Mr. Wilson counts the money every day after he closes the store. Then on Fridays his father takes all the money to Ridgewood and puts it in the bank."

"The bank? Why does he put his money in the bank?"

"I don't know why. Nigel didn't tell me why."

"Father doesn't put money in the bank."

"Maybe 'cause Father doesn't have as much money as Mr. Wilson does."

"Well, Father doesn't have a store."

"Maybe only storekeepers put money in the bank."

"When I grow up, I think I would like to have a store like Mr. Wilson." Koss pondered for a moment. "I wonder what the bank does with Mr. Wilson's money."

"I don't know."

"Tomorrow, when you talk to Nigel, tell him if he takes money from the cash register, his father wouldn't know who took it. Mitch and Laverne help him in the store; he will think they took it."

"No, Nigel said Mitch helps his father count the money, so his father would know Mitch wouldn't take it. Laverne is a girl, and girls don't steal. Mr. Wilson would know that Laverne wouldn't take money from his cash register."

"Still, all that money is just sitting there. Nigel could pretend to help his father count the money and take some when he's not watching. Why is Nigel so dumb?"

Some time passed before Mia heard more discussion about the money in Mr. Wilson's cash register.

"I want you to tell Nigel to take money out of his father's cash register and give it to you. Then I will take over from there." Koss spoke with confidence. "Listen and I will tell you my plan.

Mr. Wilson counts his money after he closes his store. When we get the money from Nigel, we will go to the store the same day and spend it before his father counts it. When Mr. Wilson counts the money, it won't be missing; it will be back in his cash register." Koss beamed when he spoke.

"Koss, you get such brilliant ideas." Jacob was ecstatic as he looked at his older brother in amazement. "I will talk to Nigel. Where do you get such brilliant ideas?"

"Well, I am older and smarter than you are." Koss radiated with pride. "That is why Mother says you all have to listen to me and do what I tell you."

"Did you tell Kassie about your idea?"

"No, I didn't tell her yet, but I will. You know, Mother does say I could figure things out very well for myself. She is proud of me and says I am the smartest of all of you."

"Can you imagine that? Nigel will take money from his father's cash register, and we will bring the money back and buy candy for it before he counts the money. Boy, he wouldn't even know it was his own money we would be using to buy candy from his store. What a brain you have, Koss—what a brain!"

Although Kassie and Koss included Jacob in their schemes, they were also heard whispering and scheming between themselves.

Hilda disapproved. "I will tell Mother what you are planning to do. Laverne is Sarah's and my friend. If Koss does anything to jeopardize our friendship, Mr. Wilson will forbid her to have anything to do with us."

However, Nadia laughed off the techniques of treachery Koss cooked up.

"We have to admit that Koss is very smart to have thought of that. If he can pull off a stunt because the neighbors' kids are not as brainy as he is…well, the better for him. Koss is very shrewd. He will do very well for himself in life." Nadia smiled, preening proudly.

"Still, he is asking Nigel to steal money from his father. What will Mr. Wilson say when he finds out Koss is involving Nigel in something so shady?"

"Well, Koss is not the one who will be taking the money from the cash register, so they can't accuse him of stealing." Nadia laughed at her oldest son's cunning scheme. "I will have a talk with Koss. If Mr. Wilson accuses Koss of being involved in the prank, Koss can deny he had anything to do it."

Hilda approached Kassie irritably about the trickery in the family. "Do you know what Koss is scheming to do?"

"Yes," Kassie cautiously answered with a titter.

"Are you involved in this scheme too?"

"No, Koss only tells me about his plans."

"I don't believe you. You and Koss have always been very underhanded. It is not right that Koss should manipulate others like that. I am going to tell Father what you are plotting."

"Mother said she didn't care if anyone tells Father about having Nigel take money from the cash register, but we shouldn't tell him about the rest."

"The rest?" Hilda looked at her sister as if she couldn't believe there could be more. "The rest?" she repeated. "There is more? What else are you scheming?"

"Oh, it is nothing. You know Koss; he talks lots and comes up with brainy ideas." With that, Kassie brushed Hilda's question off.

"What else is he scheming?" Hilda repeated insistently. Kassie evaded her sister's questions.

Later that day, as they were around the supper table, Father spoke to them sternly. He warned them of the harsh penalties if there was a need for them. The underhanded way Nadia brought the children up was not acceptable to him.

Koss and Kassie shrugged off their father's threats and hid their snickers when he wasn't watching. The intended scheme they were planning would not be stopped by their father's interference. Greed and money were the roots of their evil plans.

Mia was tired. She sat at the table with her siblings listening to her father lecturing them. She was unaware of the circumstances she was caught in, not realizing that she was endangered by the schemes Koss and Kassie were concocting. Sarah was not at home to tuck her into bed at night. Hilda and Kassie were there to protect her as she slept.

CHAPTER ELEVEN

The colluding continued as time passed, and once again their father confronted them at the dinner table. "I have been hearing things, and I want to know what is going on in this family. What is Koss up to?"

He looked at his offspring sitting around the table. Koss and Kassie lowered their heads; Jacob followed suit.

"Are you involved in illicit schemes?" He looked from Kassie to Jacob. They didn't answer.

Later, Kassie whispered to her brother, "Did you talk to those boys?"

Koss snickered.

"Are we still going to go through with it?"

His heavy lips turned into a smile, and he nodded.

"Even if Father is on to something?"

"Mother will defend us."

It was early spring, and everyone except Sarah was sitting around the dinner table. Sarah was not around much of the time. Her father forbade her to babysit for Hanna and would not allow her to see Baily unchaperoned anymore. Where was Nadia allowing Sarah to spend her time?

Mia watched her father and wondered why he sounded so irritated and looked so stern while he lectured. Kassie and Koss told her she was not supposed to cry when her father scolded them at the table. They told her he was not scolding her and if she cried, her father would become angrier with them. In turn, they would punish her. Kassie, Koss, and Jacob sat with their heads lowered.

Hilda set the food on the table and told Mia to have her dinner. Obviously, she knew there would be some disagreements around the table that evening. Hilda was waiting for her father to vent his anger before she sat at the table with her younger siblings.

Kassie and Koss were unable to scurry out of the house before their father targeted them with his anger. Nadia turned her back to the table and angrily busied herself around the cast-iron stove while her husband confronted the children.

Mia continued to eat as Hilda instructed. Her father scolded her older siblings, but she was unable to grasp the meaning of his anger. Mia picked small amounts of food up on her fork and stuck them into her mouth, blocking out the sounds of her father's raised voice.

"Why are there boys lurking around the house and in the bushes after dark?" He aimed his anger at Kassie and Koss. Looking at Kassie, he didn't wait for an answer. "You know that you are not allowed to go outside after dark."

"She doesn't go outside after dark. How do you know there is somebody there? How do you see anybody if it's dark?" Nadia's eyes blazed as she retorted indignantly.

"They are there; I hear them in the bushes. Sometimes I hear them running away when I go out; other times, I see movements. When I call out to them, they don't answer, but I hear snickering when they hide there. I want to know why they are there and who they are waiting for."

"How should they know? Do you always have to scold the children at the table? They are growing children. They need their nourishment, especially Koss; he's a growing boy. He can't eat when you scold. He is still hungry when he leaves the table; he goes outside and cries."

Mia glanced at Koss as he sat at the table with his head lowered. As his mother spoke, his beefy lips quivered as if he was about to cry. Jacob sat beside Koss; his scrawny body looked pathetically ill-nourished next to his brother. Kassie also looked like a string bean sitting on the bench beside Koss. Mia wondered how Koss could be hungry when he was so fat. *Do fat people get hungry?* Mia mused. She decided she would have to ask Sarah or Hilda if they did.

"They are up to something." Her father's voice was bitter. "Whatever it is, I am going to get it out of them. If they were not hiding anything, they would ask their friends to come to the door. They would have their friends knock on the door properly to ask for them."

"Their friends are afraid to come to the door; that is why they sneak around in the bushes."

"Afraid? What are they afraid of?"

"They are afraid of you!"

"Why are they afraid of me?"

"Because you are always scolding the children!"

"After what you have done to these children, I would like to get them on the right track. Their friends would not be afraid of anybody if their intentions were good." Then, turning back to the table, he aimed his words at Koss and Kassie. "I don't want any of your friends sneaking around in the bushes after dark. I will talk to Mr. Wilson and the other fathers in the neighborhood. I will tell them if their children want to come to visit, we will expect them to knock on the door to announce their arrival. There will be no carrying on outside in the bushes after dark. From now on, I expect your friends to visit with you in the house."

Perhaps Mia's father detected something in his children's or his wife's actions when he scolded them that evening. He told Hilda to put Mia to sleep in the bedroom and sit in the living room to make sure nothing happened to her.

"I don't want to sit in the room alone; there should be two of us watching her," Hilda said. "I don't want to take the sole responsibility of watching her alone again. The last time you told me to watch her, somebody snatched her from the bed when I went to the privy. It was not my fault; I was not gone for long. You were so angry with me you even slapped me. I don't want that to happen again."

"Yes, Hilda is right. Since Sarah isn't at home, Kassie should sit with her too," her father agreed. "Things are very unstable here, and I just can't seem to get them under control." Turning, he spoke to both girls. "I am going to leave you both in charge of watching over Mia tonight. There will be two of you taking turns watching her, so there will be no excuses. If anything happens to Mia, you will both be responsible."

Mia blocked out the horrors that submerged her. It was early, but she was tired and obediently went to bed when they told her to.

"If either one of you sees anything suspicious, I want you to tell me right away," he advised them as he left the room.

With Hilda and Kassie sitting in the next room and her parents in the kitchen, Mia felt secure. She fell into a sound sleep. Then, as if she were a zombie in a dream, she heard whispers.

"How did you get in?" It was Kassie's voice.

"Didn't you hear me? I came in through the bedroom window." Koss giggled.

"Where are you taking her? It's still light outside."

"I'm taking her outside. They're here already."

"Well, hurry. Hilda said she wanted to go to the privy before it got too dark. If you don't hurry and get her out of here before Hilda gets back, we will be in trouble."

"Yes, I know. I saw her go out the back. That's why I sneaked in through the window to get Mia now." Koss snickered. "Look how easy it is to control Mia; she even listens to me in her sleep. Look at her. When I talk to her, she does what I tell her to do."

Mia was subdued in sleep. When her brother spoke, she felt herself standing beside him. He was supporting her as he ordered her to do what he told her. Weary with sleep, Mia was hypnotized by her brother's demanding words.

"Walk. Walk with me. Lift your foot; take another step and another. Walk quietly with me."

Koss snickered again, and Mia drifted into a hypnotic state. She wore only a flimsy slip.

"Well, get her out of here quick, or I will get in trouble. Father said if I saw anything, I was to call him."

"Turn around and you won't see anything." Koss snickered. "You won't see me taking her out the door, and then you don't have to lie to him."

Mia spontaneously opened her eyes. Hilda and Kassie were both supposed to be sitting in the living room, but only Kassie was there. Was she dreaming? She was able to determine that even if she was dreaming, she should ask her sister for help. The child turned to Kassie. Kassie turned away.

Mia opened her mouth and tried to call out to her sister, but she felt Koss clamp his hand over her mouth.

"Shut up," he hissed. Then, turning to Kassie, he whispered, "They are here. They are waiting." With those words, he rushed the half-sleeping child out the door.

It was as if the whispers between Koss and Kassie weren't exchanged. Was it a dream? Now she was outside. The cold air rushed at her and roused her. The eeriness of dusk surrounded her. She could see the bleakness of the bare trees and the tall dried weeds.

Just a few days before, traces of snow still lingered in odd patches along the trees. Why was she outside? She felt cold; she was barefoot. Was she dreaming?

"Why am I outside?" the child whispered, groggy from fatigue.

"Shut up!" Koss spat the words at her like a viper. "You aren't outside; you are having a nightmare."

"I want to go into the house. I am cold." The flimsily clad child stood shivering. She closed her eyes as she spoke, thinking if sleep overcame her, she would find herself safe in her bed again.

"You don't have to sleep in the house; you can sleep outside. Sleeping outside is fun. Jacob and I don't sleep in the house; we sleep outside." Koss smiled sickly as he tried to convince the child. "Sometimes Kassie sleeps outside too."

"But I don't want to sleep outside. I'm cold."

"You can't go back into the house. If you do, Father will be angry with you because you're not supposed to be outside."

"But why am I outside?" The cold made her feel the reality of the situation. She continued to shiver.

"I will give you my coat to cover up with if you lie down in that dip you like to play in. You will be warm there. I will take you back in the house later, before anyone goes to sleep. They won't even know you were outside, and Father won't be angry with you."

"No, I want to go back now." The child shivered uncontrollably. She hoped Koss would let her go back inside.

"If I take you back now, Father will be angry with you. Remember how angry he was at the dinner table? If I take you back later, I won't even tell him you were outside."

Koss gave the child his jacket; she wrapped it around herself, curled up in the dip scratched out by the chickens, and fell asleep. But Koss's jacket was not keeping her warm anymore. The only warmth she felt was from someone's body covering hers. The person did not hurt her. The body kept her warm, and she wanted to sleep. Then it was gone.

Lying on the cold ground, the child shivered and lost control of her bladder. For a moment, the urine she lay in warmed her cold body. Nearby, she heard faint whispers.

"OK, it is your turn now."

She stirred in a delirious sleep, not knowing to whom the words belonged. She could only feel the numbness and cold as she lay on the wet ground.

Somebody was beside her, and then a high-pitched voice pierced the silence. "I don't want to do it. She is wet. She pissed herself...she pissed herself! What do you think I am? Look, my pant leg is wet and dirty; I have to wear these pants to school tomorrow. Give me my money back. I am going home!"

She recognized the voice of Davis Stephenson. She did not know Davis and only occasionally heard his voice from afar. The Stephenson children and their speech impediments were the targets of Nadia's insults.

"Shut up. Don't talk so loud. I will not give you your money back. A promise is a promise. I didn't break my promise to you, and nobody breaks a promise they make to me," Koss's voice spat angrily in the dark. "Grab her arms, Jacob, and drag her out on the grass. I will not give you your money back!"

Mia heard the sounds of angry voices as she lay in the dark. Feeling paralyzed and in shock, she could only whimper. They ravaged her and bruised her little body. With the physical act, they ripped out the soul of the innocent child. Mia could see the light shining through the kitchen window in the house. She reached out to it, but she could not move; she couldn't get up.

"Help me, Jacob. Help me please," she begged. "I want to go to the house, Jacob. I can't get up. Please help me, Jacob," she could only whimper.

"Where is Nigel?" Koss demanded.

"Nigel has gone home, don't you remember? He was the first." Mia recognized Baily Stephenson's voice.

"Why do you want Nigel? He said he wanted to go home. He didn't want to stay around here any longer."

"He gave me five cents, and I didn't have any change, so I told him he could do it to her twice."

"You didn't have the change? I gave you two cents, and Davis gave you two cents. What do you mean you didn't have the change?"

"He gave me the nickel before you paid me. I didn't have any change when he gave me the nickel."

"What kind of sick animal are you?" Baily's whiny, nasal voice rose in anger. "You are sick! Let's get out of here."

"Jacob, help me," the child begged feebly. "I am frightened. I am so cold." As she lay on the ground, she could only stretch her arm to her brother.

"No. Jacob, hold her down. The other two boys didn't come, and it's our turn."

"You are sick; she is your little sister. I should go into the house and tell your father what you are doing," Baily fumed.

"I can do anything I want to her because she is my sister and so can Jacob. You will not dare tell Father. Not after you did it to her too. You would be in as much trouble as the rest of us—even more because you aren't her brother, and you are older than we are."

"You are mentally sick," Baily replied angrily.

"What about Sarah? What did you do to our oldest sister? She had to have an abortion because of what you did to her. My father would beat you if you went to the house to tell him anything. Remember, you're not even supposed to set your foot in our yard!"

"I am going to go into the house and tell your father what you are doing!"

"You don't have to tell Father. He knows what we do, and he does not care."

"I don't believe you. Your father would be very angry if he knew what you're doing."

"Well, I dare you to go to the house and tell him then. I dare you. If you tell Father, I will tell everybody about Sarah and the abortion. You know Sarah just about died. If she had died, it would have been your fault. I will tell everybody about what you did to Sarah."

"You are a sick animal." Baily's high-pitched voice sounded close to tears. "Come on, Davis; let's go home."

Mia did not know how much longer she lay there after her brothers also ravaged her. In shock and drifting into deep pits of blackness, with hypothermia setting in, she did not feel the cold anymore. The young child drifted in and out of delirium, sometimes hearing snatches of whispers, and only then did she realize she was still outside. Then she felt she was alone. The child no longer had fear of the dark or the demons. She only feared her brothers and the other beasts that hurt her. Only the darkness of the night could protect her. She dragged her torn body away from the light of the house. If she lay in the path of light coming from the house, Koss might see her. Danger lurked in the shadows between her and the light. Darkness was a safe place; it could swallow her up, and she could hide in peace.

Mia inched herself toward a furrow at the edge of the vegetable plot. The plow had left the furrow when her father worked the soil in the fall. The spring runoff trickled into the furrow and left a watery puddle, where she played earlier that day with Yuri. Now, as she dragged herself along the same furrow, she realized she was in the puddle of icy water; she lay there, not able to pull herself farther.

She could no longer feel the cold. Was it the furrow she lay in that protected her, or was it the branches that hung over her that reached down to the cold ground? Who was protecting and watching over her as she lay waiting for sleep or death?

The child drifted into a state where she felt warmth and peace, although she knew nothing of God. Even though Nadia held herself up as a staunch churchgoer, there was no room for God in the woman's life. It was only the fourth commandment that ruled in her household—that, along with the demons and the legacy of a mad woman.

Mia drifted off into a pit of darkness. Unconsciousness took over her scantily clad body as hypothermia set in. There was a calm warmth enveloping her.

Voices! They were looking for her. She was numb with fear. Were they alone, or were others with them—the ones Koss was angry with because he told them to come and they didn't? Why were they looking for her? Their voices were coming closer.

"Where is she? We left her here."

"Where did she go? The damn brat!"

They were looking for her; she couldn't stop them from hurting her again. Her body was no longer part of her—it was an empty shell. She felt like a lifeless rag doll in the furrow. She wanted to be left in peace, to drift away forever…

"Do you think she went into the house, Koss?"

"No. We would have heard her if she did. Keep on looking. Damn it."

"But, Koss, I can't find her. Maybe somebody else found her and took her into the house."

"No, I told you to keep on looking. Damn the brat; she couldn't have gone far."

"Maybe Nigel or Baily came back and took her to their place."

Their voices were coming closer. She was partly protected and hidden in the furrow. She drifted into oblivion, and then Jacob's voice brought her back to reality as he stood over her.

"Here she is. I found her, Koss!"

Mia was barely conscious. She could not find the strength to stir or utter a word.

"How did she get there?"

"What's wrong with her?"

"We should carry her into the house." Koss motioned to Jacob as he pulled on her arms.

"I can't lift her," Jacob complained. "She is so heavy."

"Why is she so heavy? I can't carry her. Help me, damn it!"

"Couldn't we just leave her here?"

"No. If they find her here, Father will know what happened to her. We have to get her back into the house. Go and get Kassie. Tell her we need help."

Mia was unsure how much time passed; she struggled to regain awareness. More whispering occurred.

"I couldn't talk to Kassie because Hilda is sitting in the room with her." Jacob's voice filtered in.

"Well, damn it. Go and watch them through the window; if you see Hilda walk out of the room, go in and tell Kassie we need help."

More time lapsed. Then Mia felt the sensation of being dragged. The uneven frozen ground ripped through her stiffening body. Kassie and Koss dragged her by her arms, and Jacob held her legs. She couldn't moan or cry; if she did, they probably wouldn't have heard her. They whispered and snickered back and forth as they dragged her.

"Let's hurry; we have to get her into the house before Hilda comes back in the room."

"I couldn't leave until Hilda left the room." It was Kassie who whispered now.

"Remember, when we get to the door, Jacob must look through the window and tell us if Hilda is back. If she isn't back, he will open the door, and we'll carry her across the floor to the bedroom."

"We must be careful not to drag her over the floor. Father will hear us."

"Yes, the last time he caught us, there was big trouble. I don't want him to catch us again."

Kassie giggled "Jacob, open the door real wide and hold it so it doesn't swing back on us. We have to get her through without bumping her into it."

"Yes. Remember the time the door swung back and hit her in the head. She woke up and started to cry. Father was so angry with us." Kassie and Koss snickered.

"We have to walk quietly and step together. If Father hears more than one set of footsteps, he will get suspicious and come to see what's happening."

Mia felt herself lying between bed covers, but she did not feel the warmth of the bed. The coldness penetrated her body, and she shivered uncontrollably. The whispers in the room faded as she slipped in and out of pools of darkness.

"How much money did you get?"

"Nine cents."

"Oh, that will make three cents for each of us."

"Where is Jacob?" Koss asked.

"He didn't want to come into the house. He said he wanted to go to the shack and sleep."

"Well, maybe we don't have to split the money with him then."

"You know we have to. We have to include him in this so he doesn't squeal on us," Kassie reasoned.

"OK, I will give him his three cents tomorrow."

"Don't forget. Give him the money when he wakes up tomorrow morning before Father gets you out of bed to help with the chores—not tonight because he might not remember that you gave him the money."

"OK."

"How many boys were there?" she asked.

"Only three came. I asked Zachary Danielson's brothers to come, but they didn't."

"I wonder why they didn't come."

"I don't know. But I am going to have a talk with them." Koss spoke in his arrogant, controlling way. "They didn't promise to come, but if I told them to come and they said they would, that was just as good as a promise."

"Who were the boys that came?"

"Nigel, Davis, and Baily."

"Baily? Why did he come? Father forbade Baily to have anything to do with us. Even if Sarah and Baily still like each other, Father does not allow us to have anything to do with him. Why did he come here?"

"Well, I asked Davis to come, and he said Davis would have been afraid to go home in the dark. That's why Baily came with him."

"Baily? Well, did he…you know. Did he?"

"Yes, he did."

"Baily? But he's Sarah's boyfriend. Father said he would give him permission to marry Sarah when they are older. That means he's still Sarah's boyfriend."

"So what if he is? He paid me two cents. What does it matter that he is Sarah's boyfriend?"

As Kassie and Koss whispered, Mia drifted in and out of consciousness. During the times she emerged from the pits of darkness, the whispers still carried on.

"Do you know what we could do?" Koss's voice was excited. "There are lots of boys in the neighborhood. Do you know how much money we could make if they each paid two cents? Twenty-three boys…that sure would be lots of money."

"You know what I would like to do?" Kassie whispered. "I would like to get a curtain with big pink and red flowers on it and drape it around the bed in that corner just like in the movies. When Mother and Father aren't at home, I would like to lie on the bed behind the curtain and have those boys come to me. You can speak to the boys; you can tell them that I am waiting for them. You can deal with their payments." Kassie spoke longingly of the crazed ambition she would like to fulfill.

"You know, if you could get a curtain up around that bed, we could have Mia go to sleep there. We could tell her it's her own room and she should go to sleep behind it. You know how easy it is to fool her. After she falls asleep, we could get the boys to come into the house. We wouldn't have so much trouble bringing her back in. What do you think?"

"We can't do that. She would cry, and Father would hear the boys coming into the house."

"Well, you said you didn't hear me sneak in through the window. I can get them to sneak into the bedroom the same way."

"No, it wouldn't be safe. You know that even if Mia is sleeping, she still wakes up and cries. Father would hear her. Mother doesn't care what we do, but Father gets so angry. We'll just have to wait until he isn't around."

"Can you imagine twenty-three boys," Koss gloated, "times two cents?"

While Mia lay on the bed that night, the conversation between Kassie and Koss filtered through to the child's subconscious mind.

The damage was more than physical; it destroyed her very soul. It would be five decades before the door to her subconscious mind would begin to open and reveal the secrets of her childhood and of that night. Only then would Mia recall with horror those parts of their conversation repressed since she was a child. She would begin to remember the horror of a mad woman's legacy.

Sever My Earthly Ties
I look at the heavens and wishfully sigh,
Oh, God, give me wings so that I could fly,
So that I may leave worldly troubles behind,
Soar with the wind, look down at mankind,
Not know life's sorrow, not know life's pain—
Sever my ties of all earthly aim.

CHAPTER TWELVE

Mia withered into a catatonic state. How many days passed? She floated in and out, and when she edged toward a more conscious condition, she felt smothered by a tight binding wound around her neck like a noose. Her chest was compressed by a tight binding; her body ached and burned with fever. She thirsted for water, but no one gave her any; somebody lifted her head and spooned a heavy, warm broth into her mouth instead. She gagged at its greasiness. It hurt her throat; she could not swallow, and it dribbled out of her mouth.

Sarah was beside the bed. Mia was not coherent enough to talk. She wanted to tell Sarah to take the binding off her neck and give her water. All she could do was tug feebly at the binding as she sank into a fevered sleep. When she hovered back into consciousness, she found the binding still smothering her.

She heard Sarah. "She keeps tugging at the binding as if it is too tight; maybe we should loosen it."

With some argument, Nadia allowed the binding to be loosened. The child rasped hoarsely as she tried to make them understand she wanted water.

"No, she can't have water; it will only make her throat worse." Nadia opposed the suggestion.

Mia could only whimper in anguish, her body drenched in fever. Her cry was raspy; it only brought more pain to her body.

"You are not to cry," someone demanded of her. "You will only get worse if you do."

Her raw, parched throat hurt her, and her chest felt tight. She opened her eyes and saw the bowl of broth still sitting on a chair beside her bed. A glass of water sat next to it. Feeling feverishly dehydrated, she tried to point to the water to make them understand what she wanted.

"No, you can't have water. You have to eat the broth first if you want to get better."

Closing her eyes, she tried to block her fevered thirst with sleep. Maybe she would feel better when she awoke; maybe they would give her water when she did.

"We should give her some water if she is thirsty." Mia recognized Sarah's voice in her unresponsive state.

"No. Mother said she could only have broth until she gets better."

"If she is thirsty and wants water, then we should give her water."

"Her chest is congested, and her throat is inflamed. Mother says we shouldn't give her water."

"Still, Father says we should. She is feverish, and if she's thirsty, the broth won't quench her thirst."

She drifted off again into a fevered sleep. Her sisters were still talking when she emerged back into consciousness.

"She only keeps asking for water."

"Well, if she wants water, I am going to give her some. Mother won't know that I did," Sarah decided.

Someone held her head up and brought a glass of water to her lips. Mia gratefully took a sip and then gagged and sputtered. The ordeal of trying to swallow cut sharply through her swollen throat.

In pain and rasping, her sore body convulsed, and she tried not to cry.

"There, that will teach her," somebody snapped.

Mia slipped back into a bottomless pit. In her fevered sleep, she heard her parents' voices as Nadia lifted her upper body into a painful reclining position and roughly tightened the binding around her chest.

"Who did this to her?" Her father's voice was furious.

"Some boys did," Nadia said, trying to avoid her husband's question.

"Boys? Then you know who it was. Was it Koss and Jacob?" Her father's voice was hushed but peppered with anger.

"No, I didn't say that. I said some boys did. It's apparent it was boys who did this to her." Nadia spat the words at her husband.

"You know something, and you are hiding it from me. I want you to tell me what it is," he fumed back. Their voices rose in fury as they left the room.

Mia lapsed in and out of consciousness. When she felt someone gently massage her chest, she knew it was Sarah. She was comfortable and warm because Sarah didn't remove the bed cover when she massaged her chest. Hilda's touch and manners were much harsher than Sarah's.

It was shortly after she felt Sarah massage her chest that Mia was resting and felt someone slip off her bedcovers. She stirred as she felt the shock of coolness over her fevered body. Wanting to be left alone, she moved uncomfortably and shivered. Someone roughly and hurriedly rubbed her half-naked body, and then someone else entered the room.

"What are you doing?"

Even though she was barely conscious, panic gripped her when she recognized the hiss of Koss's voice.

"Sarah told me I could rub her chest," Kassie replied defensively.

"Jacob and I want to help. We want to rub her chest too."

"No. They said they wouldn't allow you in the same room with her."

"Well, nobody will know we were here if you don't tell them; besides, I don't think you are supposed to be here either."

"I asked Sarah. She said I could learn to take care of her too. When Hilda and Sarah are busy, I can rub her chest and take care of her. I think you should get out of here before someone comes in and catches you here." Kassie's voice was tense.

"We will help you. We know Sarah and Hilda won't be coming into the house for a while. It is getting dark outside, so we could sneak out the back door if we hear Father coming."

"No. If they catch you in here, I will be in real trouble."

"Well, Hilda and Sarah said we hurt her. We only want to look at her private parts, and then we'll go."

There was some bickering between Koss and Kassie, and then Mia shivered as she felt her body exposed to the cold air.

"Look, there is nothing wrong with her. She is not bleeding." Koss sounded irritated. "Sarah and Hilda lied to us. They said we hurt her. We didn't hurt her. Why did they lie to us?"

Kassie covered Mia's body. "Now get out of here quick before someone comes in and catches you here. We will all be in trouble."

"We know you're not supposed to be here either. You are afraid you will get caught here, too, aren't you? If you tell anyone we were here, we will tell them you took the covers off her and showed us her private parts."

"I didn't do that; you did. Get out of here now and I won't tell. I am going to sit beside her. I will tell them I only sat beside the bed and watched her—if you go now."

Some time elapsed, and Mia drifted between restless pain and bits of sleep. She heard Hilda talking with Sarah.

"Kassie told me what happened when she was sitting with Mia. She said and Koss and Jacob came into the room. You must realize there is something is extremely wrong with Koss. We have to watch him; he's mental. He does not realize Mia is hurt and is very sick. I am afraid he is likely to sneak into the house and hurt her again when we're not here," Hilda muttered.

"We have to take turns sitting in the room with Mia while she is recovering."

"We can't allow Kassie to be alone with her either. She is weird too. Why did you allow Kassie into the room to rub Mia's chest?"

"I told Kassie she could sit beside Mia's bed, but I did not tell her to massage her chest. I just finished massaging Mia before she came in. You know, Kassie is very manipulative; she weasels her way around and does not tell the truth. I told her to watch Mia and to watch out for Koss too.

"We cannot trust Kassie; she is as sick as Koss and is always conniving with him."

"Well, she can't harm Mia the way Koss and Jacob can."

"Did you find out what happened that night?"

"No, I didn't."

Mia slowly recovered from the brutality of that night. As she lay in bed, she didn't have any desire for the food they placed before her. The glass of water beside her bed was warm and stale. Then, with Sarah no longer beside her bed to soothe and take care of her, Hilda was left to care for Mia alone.

"If Mia doesn't want to eat, she won't get any water either. I am not going to pamper the brat like Sarah did. If she is thirsty, she will have to get out of bed and get her own water," Hilda angrily complained to Kassie as they walked about the room. "Maybe if she got out of bed and walked around, she would get better and work up an appetite."

If her sisters would not bring a glass of fresh water to the bed, Mia realized she would have to get her own. Still weak and in much pain, she made her way out of bed. Each step she took cut through her body. She silently made her way toward the kitchen. Her throat was better. The heavy wrap hung loosely around her neck as she quietly stood beside the water pail, quenching her thirst. Her sisters were in the kitchen and continued their conversation without realizing she was even in the room.

Now that she was able to get her own fresh drink of water, she wouldn't beg her sisters to bring her some. The water pail was just inside the draped door that separated the living room and kitchen. Feeling refreshed, Mia fell into a restless sleep.

"When is Mia going to come outside to play again?" Koss repeatedly pestered his sisters.

"Leave Mia alone," Hilda seethed at Koss "She won't be going outside for a long time."

"She has to get better soon; her friends are asking about her," Mia heard Koss tell Kassie.

Mia wondered who was asking about her. How did anyone know she was ill?

"Did you hear what Koss said?" Kassie asked her one day. "Your friends in school are asking about you."

"I don't have friends in school. I don't know anybody there. How do they know I am sick?"

"Yes, you do have friends. Everybody in school who is our friend is your friend. They know you are sick, and they want you to get well soon. You have lots of friends; even boys are asking about you," she added. "They want you to get better."

Mia looked at Kassie doubtfully; there was something shady about her words. When her siblings spoke of school, Mia did not get the impression they were very friendly with many of their classmates.

Mia did not like boys, and she had developed a fear of them. She didn't have any playmates her own age. Sometime her cousin Hella came along when Aunt Elana visited her mother. Hella was a destructive child, and Mia was forced to put up with her dominance. Mia found Aunt Kathryn's children more pleasant than Aunt Elana's. However, Aunt Kathryn and Uncle Philip rarely brought their daughters along when they came to visit. Mia would have preferred their company.

"Tell Mia she has to get out of bed; somebody wants to come see her," Koss persisted as he spoke to Kassie.

"Did you hear what Koss said? He said you should get out of bed because somebody wants to come and see you."

"Who wants to come to our place? Is it Aunty Kathryn or Aunty Elana?" Mia lay listlessly in bed, wondering who wanted to see her.

"No, it's not them. It's someone from Belcourt," Kassie answered.

"Marcy?" she asked. Although Marcy was younger than Mia, Mia was lonely and would have liked company. "Is Jana coming with her too?" Jana was slightly older than Mia. However, Kassie considered Jana to be one of her friends, and she didn't like to share her friends.

Sometime later, Mia lay in bed, getting stronger. She eagerly waited for the day her company would appear.

"When are they coming?" she quizzed Kassie from her bed.

"Your visitors will come when you are better. That is why you have to get up and start walking around. They will come after you can get out of bed."

"I would like Jana and Marcy to come and visit now." She thought of Marcy with her black hair and dimpled cheeks. "I could sit up against a pillow, and Marcy can sit on the side of the bed and talk to me. If Marcy came, it would make me get better faster."

Mia woke up one evening after that to find she had slept through her dinner. Food still didn't appeal to her, but her thirst for water couldn't be quenched. Lowering herself from the bed, she quietly took the labored steps toward the kitchen. The drape between the two rooms was drawn. The dim light from the coal-oil lamp lit the kitchen and illuminated the drape fabric. She stood at the drape, gathering the courage to make her way through it and hoping she would not draw attention to the fact that she was up lest her sisters force her to have food instead of the water she craved.

Mia stood at the drape for a moment, listening to Hilda and Kassie as they did the dishes. She looked through the side of the curtain; their backs were turned to the doorway.

"Baily Stephenson," she heard Hilda exclaim in shock. "You mean he was one of the boys? Who told you it was Baily?"

"The kids in school did," Kassie answered with hesitance.

While Hilda and Kassie were absorbed in their conversation, Mia slipped through the drape and silently took a drink.

"But Baily? He's still Sarah's boyfriend. Father said he would allow them to marry when they are older. Baily should know better than that. Why would he do that to Mia? She is our little sister, and she is Sarah's little sister too."

"It is Father's fault. He wouldn't allow him to see Sarah without a chaperone. If he had, Baily wouldn't have done that to Mia."

"Would you take a roll in the hay with Baily if he asked you?" Hilda turned to Kassie as she spoke.

Mia noticed Kassie lower her head; she did not reveal the rest of the horrid secret of that terrible night, nor did she take any responsibility for being a part of it. Mia lowered the dipper soundlessly into the bottom of the pail. The rest of Hilda's words followed Mia as she slipped back into the bedroom unnoticed.

"Well, I wouldn't care if Baily is Sarah's boyfriend. I would have done it if it saved Mia from the horror of being molested by him. Don't tell Sarah I said that, but see what it has done to Mia? She has been in bed for so many days. How long will it take her to recover from this?"

"She will forget about it. She always does," Kassie said idly.

Mia sank back into the bed and fell asleep. She was slowly recovering from the horror she endured at the hands of her brothers and their friends. She felt an uneasy fear of her brothers but couldn't connect it to the conversations she was hearing about herself.

The next day, Mia was feeling stronger. It was midmorning when she got out of bed. When she went into the kitchen, some breakfast dishes still sat on the table with remains of food on them. Her older siblings had gone to school. The child picked up a morsel of food and put it in her mouth; surprisingly, it tasted good. She ate it hungrily as she sat on the floor. She felt refreshed by the sun and cool spring breeze flowing through the open kitchen door.

She heard the children in the schoolyard before they were called to their studies. Yuri toddled around the house and then wandered outside to where Nadia's voice nattered in the yard. Mia picked up her father's voice as he spoke to Nadia. Then his voice exploded in rage.

"Baily? Who told you it was Baily who did that to her?"

"Hilda and Kassie found out about it. They were talking about it, and Kassie told me."

"How did they find out it was Baily?"

"I don't know. Maybe somebody told them at school."

Mia crawled back into the bed, where she felt safe. Her parents' voices got louder as they got closer to the house; their arguments were frequent and vicious.

Although her father was a gentle person, he was afraid to show his children affection. It angered Nadia when she saw a bonding between her husband and their children. As if possessed, his wife rained accusations of improper behavior on him. She accused her husband of doing exactly what she was doing. In her manipulative way, she accused him of being the one who incestuously abused their children.

Surprisingly, Mia never witnessed physical blows between her parents. Her father was a stern-looking man who carefully controlled his actions.

Mia dealt with stress the only way she could. She crawled into her shell and stayed there until her parents' arguments were over. She learned to deal with any hurt and unpleasantness in the same manner.

Now her father's voice was belting out furiously. "The little bastard! The scum. I am going to school right now; there is no telling what I will do to him. I am going to get my hands on him and break every bone in his body!"

"No. You can't do that; you will create a scandal. If I knew you were going to react this way, I wouldn't have told you. I only told you so you would stop blaming Koss. It was not Koss; it was Baily."

"Well, then how did she get outside? Hilda and Kassie were in the next room. Why wasn't she asleep in her bed?"

"I don't know. Maybe she was sleepwalking and slipped by them without being noticed."

Mia heard her father groan in dismay at Nadia's lies.

"I'm going to rip that boy to shreds. I will go to school and get some answers from that little bastard. I will have a talk with him in front of the teacher."

"No, you can't do that. Everyone will know."

"If you wanted me to confront him when he was alone, why didn't you tell me about it before recess was over? I could have confronted him in the schoolyard. I could have had this talk with him after everyone went into the school."

"No, you can't confront him at school; it would only cause a scandal. He will tell everyone about Sarah and the abortion. If you want to talk to him, do it after he goes home from school, maybe in the evening."

Mia slept through the lunch hour and didn't see her sisters until they came home after classes were over. When they coaxed her out of bed, she sat listlessly in the kitchen, unaware of her sisters' chitchat and whispers. They appeared to know that there was going to be a reckoning between their father and Baily Stephenson, but Mia remained unaware of her circumstances and of why her father would want to confront the boy. Yuri ran about the room, unaffected by the tension around him.

"Father is back." The words were hardly more than a harsh whisper.

He walked into the house, a defeated man drained of anger.

"Well, what did he say?" Nadia sounded loud and shrill as her voice cut through the silence of the darkening room.

"He admitted it."

"What else did he say?" Her voice crackled.

"Nothing. He wouldn't tell me anything. He sniveled and blubbered like the runny-nosed wimp that he is, yet he would not tell me anything else."

"Did you hit him?"

"God, I wanted to. I wanted to break every bone in his scrawny body. I wanted to kill him, yet I did not. He is a child. I couldn't hit a sniveling child."

"Why was he crying?"

"Because he is a wimp. He just stood in the middle of the yard and bawled like a baby."

"Why didn't you go into the house to talk to him? You know the neighbors shouldn't hear what you talked about."

"Nobody heard anything except his father."

"Mr. Stephenson? He heard you scolding his son?" Nadia blared irately.

"Yes, he stood in the yard with us; he was angry with the boy and begged him to tell me what he knew. All he did was snivel and bawl." Her father paused, exasperated. "I told that boy and Mr. Stephenson that I forbid him to ever speak to any of my children again. There will be no association between any of you and that boy ever again. Do you understand? I stopped at the school, and I spoke to the teachers about it too."

"You spoke to the teachers about this? How dare you?" Nadia's cold eyes blazed with disapproval.

"Yes, I did, and they agreed to keep that boy in line. There will be no communication between any one of my children and Baily

Stephenson. If he so much as looks at Sarah or the other girls, there will be all hell to pay, and I mean it. Mr. Stephenson also agreed it was the right thing to do, and so did the teachers."

"But he might tell everybody about Sarah and the abortion," Nadia said, displaying her only concern in the matter.

Mia sat unaware of the cause of her father's anger and the reason for her parents' conversation. She was sick and despondent. She was filled with fear and revulsion toward her brothers, Nigel, and the Stephenson boys—a fear she could not determine the cause of. Her mind blocked off all memory of the night that Koss took her out into the cold night to be ravaged by them. She could only retreat into the shell where she felt safe.

CHAPTER THIRTEEN

Mia lived in a trancelike state. She was not allowed to lie in bed, where she could cower under the covers and feel safe, so she sat aimlessly in the house. If she heard footsteps approaching, she panicked and wanted to hide. Sarah still attended school nearby, but she did not spend much time at home. Mia felt safest when Hilda was around, but her fears mounted knowing that Koss and Jacob were also at home. When they expected her brothers in the house, she stayed close to Hilda.

"What is wrong with the brat? Why does she always follow me?" Mia's constant presence aggravated Hilda. "I cannot take a step without her being at my feet; whenever I turn around, she is right behind me."

"Koss and Jacob will be coming into the house for dinner soon; she must be afraid," Kassie offered.

"Well, she should be over that by now. Why doesn't she ever latch on to you?" Hilda snapped. Then, turning toward the child, she lashed out angrily. "Get out from under my feet, or I will belt you!"

Mia sat at the far end of the room, hoping that Koss wouldn't notice her when he came into the house. He eyed her smugly with a sneer; she lowered her head and pretended he was not there.

Later, Mia was at the water pail having a drink when Jacob came into the house and approached her unexpectedly. When he came up behind her, her first instinct was to drop the dipper into the water pail and run to Hilda for cover.

"Why are you afraid of Jacob? He will not hurt you," Hilda said sharply. "Can't you see he only wants a drink of water?"

Mia returned to continue her drink; Jacob stood behind her, watching her.

"Do you know how many boys there are in school?" he whispered.

She didn't know why the question alarmed her. She quietly muttered, "No."

"Then guess."

"I don't know," she murmured softly.

"Twenty-three. There are twenty-three boys."

Mia took another sip of water. She didn't care how many boys there were in school. She didn't like boys. Jacob stood waiting for her to finish drinking the water. She swallowed the last sip before she spoke.

"How many girls are there in school?"

"Shame on you for asking that question." Jacob scowled at her.

Mia dropped the dipper into the water pail and burst into tears. She ran into the bedroom to hide. She didn't know what was so shameful about wanting to know how many girls there were in school. She huddled in the bedroom for the rest of the day and wept over her brother's rudeness.

"Why did you ask how many girls there are in school?" Kassie questioned.

It was as if she asked Jacob something disgraceful. The child could only hide her face and her tears. Later, when Sarah came home, she gently spoke to Mia.

"Why are you crying?"

"Jacob was angry because I asked him how many girls there are in school. Kassie and Hilda are angry too."

"Why do you want to know how many girls there are in school?"

"Hilda and Kassie always talk about boys. Everybody talks about boys. I don't like boys, and I don't want to be friends with boys. Jacob said there are twenty-three boys in school. I wanted to know how many girls there are because when I go to school, I want to have girls to play with, not boys."

"Yes," Sarah replied. "There are girls in school, and there will be other girls who will start school with you."

"What are their names?" Mia blinked away her tears and looked at her sister eagerly.

"Rebecca will be starting school, and there will be others."

Later, Mia overheard Sarah asking Hilda and Kassie, "What was wrong with Mia wanting to know how many girls there are in school? She is anxious to know if there will be girls in her class. You were cruel to Mia, and so was Jacob."

"Well, how should we know if there will be any girls in her class? I am tired of being pestered by her with questions," Hilda answered heatedly.

Mia was happy when Sarah told her Rebecca would be starting school with her. She recalled the little girl called Rebecca from the day she went to the school picnic with Hilda and Kassie—the day Sarah arrived late because Nadia wanted her to stay behind and keep her company. She remembered sitting on the bench in the schoolyard. She thought the little girl called Rebecca was special because her mother held her hand so caringly as they walked into the schoolyard. Mia wanted company of her own age, and she wanted to meet Rebecca and others.

Riddled by fear and recovering from brutality, Mia continued to spend much of her time in bed. When they told her she would have company from Belcourt, she still waited and hoped Jana would bring Marcy to visit her.

The day finally came when Nadia and her older siblings forced her out of the house.

"It's Saturday, and we will all be at home. Mother says you must go outside today," Hilda directed.

"But I don't want to go outside," the fearful child begged her sisters. "I want to stay in the house. I am afraid."

"No, Mother says you have stayed in the house long enough. It's time for you to go outside."

"I don't know if forcing her to go outside is a good idea." Sarah stepped in to voice her concern. "She was hurt, and it will take time for her to heal. She also had a serious bout of fever. To have her sit and play on the cold ground would not be wise."

"Well, it is Saturday, and Mother says she has to go outside. We can't have her underfoot when we clean the house."

"I wouldn't be in your way when you clean the house. I will stay in bed," Mia begged.

"You have stayed in bed long enough, and you will be in our way because we have to change the bedding," Hilda snapped.

"Well, then, Mia, if Mother says you have to go outside, I'm afraid you must do what she says." Sarah looked at Mia sympathetically.

"But I'm afraid," she whispered to Sarah.

"There is nothing to be afraid of. Father has some pruning to do. He will not be in the yard, but he won't be far. You won't be alone. Koss and Jacob will be outside too."

Mia lowered her head in defeat.

"How are you feeling?"

"My stomach hurts when I walk."

"You don't have to walk far. Just stay close to the house," Sarah advised. "I will keep an eye on you."

Mia slowly walked out of the house, peering cautiously around the corner. She sat under the closest window to the door; she felt it would be the safest place. Jacob came and stood beside her for a moment.

"Remember, you aren't supposed to go far. Just stay right here," he instructed as he disappeared around the house. Then she heard him talking to Koss. Their voices faded as they walked farther into the yard.

Mia knelt on the ground and dug her fingers into the soil; there was a trace of sand in it. Now, all alone, she felt weak and tired and longed to go back into the house, but they had made it clear they didn't want her there. She felt lifeless like a shadow and knew she would have to stay outside until someone called her into the house. She was hopeful that when they called her in for lunch, they might allow her to stay for the rest of the day. They might even allow her to rest in bed.

Some time passed, and she continued to kneel wearily beside the house, clenching and unclenching her fist, watching the soil filter through her fingers. Suddenly, something drew her attention toward the garden plot. There, standing beside an apple tree, was Nigel Wilson. Her blood went cold; she tensed with fear. She was forbidden to go into the house, so she sat in silence, her body trembling. Mia covered her face and lowered her head, hoping Nigel Wilson would go away. It was moments before she could slowly bring her head up to see if he had gone. He was still there, watching her. Paralyzed by fear, she could only whimper. She lowered her head again and covered her face in panic, still unable to stifle the terror she felt. She couldn't bring herself to look toward the tree again.

She thought she heard a footstep nearby and brought her head up, wanting to cry out. Maybe he would leave her be if she begged him. When she brought her hands down and looked around, he wasn't there. She looked toward the garden plot, but he was no longer there. Shaken, she sighed with relief.

She sat solemnly, not knowing why she had been shrouded in fear as if a dark cloud blanketed her. Mia felt that something traumatic had happened and left a deep psychological scar on her, but she couldn't remember what it was. She feared her brothers, and she hated Koss; he repelled her, and she felt he should be punished—for something. But she could not remember why she loathed him. She had repressed the horror of that night so she could continue to live.

She could no longer be an innocent, carefree child. She had been brutally ravaged by ones she should have trusted. Fear, uncertainty, and mistrust of humanity would be her companions to haunt and follow her for the rest of her life. The innocent child had suffered and endured more than most older women. She was alone with no one to turn to and no place to find comfort.

She sat solemnly. *If Nigel was here, had he come to see Koss and Jacob? When he didn't see them, did he go back home?* Confusion led Mia to think that perhaps she only imagined him standing beside the trees, watching her. Was the fear she felt unwarranted?

She heard her brothers' voices, and then Jacob was standing beside her again.

"Are you alone?" He glanced around as he spoke.

"Yes." Mia hid her face.

"Was there anyone here with you?"

"No."

"Wasn't Nigel here?"

"I guess so."

"What do you mean you guess so? Where is he?"

"He was standing by the apple tree."

"Well, where is he now?"

"I don't know."

"Did he go back home?"

"I guess so."

"What did he tell you?"

"Nothing."

"What do you mean nothing? Didn't he talk to you?"

"No," she whispered, her head still lowered.

"Well, what happened? Did you tell him something to make him go away?"

"No, he stood by the trees and waited," Mia said in confusion. "You and Koss weren't here, so he went home, I guess."

"Didn't he talk to you at all?"

"No." Mia shook her head.

"Then what made him go back home? What did you do?"

"Nothing. I saw him, and I got really scared."

"Well, you must have done something to scare him off. Tell me what you said when you saw him. What did you do?"

"Nothing. I didn't do anything. It scared me when I saw him."

"Well, what did you do when you were frightened?"

"I put my hands over my eyes."

"Why did you do that?"

"Because it scared me, and I wanted to cry. When I looked up, he was still there. Then I looked again, and he was gone."

Mia sat detached from her surroundings, unsure of Jacob's reason for questioning her. Koss approached Jacob.

"What did she do?" he hissed angrily.

"Nigel was here. She saw him and put her head down to cry, so he went back home."

"Brat! Damned brat! Damned little fool brat!" Koss spat at her hatefully, his face discolored with rage. "We told you somebody from Belcourt was going to come to see you when you got better. Stupid little fool! Who did you think it would be? Didn't you know it was Nigel?"

Mia cringed. She lowered her head and tried not to cry. She wished her father would punish Koss and Jacob; they were such terrible boys. Why were they angry with her now? She waited for her sisters to tell her she could come back into the house.

Koss continued talking to his younger brother as they walked off in the direction of the road.

"Damned stupid brat! I had it all set up, and she scared Nigel away. I told him I will not give him his money back. He knows that I spent it already."

"Look, Koss. There is somebody coming down the road," Jacob interrupted.

"Wonder who it is."

"I don't know. Looks like it's two big boys."

"Oh, it looks like Mitch Wilson, and there is someone with him."

"Is it Mr. Wilson?"

"No, I don't think so. Mr. Wilson is not that tall."

Mia watched her brothers. Koss strained his neck, trying to make out the approaching figures.

"Oh, it must be Adam. Nigel did say his oldest brother was getting a few days off and would be coming home; he must have come last night."

"Koss, why are they coming down the road? Do you think they are coming here?"

"Well, what do you think? Of course they are. Nigel must have told them. You know Adam should have lots of money, and so should Mitch. We can get more money from them than from any other boys around here. Let's go and talk to that brat. She'd better not start sniveling this time, and she'd better not go into the house."

Mia was still sitting beside the house.

"Look here," Koss demanded sharply. "Two boys are coming down the road, and if you start sniveling and crying like you did with Nigel, I will deal with you my way. Mother will be angry when I tell her, and I'll tell her to beat you too. All I have to do is tell her you don't do what I tell you, and she will beat the hell out of you."

Mia was intimidated by her eldest brother.

"If you do what I tell you to do, everything will be OK. You don't have to be afraid of the boys, and you are not to scare them away like you scared Nigel. It is not nice to scare people off when they come to visit us; we have to be nice to them." Koss controlled the child with the power and the authority given to him by Nadia.

"Remember, when those boys come into the yard, all you have to do is sit and smile at them."

"But I can't smile. I'm afraid of boys," the child whimpered with her head lowered, afraid to look up at Koss.

"If you don't do what I tell you to do, I will hurt you myself. I will also beat you after they are gone. Just remember that. Now I want you to look up at me and show me how you are going to smile at them."

Mia looked up at her brother. The sight of him frightened her; she couldn't smile.

"I told you to smile," he hissed.

"I can't." Covering her face, she struggled to hide her fear.

"Maybe if she just showed her teeth, they would think she is smiling," Jacob suggested.

"OK. Look at us and show your teeth."

Mia lifted her head, closed her eyes and showed her teeth

"OK, that is better."

"But she closes her eyes."

"They probably won't see her eyes are closed if they see her from far away. Besides, did you notice when Kassie is real happy and smiles hard, it looks like her eyes are closed? Now you also have to get up off your knees and squat down with your knees apart."

Mia didn't know why she had to pose so awkwardly and show her teeth.

"We'll have to get Kassie to teach her how to sit when there are boys around. It would be best if she showed Mia how a girl acts in front of boys and what we expect of her. Those boys are coming closer. Let's leave her now. If we stand beside the gate, they will stop and to talk to us. When they stop to talk to us, you can ask them how much money they have," Koss advised his younger brother. "Remember," he sputtered at the child, "when they come in, all you have to do is hold your face up and show your teeth."

Mia squatted beside the house and turned her attention to the sandy soil in her hands. The two big Wilson boys came down the path, through the little gate that led into the yard. As they stood at the gate and spoke to her brothers, Mia noticed Koss shoot a mean glance her way. She fearfully exposed her teeth as she was told. The child wondered why the voices that were coming her way sounded so angry.

"She is a mere baby," the taller one, who she later learned was Adam, spat out at Koss. "What are you doing to her? What are you doing to your little sister? You should love her and take care of her." As Adam spoke, his voice sounded as if it was ready to break.

Koss turned to run away from the Wilson boys, but, in one long stride, Adam reached him and grabbed him. He brought him back by the scruff of the neck. Enraged, he lashed out at Koss as he looked toward the little girl beside the house.

"Look at her—she is a baby! Look at your sister. How old is she? Is she three? Is she four?"

"She is a little older than Marcy." It was Mitch who spoke.

Mia couldn't help but hear the anger in the Wilson boys' voices as they scolded her brothers.

"We didn't come here to punish you; it is up to your father to do that. We only came to talk to him. Where is he?"

She wondered why the Wilson boys were asking how old she was. Nadia didn't make a fuss over her children's birthdays; only Kassie and Koss made a big fuss over theirs. However, they would not tell her when her birthday was or how old she was. When she asked, one of her sisters told her she didn't have birthdays, and another sister told her it had passed.

Koss squirmed angrily as he tried to fight his way out of Adam's grip. Koss looked big and fearless when he bullied his way around her, but, beside Adam, he looked very short and pudgy. His face was red, and he looked like he might cry. He was powerless and not in control.

Adam looked as big as her father and had no problem restraining her brother. She would have liked her father to grab Koss by his neck and scold him when he misbehaved just like Adam Wilson was now doing.

"I want to talk to your father," Adam lashed out. "Where is he?"

"You can't talk to him," Koss sassed as Adam tightened his hold on him.

"Where is he?"

"He's not at home," Koss snapped back.

"Did he go to Ridgewood this morning?"

"No, I don't think he did, or I would have seen his car drive past," Mitch answered his brother.

"Well, then he must be around somewhere." Redirecting his question, he turned to Jacob. "Is your father at home?"

"Yes."

"Where is he?"

"We don't have to tell them, Jacob. They don't have to know." Koss snapped at his brother. "Don't tell him anything!"

"Go and get your father, Jacob. Tell him we want to talk to him."

"No!" Koss struggled to free himself of Adam's hold. "If you let me go, I will get him. I am older than Jacob. Let me go. I will get him." His body jerked in exasperation as he tried to shake free of Adam's hold.

"No, you won't, you slimy little punk. Do you think you can trick us into believing you? You will stand right here with us. I will not let go of my hold on you. Jacob will get him." Adam held Koss sternly by the scruff of his neck, totally in control of the situation.

Mia continued to sit beside the house, still waiting for one of her sisters to tell her that she could go into the house. The Wilson boys stood waiting for Jacob to return with his father. Adam didn't release his hold on Koss while they waited.

Soon, one of them said, "Look, there they are."

The Wilson boys pushed Koss in front of them as they walked around the corner of the house and out of Mia's sight. Mia heard angry voices. Was her father going to beat Koss? Although violence disturbed the child, she wanted her father to scold Koss like Adam said he should. Adam said he would leave the punishment to her father. Mia wanted him to punish Koss for the unknown violations she felt.

Mia remained where she was, listening to the angry voices, until she could no longer curb her curiosity. She stood up and cautiously made her way toward the gate, wanting to see what was taking place around the corner.

Her father and the Wilson boys stood in the yard. Koss and Jacob stood beside them in angry confrontation. Adam was no longer holding Koss by the scruff of his neck, but he had his head lowered as if he were the target of their fury. Jacob was looking up at them. Mia knew they were sorting out some sordid matters. She felt better as she anticipated punishment for her brothers. Things would be better; Koss would stop manipulating and violating her. She watched them for a moment and then cautiously made her way back to sit beside the house.

After a while, she heard a further flow of anger from the other side of the yard. Then the voices simmered down. She didn't hear any cries from Koss. Didn't their father punish him as Adam said he should? Maybe he took him into the shed to punish him. Where were the Wilson boys? Mia could no longer hear their voices. She hadn't seen them walk down the path and leave, but neither could she hear their voices anymore. Did they leave the yard unseen by her?

Mia needed to satisfy her curiosity. She felt that so much depended on the outcome of what took place between her father and the Wilson boys that day. She slowly made her way to the gate again, wanting to see if the Wilson boys were still in the yard. They were still there.

What had started as an angry confrontation now appeared to be a grave discussion. She watched her father, Adam, and Mitch. They stood in the yard, and it appeared they were having a very solemn discussion. As they spoke, they occasionally lowered or lifted their heads. Koss and Jacob were no longer with them.

She was elated as she took the steps back toward the house. They would sort things out; everything would be OK. With the thought of not being abused again, she happily walked back toward the house and ecstatically skipped a happy step. Pain ripped through her lower abdomen. She tried not to cry. The pain was unbearable, and she fought to stay on her feet. She was told to sit beside the house; if she lay right there on the ground, they would see she had wandered farther than she was allowed. Nadia would surely punish her for disobeying. If she spanked her mercilessly, it would aggravate the pain in her lower abdomen. Holding on to her tears and her lower abdomen, she painfully made her way into the house.

Curling up in a fetal position on the kitchen cot, she couldn't stop shivering; the sharp pain continued until she could no longer control her silent sobs.

It was Sarah who walked into the kitchen and found her. "What happened?" she anxiously asked the child.

"I only wanted to see if the Wilson boys were still here. I hurt my stomach when I was coming back. Sarah, it hurts so much." Her body quivered as she shivered in shock.

"I will cover you with a comforter to keep you warm; it will make you feel better."

"What happened?" Hilda took in the situation as she entered the room. "Did they—"

"No, she hurt herself when she was walking back to the house."

"God forbid. If they had hurt her again, I would have had it out with Mother myself." Hilda spoke with indignation. Her fiery temperament matched Nadia's caustic psyche.

"She is our mother." Sarah spoke quietly. "We have to respect her."

Later, when Mia was able to walk without much pain, Sarah helped her into the bedroom to lie down on her own bed. She was surprised to see Nadia lying on the other bed. The child stopped short, unsure if she should enter.

"But why is Mother here?" Mia whispered and paused as she held back. "I might wake her up; she will be angry at me."

"It's OK. Mother is only resting on the bed."

Mia noticed that Nadia's vacant eyes were opened and affixed on the ceiling as if she was in a trance. Dried tears on the side of her face were visible. It was as if Nadia were in mourning. Mia backed away from her and quietly lay down on the other bed.

After the Wilson boys left, Koss moped around angrily in a sulky mood. It upset his mother to see her son in such a downcast state. To add to Nadia's and her son's insult, Mr. Wilson forbade Nigel to speak to or have any association with Koss or Jacob.

CHAPTER FOURTEEN

"I will get that Nigel for snitching to his brothers and his father. It was our secret. He shouldn't have told them." Koss conveyed his anger to Jacob. "And I will not give him his money back either."

A short while later, their father sent Koss and Jacob to an old abandoned shack to fix some storing crates needed for their abundant crop later in the season. When they returned, Koss spoke enthusiastically with Jacob.

"I sure got even with that snitch today, didn't I? Did you see the look on his face? It was a good thing we had a chance to hide when we heard him coming down the path."

"It was my idea to hide behind the crates," Jacob boasted. "It was a better idea to scare him like we did. I don't think bashing his head with the hammer would have been wise."

"Well, I wouldn't have bashed him hard."

"It was a better idea to take the hammers and point the steel handles at him and pretend they were guns."

"Yes, and my hammer had an open base, so it really looked like the barrel of a gun."

"We should have told him to put his hands up or we would shoot him like the gangsters in the movies do," Jacob said.

"He said we only scared him because he didn't expect anyone to be there. I think we scared him because he thought we had real guns."

"He said he recognized your voice. If you had spoken in a deep voice, you might have made him believe you were a military policeman like Uncle Tom."

"Too bad Uncle Tom hasn't come to visit us yet. He keeps his gun in the trunk of his car. If we had taken it, we really could have scared Nigel with it, Mr. Wilson told Nigel he wasn't ever supposed to talk to us, and he did. If I threaten to tell his father that he spoke to us, we can probably get Nigel to do what we want him to do again," Koss said with a pout.

When their father came in for lunch, Koss and Jacob sat smugly at the table. There was no mention of the prank they had pulled on their neighbor. They were not to be outwitted or ordered about by Mr. Wilson or any neighbor who disagreed with Nadia's devious ways.

The crimes carried out by Nadia against her children concerned the neighbors who knew; however, those neighbors who knew were helpless. They couldn't stop the dysfunctional acts in Nadia's house. What could be done about such a shocking crime taking place in this remote little settlement? It was the Depression years of the 1930s. There was no protection for the young and innocent.

Parents conceived, gave birth, and were left to raise their children as they chose. As long as the child was registered at birth and attended school until the age of fifteen, and the parents were not deceased, they remained under the care of their parents. In Europe, the dark clouds of war were looming on the horizon. Mia listened to her father and Nikola when Nikola and Rachel came to visit. Her father and Nikola hashed over the latest crises in far-off war-torn countries, while Rachel sat and quietly chatted with Nadia.

Mia loved to sit and take in Rachel's calm, soothing voice. Nikola and Rachel didn't allow Nadia to shoo Mia off like she did when her sister Elana came with her upsetting attitude. The child sensed Nikola and Rachel's compassion and silently relished the shelter of their company.

Whether the violations took place in war-torn Europe or in Nadia's house, the crimes against helpless children and humanity continued. The neighbors who knew of the abuse in Nadia's house could do nothing to stop it. They were just as helpless as the people in Europe, where women, children, and all of humanity were being violated. There, the violators were enemy soldiers under the leadership of a ruthless dictator; in Nadia's home, the violations were carried out by children under the leadership of the ruthless woman who bore them.

When her older siblings were in school, Mia sat in the house and listened to Nadia as she madly raved about the Wilsons.

"What kind of people are they? I will talk to Mr. Wilson myself. What kind of upbringing did he give that boy? To think he would have the nerve to butt into other people's affairs. He had some nerve to come into my yard and scold my sons. The nerve of him telling us what to do! He himself is a heathen, but he is going into the ministry to preach to heathens."

Mia liked Mr. Wilson. He was a pleasant man, and although Mia was a shy, withdrawn child, he showed patience with her whenever she was sent to his store on an errand.

Mia's father had gone to Ridgewood. When he returned, Mia heard him enter the house and calmly address Nadia.

"I saw your sister Kathryn in town today."

"Kathryn?" Nadia asked. "I haven't seen her for some time. Did you talk to her?"

"Yes, I did."

"Well, what did she say?" Nadia looked at her husband, anxiously waiting to hear more.

"Kathryn said she would like to come down and have a talk with you."

"A talk with me, not a visit? What does she want to talk to me about?"

Mia noticed that Nadia seemed upset because her sister wanted to talk to her.

"I didn't speak to her for long. She said there was talk among the congregation in her church on Sunday, and it disturbed her."

"Her church—with all those heathens and their beliefs? What a bunch of rubbish. Our father would be turning in his grave if he knew she changed her religion to one headed by the demon himself—that Mr. Gabriel." Nadia spat the name in hate. "Is that all she said? Did she tell you what the talk was about?" she questioned her husband again.

Mia was quiet as she listened to her parents discuss the matter. A slight knock on the door interrupted them. She was surprised when Mr. Wilson entered the room; he wasn't a common visitor in their house. He glanced in Mia's direction before he started to talk. His eyes looked bright and glassy as if he had been crying. He didn't take time to explain his visit but came straight to the point.

"What is happening in this house? What are you teaching your boys?" Mr. Wilson took a deep breath and a moment's pause before he continued. "Not only are your boys teaching my children things they shouldn't know, but they are also teaching them to steal from me. I am their father, and your sons are teaching my children to steal from me and lie about it." Mr. Wilson's words were spoken softly.

Nadia, who earlier damned Mr. Wilson and angrily spoke of confronting him about the upbringing of his children, did not utter a word. Mia's father didn't speak either. Mia sat and watched as Mr. Wilson seemed to fumble and falter as if he couldn't speak anymore. As he turned to leave, she saw tears rolling down his cheeks. Her father followed him out the door.

When Mia's father returned, Nadia continued the conversation as if there had been no interruption by Mr. Wilson.

"Well, did Kathryn say what she wanted to talk to me about?"

He was slow to answer, but his words were deliberate. "She wanted to talk about exactly what Mr. Wilson had to say."

Nadia looked flustered. For the rest of the day, she seemed taken up in thought and didn't talk much. When the older children came home from school, Nadia demanded a discussion with them.

"We will be having company this evening," she forewarned them. "When Aunt Kathryn and Uncle Philip come, I don't want you to go off and hide in the other room like you always do. I want you to stay in the kitchen while they are here just like their children do. I want you to face them and look them straight in the eye. When they mention fault about you, pretend you don't know what they are talking about; act innocent. Make sure to include Mia with you. I don't want them to say we mistreat her or treat her differently because she is young."

Later, when their aunt and uncle arrived, Sarah and Hilda were free to do as they pleased. Mia was called into the kitchen to join her three other siblings. Koss made a demanding motion to Mia to stand beside them where Kassie made room.

"By the stories we have been hearing about your children, especially Koss and Kassie, there have been some dastardly acts carried out here." Aunt Kathryn's voice was strong. She came to the point without delay.

"We haven't heard anything. My children are good children. Who has been making up stories about them?" Nadia acted as if her sister's words took her by surprise.

"Everyone is talking about what is happening in this house," Kathryn explained.

"What kind of criminals are you raising?" Uncle Philip cut in sharply.

"What do you mean criminals? We are not raising criminals," Nadia flared back at her brother-in-law.

"Well, from the talk in the school and the talk brought to the church, they are involved in some very wicked acts. Do you realize the shocking things they have been doing? Do you also realize the long-lasting consequences are going to stick with you and your family name for the rest of your lives and their lives?"

Mia often heard Nadia ridicule Uncle Philip. She would claim he didn't have a brain in his head and if it weren't for her sister, he would be picking garbage out of the dump. Now Mia looked at Nadia sitting in her chair, her fists clenched tightly on her knees, her mouth set in anger. She sat like a child who was caught for some unforgivable deed, sulking for being punished. She did not respond or look anyone in the face.

Uncle Philip spoke sharply, his voice rising. Mia watched the tall, slender man, his hands clasped behind his back as he paced about the room. He spoke sternly to Nadia and her husband. Although the point of his lecture was lost on the young child, he sounded like an intelligent person. *Uncle Philip doesn't sound like a nitwit like Mother says he is*, Mia thought.

"I am not worried about my name," Uncle Philip continued. "It is not my name that is degraded by your sons; it is your name being degraded. Your name," he repeated angrily, his look focused on Nadia and then on her husband. The man's words seemed to send a stinging message through the quiet room.

Nadia sat unmoving, her expression vacant.

"The things your boys are doing are criminal! You gave those boys life, and they carry your name. If you can't control them now, what is going to happen to them later? Don't you want them to carry your family name forward with dignity? Your family name is something you do not outgrow and throw away." With those words, Uncle Philip's gaze rested on Koss and Jacob. "When you die, you end in a grave, but your name lives on. When you die, they carve your name in marble on your headstone. There it lives forever."

He stopped for a moment and looked at Kassie before he continued.

"Maybe she won't have the family name on her headstone—that is, if anyone will want her for a wife. Maybe one day she will meet a simpleton who will marry her." He paused and gave Kassie a searing look before he continued. "This will live on long after you are gone. People will look at your graves and remember. They will keep talking about you and your family and the things you did in your lifetime."

The anger in her uncle's face was obvious as he directed the words at her siblings. They were accompanied by a harsh and lengthy stare. He turned and looked down at Nadia. Then he directed a harsh and lengthy glare at those around him. Mia watched Kassie and Koss shuffle their feet uncomfortably and lower their gaze; Jacob followed suit.

Aunt Kathryn sat quietly while her husband spoke. Nadia did not say anything either. Mia looked at her father. He sat with his head lowered, cupped in his hands. Everyone was silent as if the words their uncle spoke were distasteful. When Mia's father spoke, he sounded like a broken man struggling to keep from crying.

"I have tried. God help me, I have tried, but I can't stop the inhumanity in this family. I have tried to keep my family name clean and honest like my father did. Nobody can say I did anything to tarnish my father's name. My father was a respected man; he carried his name with dignity, and he was proud of it. I feel the same pride, but my sons…my sons. What are they doing to my name? I admit I can't control what is happening in this family. It is happening, and I can't do anything to stop it. It is not in my hands. They don't listen to me. They listen to her, and I can't stop it."

Nadia sat motionless. A look of contempt crossed her face before she once more assumed a vacant stare to mask her anger. As Mia watched her mother listen to Philip's biting words, she occasionally detected a look of embittered hatred at being exposed. Still, Nadia did not speak.

Mia looked at the three siblings standing around her. She didn't understand the full meaning of what was going on. She only knew it hurt to see her father upset, a broken man on the verge of tears.

"Why does Father want to cry?" Mia looked up at her brothers and sister for an answer.

"Shut up," Koss muttered under his breath.

"Why is everybody so angry? Are you all going to die?" Mia whispered to Kassie.

"No," she hissed back at the child.

"Then why did Uncle say they will put your names on your graves?"

"Be quiet. We will tell you later," Kassie hissed again.

"Why did Uncle scold everybody? What happened in school?" Mia continued.

"Nothing."

"Then why did Uncle Philip say everybody in school is talking about what happened?"

"Because we did something bad in school, that's why."

"What did you do in school?"

"We stole an eraser; that's what we did."

"Oh, that is bad. Is the teacher going to strap you for stealing it?"

"Yes."

"Is that why Father wants to cry?"

"Yes."

"Tell the brat to shut up," Koss hissed under his breath.

After Uncle Philip and Aunt Kathryn left, Nadia condemned and damned her brother-in-law. "He had no right to scare my children. He had no right to tell them their gravestones will be marked with their names," she blazed angrily. "Now they are afraid because they think they will die."

"Who is afraid?" her husband lashed back. "They don't look like they are afraid. Which one of them looks like they have fear, shame, or remorse?"

"Well, the younger ones are afraid." Nadia paused. "Jacob is afraid. He asked me if he is going to die."

It was some time later, when Nadia was preparing the noon meal and her father was working in the orchard, that Mia heard the older children's infuriated voices as they entered the yard for lunch.

"They are all laughing at Jacob and me," Koss raved in a fury of tears.

"I don't know what you are talking about. It wasn't me. I didn't tell anyone anything," Hilda shouted back at her brother before they reached the door.

"It was you or Kassie who did. Jacob said he didn't tell anyone." Koss burst into the house in a fit of anger and fresh tears.

"What have you done to upset your brother?" Nadia turned on Hilda with visible irritation.

"I haven't done anything. I didn't say anything to anyone, and nobody said anything to me."

"Yes, you did, and I'm not going to school after lunch; I am never going back to school," Koss exploded angrily in a fresh round of tears. "The boys are all making fun of and laughing at me now."

"What did you do? Why are the boys making fun of Koss?" Nadia was furious.

"Nothing. I didn't do anything. I didn't," Hilda protested.

"Yes, she did. Now the boys are teasing and laughing at me. You said we were not supposed to tell anyone our secrets." Koss blurted the words out and burst into another flurry of tears. "She told everybody. Now they're making fun of us."

Nadia's sweaty face turned crimson with rage. She turned on Hilda and shrieked like a demon. "You told them! You told them what happens in the privacy of this house? How dare you?" In a wild frenzy, she ripped the heavy leather strap from the hook on the wall. Whipping it toward Hilda, she wailed, "How dare you carry things of that sort out my door? How dare you?"

Mia sat huddled on the kitchen cot with Yuri. She cringed at the sight of Nadia's crazed behavior.

"I didn't say anything." Hilda shook with fear as she screamed back at her mother. "I didn't!"

"Take your clothes off! Take them off right now!" The leather strap whipped through the air and caught Hilda on the arm.

"No, I didn't tell anyone. I wouldn't tell anyone! If I did, Josh would hear about it, and I don't want Josh to know what is happening in this house. What would he think of me if he found out you make us sleep with our brothers?" Hilda was crying hysterically. "Kassie...it must have been Kassie who told them."

"No, Kassie promised that she wouldn't tell anyone; she promised that she wouldn't. Why would she tell them about it in school?" Nadia screamed at Hilda.

"Kassie is jealous because Sarah and I have boyfriends. If she told everyone in school she was sleeping with her brothers, it would make her more popular with the boys in school."

Nadia lowered the strap and leveled her gaze at Hilda. "You are right; you wouldn't want Josh to know. It must have been Kassie. Even though she promised she wouldn't give our secret away, it must have been her. Where is she? Where is that girl?" Nadia bellowed, turning her maniacal madness toward her absent daughter.

"She said she had to step out to the privy before she came in for lunch."

"Kassie…it must have been Kassie who carried my secret out the door. Go get her!" Nadia's voice echoed throughout the house.

Without any forewarning, Kassie flounced into the house, smiling, unaware of what awaited her. She stopped short when she saw her enraged mother standing before her, strap in hand.

"You told them about our secret," Nadia shrieked. "Take your clothes off!"

"No!" Kassie cringed.

"You told them. Take your clothes off."

"No, I didn't do it. I didn't tell anyone."

"Take your clothes off now!" Nadia lashed the strap at Kassie as she raged. "Take them off, or you will be going back to school with blood dripping off them!"

"No, I didn't tell anyone. I didn't!"

"Take her clothes off now!" Nadia shrieked the command at Hilda.

Mia watched Hilda go up to Kassie and try to undo her sister's blouse, struggling with one button at a time, while Kassie held her off, enraged and in tears.

"I didn't tell anyone. I wouldn't." She struggled to keep Hilda from unbuttoning her blouse. "Honest to God, I didn't tell anyone!"

"Get that blouse off her," Nadia screamed. "Or I will lash this strap on whoever it lands on. Then you both will be going back to school with bloody clothes."

Hilda continued an attempt to follow Nadia's orders.

"No, no, please...it wasn't me. I didn't tell anyone." Kassie begged for her mother to stop. "I didn't tell anyone. I didn't tell anyone!"

All hell broke loose. Nadia shrieked demonically. Koss kept snarling, playing up his wounds. Kassie's screams were pathetic to Mia's ears. Hilda, in exasperation, struggled to strip her sister of her clothing, all the while trying to keep out of Nadia's way. Mia huddled on the kitchen cot, trying to protect her young brother, Yuri, from the madness around them. When Hilda finally had Kassie stripped down to her underclothing, Nadia whipped Kassie while bellowing wildly. Kassie's relentless screams were inhuman.

"What is going on here?"

Mia looked up at the tall, lanky figure of her father standing in the doorway. Amid the bedlam, no one heard him enter the house.

"What is going on here?" he repeated sharply. "I could hear the screams up to the far end of the orchard. I am sure the neighbors heard them too. What is going on?" He looked at Nadia as he waited for an answer.

"Keep out of this. This is not for you to interfere with," Nadia lashed out at her husband. "I am whipping her. *I* deal with the children! She defied me, and I must punish her. She told everyone in school the things that are not supposed to be spoken of outside of this house. I must punish her for doing it. You keep out of this. I will deal with my children my way!"

Kassie continued screaming. "No, I didn't. I didn't tell anyone!"

"Put that strap down and leave her alone."

Everyone's eyes were drawn to the figure still standing in the doorway.

"She didn't tell anybody anything. I did." His voice was intense.

Nadia's face flushed, bathed in sweat and anger. "You told them? *You* told them? I don't believe you. You are covering up for her like you cover up for Hilda. I don't believe you!"

"No, I am not covering up for anyone." His bitter look held his wife's angered gaze. "It was I, not Kassie, who spoke out about what is happening in this house."

Nadia stood in pent-up fury, the heavy strap held tightly in her hand. Mia wondered if Nadia would turn the strap on her husband and use it on him as she did on Kassie.

"You went to school and told the children about what takes place in my house?" Nadia repeated, her voice penetrating the silenced room. "I don't believe you." She looked at her husband icily. "You only want to protect her. You did not go to the school to tell the children. I don't believe you," she repeated hoarsely. "When did you go to school? You've been working in the far orchard the whole morning. I would have seen you go to the school. I don't believe you," Nadia repeated.

"I didn't go to the school. I told Adam and Mitch."

"Adam and Mitch? When did you tell them?" Nadia held her cold gaze on her husband as she spoke. Her pale, vacant eyes pierced him without leaving his face.

"We stood talking in the yard when they told me about what Koss was doing. I had to tell them. I couldn't hold it back any longer. I had to tell someone. How much of this agony do you think a man can take?"

"But that was two weeks ago. Why didn't they say anything sooner?" Nadia's voice was cynical. Then she turned and lashed out at her husband. "You are going to go to the Wilsons' right now before you sit down to lunch. You are going to Belcourt to tell Mr. Wilson that what you told Adam and Mitch was not true." Nadia directed her husband without taking her icy gaze from his face. "Go. Go right now," she uttered coldly. Unemotionally, she ordered her husband as if he were a child she was disciplining—a child she might lash with the strap that she still held in her hand.

"No, I will not go before I eat. I will sit and have my lunch first." Mia watched as her father sat in his place at the table.

"What will you tell him?" Nadia glared down at her husband, her face tense. She still grasped the strap in her clenched fist.

"I will think of something."

"You must tell them it isn't true. You must tell them it is a lie. If the boys in school don't quit making fun of Koss, so help me, I will go to Belcourt and talk to the Wilsons myself. So help me, there will be hell to pay," Nadia hissed, her eyes blazing with anger.

Were the stories of the evil deeds in Nadia's house squelched by the tall, slender man who fathered Nadia's unfortunate children? Or was it the fear of Nadia's wrath that held the neighbors' tongues in check?

CHAPTER FIFTEEN

The daily conflict between Nadia's elder offspring escalated with the most intense brawls taking place when Nadia and her husband were absent. As in any dysfunctional family, animosity festered and grew.

Mia dreaded when her parents left home on trips. Some of the trips were made out of necessity; leaving in the morning, they returned late at night. At other times, they spent the night away from home. It was when their parents were absent that the intense disputes erupted. It was a free-for-all among the older siblings.

Sarah was away from home. Nadia protected her eldest daughter. Was sending Sarah away from this type of environment a way of protecting her from the rivalry among the other offspring?

When Nadia and her husband were preparing to leave, she assigned the work to be done in their absence. Then, turning to Mia and Yuri, she warned them to mind the older siblings and not to interrupt them when they were at work. The youngsters were sent outside and forbidden to enter the house until they were called. It was a long, grueling day for them. When they didn't see any signs of the older siblings for long periods, they thought they had been abandoned.

Hungry and thirsty after the long day in the blistering heat, they would wander into the house to find no one there. They were overwhelmed with loneliness and gripped with fear. At times they would spot Kassie running from the house carrying food and disappearing toward the forbidden shed. When they called to her, she did not answer.

One day, Nadia gave her usual orders to her older offspring before leaving on a trip. "After you have done what I told you, Jacob can bring the cows in for their five o'clock milking. Cool and bottle the milk." Then, turning to Mia and Yuri, she added, "Don't interrupt your brothers and sisters. They have work to do in the storage shed."

The storage shed was a forbidden area to the two youngsters. It stood in isolation at the far end of the yard. To the children's eyes, there were no windows in the mysterious building, only a chunky door facing the opposite direction.

"What are you going to do in the shed?" Mia looked at her sisters and waited for an answer.

"They are going to shell peas," Nadia blurted at the child, half in anger.

"Can Yuri and I help them?" Mia begged.

"No, you can't."

"Then can I help? I am older than Yuri. Yuri can sit and watch us shell the peas."

"No, you can't. You will only break the pods and mush the peas," Nadia answered.

"But Yuri and I are scared when we are left alone. I will be careful if they let me help them. Kassie lets me help her shell peas for dinner."

"No, you can't," Nadia snapped again, her increasing irritation with the child was obvious.

The afternoon lagged, dreary and unrelenting, and the youngsters were feeling dejected; they hadn't eaten and were hungry. By late afternoon, they decided to trudge toward the storage shed to see if their siblings had finished shelling the peas. Mia walked around the building, expecting the door to be open, but it was closed. She realized the windowless shed would be dark with the door closed, making it difficult for them to work inside.

"They must be finished shelling the peas. That is why the door is closed," she speculated. "You wait here, Yuri. I will go to the door and ask them to give us some peas," Mia reassured her brother.

"Get me lots of peas, Mia. I am so hungry," Yuri somberly begged his sister; his dirty, tear-stained cheeks revealed the lonely day they'd had with the fear of being abandoned.

There was a huge rock beside the door. Mia crawled onto it and tugged at the latch, and the heavy door opened, swinging on its hinges and past her. She stood looking into the darkened building, but there were no baskets of peas and shells in the shed as she expected.

Kassie and Jacob lay on their stomachs on a lower wooden bunk. They were looking up to the gable end of the opened loft. Mia's entrance caught her older siblings by surprise.

"What are you doing here?" Kassie lashed out, astonished to see the child.

"Who opened the door?" Hilda's angry voice came from the loft area.

"It is Mia," Kassie answered in annoyance.

"Where are the peas?" Mia looked around in surprise. "There are no peas here. Why are you and Jacob lying down on the bunk? Yuri and I are hungry, and we want some peas."

"Get the brat out of here." Hilda's angry voice floated down from the loft.

Mia looked toward the opened loft where Hilda lay with Koss.

"Why is Hilda up there? How did she get there?"

"Get the brat out of here," Hilda lashed out again. Then, in a quieter voice, she added, "We are lucky the show was over; she didn't catch us at it."

"Get out of here and close the door," Kassie yelled from the bunk where she lay.

"Can we come in? We are tired and hungry, and we want some peas."

"No. This is off limits to you. You are not supposed to come in here. Get out. We will be out in a while. Go into the house and wait for us."

Mia knew that her siblings were upset with her, but she did not understand why. Nadia said they would be shelling peas. Mia did not see any peas or the remains of them. She tried to close the heavy wooden door, but it kept swinging open.

"Leave the door alone; we'll close it ourselves," someone shouted at her. "Just get out of here."

Yuri stood at the corner of the shed waiting for her. "Are they there? Did you see them?" He looked expectantly at Mia through grime and dried tears.

"Yes, they are there."

"Then why didn't you bring me some peas, Mia? I am so hungry."

"There aren't any peas in the shed. They are angry, and they said we should go into the house."

The agony of being left alone was not over. Not only were the two youngsters deserted for most of the day, but after the dinner dishes were done, the evening ended with one of the most terrifying battles the youngsters were to witness.

Mia could not understand what brought on the horrendous brawls. Earlier, her elder siblings had quietly isolated themselves in the shed and didn't want to be interrupted. Later, all the fury and resentment within them spilled over at each other in hatred. Even though Hilda was the eldest, Nadia gave Koss the reins of control.

After the day's activities had taken place, Koss sat composed in his father's favorite chair, looking at some family photos. Everything was calm until Kassie let out a blood-curdling shriek and lunged toward her brother with her father's sharp barber scissors in her hand. Mia was petrified by the scene taking place before her. With the scissors a few mere inches away from the back of her brother's head, Hilda sprang at Kassie and grabbed her hand. A fight ensued, and Hilda got the scissors from her sister. But Koss thought Hilda was going to stab Kassie and took it upon himself to pounce on his older sister and wrestle her to the floor.

"Grab the scissors from her," he shrieked at Kassie as he wrestled Hilda to the ground.

"No, she can't have them. Help me, Jacob. Don't let Kassie have the scissors," Hilda shrieked from the tangled mass on the floor.

Whimpering in fright, Mia wrapped her arms around Yuri as she tried to protect them both from the horror surrounding them. Scenes such as this were common when Nadia and their father were absent. It was as if all hell broke loose and the demon himself was in control.

As the tangled mass of bodies struggled against the opposite wall, they accidently pulled the flimsy curtain from the window. Fearing the dark, Mia looked at the curtainless, dark window. Moisture formed in little beads and trickled down the window pane. The flickering reflection of light from the glowing oil lamp, along with the blazing reflection of the fire in the kitchen grate, gave the child an overall impression of a shadowy movement. To her, it appeared to be the fiery face of the feared demon that had haunted and terrorized her young life; it appeared to be watching them through the window. Her terror-filled, blood-curdling scream cut through the air.

The ferocious brawl came to a standstill, but the child's spine-tingling scream endured, chilling the air. Mia's face was drained; traces of tears spattered her cheeks. Her eyes were glazed in fear as she protectively tightened her arms around Yuri and pointed toward the widow. So great was the child's terror that even the angered voices of her siblings couldn't stop her scream.

"What is wrong with her?"

"Shut up, you brat!" Koss flung the words at the child as he made an angry motion to strike her.

"Leave her alone. What happened? What is wrong with her?" Hilda took control of the situation.

"Make the brat shut up, or I will shut her up," Koss bellowed, his normally ruddy face bursting crimson under his bleached hair and pale eyes.

"What is wrong with her?"

"Maybe one of us hurt her when we were fighting."

"No, I don't think we did."

"Why is she pointing at the window?"

"The curtain is off the window; maybe she saw someone there."

"There is nothing in the window; it's dark outside."

"Well, you know she is afraid of the dark. Quick, put the curtain back over the window so she can't see the darkness."

Only when the darkness of the night was shut out did Mia's heart-wrenching scream die away to a terrified whimper.

"Damned brat. Why was she screaming? We should beat her for screaming. Mother said she is not supposed to scream." Koss made his way toward the child again.

"No, don't touch her," Hilda commanded.

Through her tears and anguish, Mia was barely able to speak. "I saw him. I saw him. He was watching you. He was watching you fight. I saw him when you pulled the curtain down. I saw him!"

"Who did you see?"

"The demon," she whispered. "I saw him. I saw him. He was watching you fight, and he saw Yuri and me because we were in the room with you."

"There was no demon."

"Yes, I saw him. Yuri and I couldn't hide from him. He saw us both sitting on the bench. He was watching us, and he was laughing."

"Who is she talking about? Do you suppose Mr. Wilson or Mr. Gabriel heard us fighting and looked through the window?"

"No, no. It was the demon! He was watching you fight; he is going to take you to hell because you were fighting, and he saw Yuri and me too. He is going to burn us in hell, too, 'cause we were in the same room with you."

"Maybe someone was passing down the road and stopped in to see what was happening."

"No, it was the demon." Mia tried to convince her siblings. "It was! He saw Yuri and me sitting on the bench, and he is going to take us and burn us in hell too," the terrified child repeated.

"What is wrong with the stupid brat? I am going to pound some sense into her," Koss threatened.

"It must have been a neighbor passing by who looked through the window to see what was happening."

"If it were Mr. Wilson or Mr. Gabriel, they would have knocked on the door or come in to see why we were fighting."

"What did the face in the window look like? Did it look like Mr. Wilson's or Mr. Gabriel's face?"

It wasn't Mr. Wilson's jolly face she saw in the window. Her mother said Mr. Gabriel was a demon, but it wasn't his face either.

"No," she cried. "It was the demon!"

"Well, what did he look like?"

"His face was skinny, and it looked dark."

"Mr. Wilson's face is round, so it was not his face. Mr. Gabriel's face is skinny, and if he were outside, his face would appear to be dark."

"Yes, it could've been Mr. Gabriel." The older children decided among themselves.

"It wasn't Mr. Gabriel." Even though Mia tried to be calm, the image shook her. Her voice quivered, and her body trembled uncontrollably.

"Do you suppose Josh came by and saw us fighting?" Hilda looked at Kassie. "If he did, what would he think of me?"

"Well, if the face looked like the demon's, it could have been Igor. He has a scary face, and he would laugh if he saw us fighting," Kassie admitted.

Mia thought for a moment. "His face looked a bit like Igor's. He had a pointed chin and a pointed beard, and I think he had pointed horns on his head, and his mouth was open. He was laughing very hard, and fire was coming from his mouth. I think his teeth were pointed and sharp. Koss and Kassie said the demon had eyes that burn like fire, and there was fire. He looked very mean and scary."

The child's voice was hardly more than a whisper. As she spoke, she cringed and hung on to Yuri. She hoped the demon didn't hear her talking about him.

For a moment, everyone was quiet, and then Hilda turned to Koss. "It was you who started the fight."

"I did not. It was you; you were going to stab Kassie with the scissors."

"I was not going to stab Kassie with the scissors. I took them away from her because she was going to stab you with them." Hilda's annoyance was aimed at Koss. Then she directed her gaze at Kassie. "Why did you want to stab Koss?"

"I didn't."

"Yes, you did. I saw you come at him with the scissors raised to his head. Did you see Kassie point the scissors at Koss?" Hilda asked Jacob.

"No. I was looking the other way. Mia was standing behind Koss."

"Did you see what Kassie was going to do?" Hilda asked the child.

Mia fearfully nodded her head.

"What did you see?"

Mia knew she must always speak the truth. She bravely looked at her siblings as she whispered softly. "Kassie was standing behind Koss." Mia shuddered. "He was looking at the pictures. When Kassie went away, I stood behind the chair because I wanted to see the pictures too. Kassie came with the sharp scissors. She screamed, and she was going to stick them in Koss's head. I think she was going to make his head bleed."

"Well, he wouldn't have bled much if I only stuck them in his head." Kassie jumped in to defend herself.

"Why were you angry with Koss?" Hilda demanded. "Are you jealous because he lay in the shed with me today?"

"No," Kassie answered readily. "He was looking at the picture of Aunt Elana standing beside Mother and Father. He said he didn't like Aunt Elana and he wished she was not in the picture. It looked like he was going to rip her out of the picture."

"You don't like her either; nobody does. So why were you going to stab him?"

"I thought he was going to rip Mother out of the picture, too, because she was standing close to Aunt Elana."

"Is that why you were going to stab him?"

"Yes. But I wasn't going to stab him hard. If a person got stabbed in their head, they wouldn't even bleed because their head is only a bone."

"Where are your brains? You should know a person could bleed to death if they were stabbed in the head."

"No, they wouldn't. You are lying. Ask Jacob. He watches Father shave and saw him cut his face, but he didn't bleed much, so if he were cut on his head, he wouldn't bleed at all."

Mia listened to them argue about stabbing people in different parts of the body. Their rowdiness was increasing again, and she hoped they wouldn't start another brawl before Nadia and their father returned. Even though the tyranny in Nadia's house never ended, she was concerned about the incident where Koss was almost stabbed by his sister. After Nadia was told what had happened, she hid the barber scissors whenever she and her husband left on trips in the future.

CHAPTER SIXTEEN

As time passed, Mia withdrew from her chaotic surroundings and isolated herself, helplessly consumed by fear. Nadia, with her devious personality, was setting her up to be the target of Koss's abuse. Sarah was usually not at home to comfort her. She couldn't turn to Hilda or Kassie because they were also trapped in Nadia's dysfunctional abuse. Mia lived in quiet desperation. Sometimes she was found her crying in the yard in pain; other times she returned to the house fighting tears and anguish. Her sisters knew what was happening.

"Did Koss hurt you again?"

Mia could only nod in answer to Hilda's question as she held on to her painfully ravaged body and lay in bed sobbing. When Hilda was there, Mia felt safe from Koss, but she was not allowed to stay in the house.

"Get out of the house and quit pestering your sisters." Nadia's manipulation was insidious.

Mia knew Koss would be waiting outside. She could not comprehend why Koss was so mean to her and hurt her the way he did.

He didn't hurt Yuri like he hurt her. Yuri was free to play outdoors. Mia liked to play with Yuri, but she feared the outdoors, where her older brother lurked in the trees and around the buildings.

Her father usually left for Ridgewood in the mornings to do his daily errands. Before he left, he would assign chores to be carried out before his return. Mia silently crept into the bedroom or hid under the bed and waited for his return. Koss was always sent away from the house, usually to the far orchard, but Nadia did not pressure him to leave the yard immediately, not the way she pressured her husband or others who stood in her way.

He lurked and loitered in the yard until his father's car was seen returning in the distance. When Sarah was at home, Mia was told by Sarah and Hilda, her that she must scream and fight when she was being attacked by Koss. If she screamed and held him off they would come and rescue her. However, it was not her sisters who came as they said they would—it was Nadia who irately slammed out of the house. When Koss heard the screen door slam shut, he got up and ran for cover while Mia huddled and sobbed in fright.

"Why are you screaming?" Nadia demanded of the child. "Can't we have any peace and quiet around here? Do you want the neighbors to come running to see who is being slaughtered?"

Mia cowered in fear as Nadia's huge bulk hovered over her. Her face was flushed with fury, and her eyes blazed with rage as she stood over the traumatized child.

"Koss was hurting me."

"You are lying. Shut up and get into the house!" Her mother angrily flailed at the bewildered child. "Koss isn't even around. If I ever hear you screaming like that again, I will come out, and I will rip you from limb to limb all by myself."

Mia had no doubt that the huge, angered woman could rip her apart. As she walked through the yard, to her disgust, she saw unsightly gruesome cadaver fragments littered about. The thought of

Nadia ripping her apart and scattering her parts over the yard like the unsightly remains there, terrified her.

Sarah and Hilda said they would come to rescue her when they heard her scream for help. They made her feel she would be safe if she went outside. Why did Nadia come? Nadia only came to scold her for screaming. Why did it inflame her mother to be disturbed by her screams? She wondered why her sisters didn't come like they said they would. The answer came when Mia tearfully confided in them. Nadia wouldn't allow them to help Mia when she was being molested by her brother.

"Mother told us to stay in the house; she wouldn't allow us to go outside. She said she would go outside and handle the matter herself."

"But you said one of you would come to help me," Mia sobbed, broken in body and spirit. "Why didn't you come?" she begged. "When Mother comes, she gets very angry and scolds me."

"We have to do what Mother tells us." Her sisters exchanged helpless glances as they spoke.

"But why didn't Mother come right away? She came after Koss ran away. Then she scolded me for screaming and said I was lying."

"Yes," Hilda admitted to Sarah. "She didn't leave the first time we heard Mia scream. She said she had to finish her work first. Then she washed and wiped her hands," Hilda recalled with uncertainty. "She didn't have to wash and wipe her hands. Why did she waste time doing that? She was wiping the dishes when we heard Mia scream, so it wasn't as if her hands were dirty."

Her sisters looked uneasy, consumed in silent thought.

"Well, why didn't you come before she came?" Mia continued.

"We have to do what Mother tells us to do." Her sisters avoided looking at each other when they spoke.

"She became very angry with me and told me she was going to rip me from limb to limb. I am afraid of her." Mia trembled as she sobbed.

"When Koss is hurting you again, just keep screaming. If Mother sees him running away, she will believe you."

Mia felt hopelessly trapped, but perhaps her sisters were right. If Nadia saw Koss running away, she would have to believe her.

Sometimes after he molested her, Koss ran a short distance before he slipped into the trees and disappeared. Other times, he unexpectedly loomed before her, wielding a club and knocking her down by striking her on the legs. Then, standing over the terrified child, he threatened to use the club on her if she uttered a sound.

"Remember, if I hear you scream before I am out of sight, I will return and finish you off. Mother doesn't like it if you scream either. She will be angry with you too." He hissed vicious threats as she cowered on the ground.

Mia cringed and held her arms over her head, trying to protect herself. She was afraid Koss would club her as violently as she had witnessed Nadia clubbing Jacob. Then she continued to scream as her sisters advised, even though her brother was no longer in sight. Once, he was still in sight when Nadia approached her, furious because she was screaming. The distraught child pointed to the form of her brother running at the far end of the yard.

"Koss hurt me," she cried. "Look, there he is." She pointed to him before he had a chance to completely disappear into the orchard. "Look, there he is," the distraught child repeated, looking up at Nadia.

Nadia twitched her head in other directions, looking at the sky and all around except the direction Mia pointed. Her behavior confused the child.

"No, there...there he is! Can't you see him?" Mia cried in frustration.

Finally, Nadia looked blankly in the direction Mia indicated. Her mother didn't say anything, but Mia was sure she would see Koss, who was still in plain sight.

"Look, can't you see him?"

"No, I can't see anyone." Nadia's face was expressionless.

Mia wanted to cry; it was hopeless. Why did her mother say she didn't see Koss?

The tormented child confided in her sisters later and waited for an explanation. They couldn't give her an answer. The next time she screamed for help when she was being molested by Koss, she hoped her sisters would come, but, as usual, it was Nadia who appeared.

"Koss hurt me again." Through her tears, she saw Nadia's flushed face. Her eyes blazed as if obsessed. Her anger was not at Koss, though—she directed it at Mia with a brutal blow.

"Shut up, or I will rip you limb from limb." She spoke through clinched teeth.

"But Koss hurt me," she sobbed in distress.

"So what if he did? I have heard enough of your whining. I will rip you to bits and pieces if you don't quit complaining about your brother." Nadia brutally rammed her fist into the child's stomach. Mia fell back, holding herself. Before she could recover from the blow and open her eyes, she felt an excruciating pain in her leg as Nadia positioned a side blow into her leg and then savagely twisted it.

"If you don't quit complaining about your brother, I will snap your leg right off."

Mia couldn't contain the blood-curdling shriek. Like a crazed animal, Nadia hung on, refusing to release her twisting grip. Overwhelmed with pain, Mia felt darkness envelop her.

Upon opening her eyes, Mia saw Nadia sitting at her feet, a firm hold still on her leg. The pain was unbearable. After all the threats, Mia expected to see blood oozing from a splintered stump. Her leg was still intact; there was only the agonizing pain.

"Get up and go into the house," Nadia snapped at the child, her face reddened with rage. "You must be punished for complaining about your brother."

Mia couldn't move. She lay in anguish, waiting for the pain to subside before dragging her bruised body away from the woman and crawling toward the house.

Sarah and Hilda were waiting for her. "What happened? Why aren't you walking? Why were you lying on the ground and screaming like that?"

Writhing in pain, Mia told them of Nadia's bizarre outburst. "Why didn't you come outside and make her stop hurting me?" Brokenhearted, she could only sob in agony. "Why didn't you come?"

"We couldn't. And besides, we couldn't see what she was doing to you." Hilda and Sarah glanced evasively at each other. "You were hidden behind her. She was kneeling with her back toward the house, and we couldn't see what she was doing. We only heard your screams."

"Why didn't you come to help me? You told me to scream when Koss hurts me. You said you would help me when I was being hurt. Why didn't you come and make her stop? Why did she hurt me? Why did she do that to me?" Mia sobbed through a blur of tears. "Did she ever try to rip you apart and try to break your leg off?"

They were silent; they could not give an explanation for their mother's insane behavior.

"Why did she hurt me like that? Why didn't you come to help me?" the confused child continued through sobs.

The Unforgiven

Now that you are getting older,
I hope you find your peace.
Dark secrets of my childhood,
I find hard to release.

A mother's touch is tender;
A mother's touch is kind.
The memories of my childhood
In terror you entwined...

As time passed, Mia's fear of Nadia continued to grow. She was afraid to go outside, and when she heard Nadia's voice or approaching footsteps, she fearfully hid under the bed, cowering.

"Don't tell Mother I am here. If she asks, please tell her you don't know where I am," she begged her sisters as she anxiously waited for her father to return home.

"Why does Mia tremble and hide under the bed when she hears Mother coming into the house? She does it even when Father is still in the yard." Mia listened to Sarah and Hilda question her behavior.

"I am so afraid of Mother," the child quietly confided.

"Why are you afraid of her?"

"Koss hurts me, but she doesn't get angry at him. She gets very angry at me because I cry. She hurt my leg so bad. I thought she broke it off, and it hurt for a long time. She said she will rip me apart with her bare hands; it will hurt if she rips me apart. Does she rip things apart when she gets angry?"

Her sisters looked at Mia questioningly. "What sort of things?"

The image of bloody parts of cadavers she had seen strewn in the yard filtered through Mia's mind. "Animals and people." She replied.

"What is she talking about? Why would she ask such a bizarre question?" her sisters asked in confusion.

"Mother was very angry with me. She said she will rip me from limb to limb, and she tried to break my leg off."

"Well, she didn't rip you apart or break your leg off," Hilda scoffed.

"No," Mia sobbed. "But it felt like she did, and my leg hurt for a long time after she did that. I am afraid of her." The child then revealed the rest of her fears. "I am scared 'cause I saw dead pieces and bones in the yard. I thought they were from dead people, but I didn't see pieces from people's hands or feet or fingers. I asked Kassie, and she told me they were not from people; they were pieces from animals. Does Mother rip animals apart because she gets angry with them too?"

"No." Dumbfounded by the revelation, the older sisters just looked at the distressed child.

"Why was the animal ripped apart in the yard? Its head was missing, and pieces of it were scattered around. Mother must have been very angry when she ripped it apart." The child could not contain her fears.

"No. Coyotes and dogs did that to the animal."

Mia sat in silence for a moment, thinking that it must have been painful for the animal to be ripped apart. "Why did they do it to the animal? Were they angry at it? Did it hurt the animal very much when they ripped it apart?"

"The animal was dead before they ripped it apart."

"Why was the animal dead? Did Mother make it die because she was angry at it?"

"The animal just died."

"Who made it die? If Mother didn't make it die, was it the demons that made it die?" Fear aligned the child's perception of her mother and the demons.

Mia's mistrust and paranoia sometimes came to the attention of her father. When questioned by her husband, Nadia would dismiss the concerns.

"You must not be frightened of Mother. She won't hurt you." Sarah tried to soothe the child's fear of Nadia.

"We must talk to Mother," Mia heard her sisters whisper. "She is going too far; it isn't right that anyone would fear their mother as much as Mia does. If anyone came to the house and witnessed that, they would quickly realize things are not right here. Mia has too much fear of Mother," they agreed. "It isn't Mother you should be afraid of," they tried to reason. "It is Koss who hurts you, not Mother. Mother only gets angry with you, but she really does love you. She doesn't have anything to do with Koss hurting you, and she will not rip you apart."

"Why does she get so angry at me? I'm afraid of her." The child was isolated in suppression. "Why does Koss hurt me?" she asked.

"I don't know."

"Why doesn't Mother scold him for hurting me?"

Her sisters continued to whisper to each other as Mia asked questions.

"Yuri isn't afraid to go outside. He says Koss doesn't hurt him. Why doesn't he hurt Yuri like he hurts me?"

The question seemed to surprise her sisters. "He doesn't hurt Yuri because he can't hurt him," Hilda answered.

"Why can't he hurt him?"

"Because Yuri is a boy."

Mia couldn't differentiate between being a boy and a girl and why that was a reason. She wondered why Koss didn't hurt Yuri because he was a boy. Yuri didn't like to play with the tea set she liked to play with, but he liked wearing her dresses. Sometimes they even fought because he wanted to wear her favorite one. What made Yuri different? She would give up the things she liked if only she could be a boy; then Koss wouldn't hurt her the way he did. She looked up expectantly to her sisters.

"Can I be a boy like Yuri so Koss doesn't hurt me? If Yuri wants, he can have my dresses, and I will wear his coveralls."

"You can't be a boy like Yuri. Even if you wear his coveralls, you can't be a boy."Sarah looked at Hilda and smiled.

"Why?"

"Because you are a girl."Hilda answered.

"But I want to be a boy. I want to wear Yuri's clothes so Koss thinks I am a boy."

"Koss knows you're not a boy, and we can't fool him." Sarah and Hilda looked at each other in resignation.

Disillusioned, Mia could not understand why she was victimized for being a girl.

Animosity flowed continually between Nadia's offspring. There was resentment between Hilda and Sarah. Kassie, like an obedient fiend, was willing to please Nadia in any way to gain favoritism. Kassie envied the close relationship between Sarah and Nadia, and Mia would often hear her mercilessly maligning Sarah to Hilda. Her oldest sister didn't strike back, though. Sarah's eyes filled with tears as she silently faced the insensitive brutality.

When Sarah wasn't home, Hilda and Kassie's fights were brought on by the most insignificant matters. If one boasted of an eloquent voice or attractiveness or made a comparison to the other, a battle-royal ensued. Their popularity with the opposite sex always brought on a confrontation. If one of them felt the other stole a prospective suitor, their battles were the wildest imaginable. It would continue until their parents returned and then resume the next time they were absent.

Hilda used Sarah's birth as a barb against her. Nadia's firstborn arrived before nine months of her parents' marriage, and, apparently, the untimely birth of that first child came as a surprise to her husband. He questioned her about it. Nadia held a lifelong grudge against him because of those suspicions; she accused him of not liking her firstborn child. It was Hilda, the second born, who was their father's favorite.

Although Sarah spent much time away from home, eruptions between the two oldest daughters prompted Nadia and her husband to consider sending one of them away. An argument arose between the parents because of the decision.

"You have always mistreated Hilda," her husband accused. "It is impossible for her to live under the same roof as you. It is best that Hilda leave home and find a life for herself elsewhere."

"No, Sarah should be the one to get out from under your roof," Nadia flared back. "You have never accepted her, and, besides, Sarah is the eldest."

"You gave birth to both, yet you do not treat Hilda in the same manner as Sarah."

"Well, you have never treated Sarah as if she were your child." Nadia's nostrils flared in anger. "You didn't accept her, and you never will."

Her father looked helplessly at Nadia for a moment before he muttered and walked away in defeat.

Later, Mia listened as Sarah spoke to Hilda. "I can't stay here. I can't live in the same house with Koss. Mother said she wouldn't force me to do what I didn't want to do anymore. Still, Koss makes my skin crawl. Why does he expect things of me? What does he think I am?"

"What about me?" Hilda lashed back at her sister. "Kassie is more than willing to do what Mother tells her to do. Why does Mother think I have a duty to Koss? I want to marry Josh. I want to get away from here as soon as possible. I want to earn some money before we marry."

"Josh? Why would you want to marry someone like Josh?" Sarah's words were laced with an air of superiority.

"Well, who do you think you are?" Hilda was incensed. "Josh said he will marry me, and I know he will. He is not a sniveling kid with a runny nose like Baily is. Josh is a man."

"How dare you bring Baily's name into this? Mother said you are not to mention Baily's name in this house ever." Sarah was close to tears.

"Mother," Hilda fumed angrily. "She lets you do anything you want to. I know you aren't my full-blooded sister." Hilda whipped the words at her older sister, rubbing salt into wounds. "You are only my half sister."

Mia helplessly watched as Sarah covered her face and burst into tears.

Later that day, Nadia angrily confronted her husband over the matter. She alone settled the decision as to which daughter would have her freedom.

"Sarah will be the one to leave this house. She has to put her past behind her. With the Stephenson family right next door, she can't forget what Baily has done. She must leave so she can make a new life for herself."

Sarah left home to work in a military parts factory. Hilda, though she was unscrupulous and mistreated the youngsters, did not molest them; she continued in the role of caregiver to her younger siblings. With support from her father, she acted as a substitute mother to Mia and Yuri.

CHAPTER SEVENTEEN

Mia missed her oldest sister. Even though Sarah spent much of her time away when she lived at home, she had a gentle personality and showed the child compassion when the other siblings didn't. Sometimes the child feared Hilda as much as she feared Nadia. Driven by the dysfunction of her family and using imaginary illnesses to get attention, Hilda used her control and brutalized her younger siblings to no end. Where would she have learned differently?

Fear and mistrust were deeply embedded in Mia, and she longed for the comfort and conversations with her eldest sister.

She remembered a Sunday when Sarah was at home for the weekend and Nadia had gathered her brood for a family picnic after church. Mia longingly stood and watched her older siblings as they indulged in ice-cream cones.

"Can I have one too?" she asked wistfully.

"No, you can't. Mother said you and Yuri couldn't have any ice cream."Kassie answered, as she indulged in her treat

"Why can't I have one? I would share it with Yuri"

"You can't have one because you don't deserve it," Koss taunted the child.

Mia watched other children greedily slurp at their cones until she felt she could no longer stand it. With her head lowered, she stepped around the corner, wanting to lose sight of the disappearing ice-cream cones. Sarah sat there quietly, talking with a friend and enjoying her treat.

"Where is Mia's cone? Didn't she get one?" Sarah's friend asked. Sarah didn't answer.

"You didn't have one?" the friend said in surprise as she took in Mia's reaction.

Mia kept her head lowered, embarrassed to expose the naked urge she felt for even a tiny lick of the sweet treat.

"You want some ice cream, don't you?" she asked Mia. "I will give you some of mine," she volunteered. "Why didn't Mia get a cone of ice cream?" Sarah's friend asked again.

"That's OK, don't worry. I will share mine with her," Sarah offered, as she attempted to cover the uneasiness of the moment. "Look, I have cherries in mine. Would you like a red or green cherry?"

Mia didn't know what cherries tasted like; she thought the red ones looked good and pointed to one. Sarah picked two tiny bits of red cherry from her cone and stuck them into Mia's opened mouth.

Even simple gestures between Sarah and her youngest sister angered Nadia and she would scold Mia for taking up Sarah's time. It was as if she couldn't bear to share her favorite daughter with any of her unworthy offspring. Isolating them from each other gave Nadia more control over everything.

During one visit home, Sarah found Mia sleepless and disoriented amid the bedlam taking place in Nadia's house.

"What is wrong with Mia?" Sarah asked Hilda.

"You know we aren't supposed to talk about what happens in this house," Hilda snapped at her older sister. "It's the usual thing, and we aren't allowed to talk about it even among ourselves."

"Tell me what happened while I was gone," Sarah urged Hilda.

"No, I have to live here. Mother would crucify me if I told anyone," Hilda snapped as she left the room.

Sarah turned to Mia. "What's happening? Tell me what's bothering you."

Mia lowered her head and dug her fists into her eyes, trying to stop the tears.

"Is it Koss? Is he still hurting you?"

Mia could only nod, and she shrank from Sarah's reach. She couldn't stand being touched by anyone anymore, not even her sister.

"Poor child," Sarah uttered soothingly. "I wish I could help you, but there is nothing I can do."

"Can you take me with you? I am afraid. I don't want to stay here," Mia whispered between quiet sobs.

Sarah looked down at Mia. There was hesitation as if she might be thinking it over.

"Please, Sarah," Mia pleaded. "Can you take me with you?"

"Maybe," Sarah muttered thoughtlessly.

The child's tear-streaked face lit up with hope as she looked up at her sister.

"Maybe when you are older." Sarah retracted the glimmer of hope for the child as she turned away. "Everyone has to live with the family they are born to. This is your family, and you have to live with them."

Mia lowered her head in disappointment as tears flowed from her eyes. "But I am so afraid of Mother and Koss. I'm afraid to live here one more day."

"You have to listen to Mother; there is nothing we can do about what happens in this family. That is the way life is, and we all have to learn to live with it."

The child trembled; the nightmare of the continuing horrors played over in her mind. Through a sleepy haze, she would still find herself outside in the dark without remembering how she had gotten from her bed yet knowing that Koss was responsible for her being there.

"But Koss hurts me, and so do his friends."

"Koss and his friends?" Sarah asked in disbelief. "It isn't only Koss? He still takes you outside during the night, and there are still others?"

Mia nodded her head and dug her fists deeply into her tear-filled eyes.

"Who? Baily?" Sarah sputtered.

Mia was silent.

"What are you doing?" Nadia's voice blared when she entered the room. "Leave the sniveling brat alone. Do you hear? Leave the brat alone. She is spoiled, and she needs her sleep. That is the reason she is in such a wretched state. Let her get back into bed and sleep her misery off."

"What has been happening to her? She said it is not only Koss who abuses her but others too. Who else? Is it Baily? I have to know."

Nadia looked from Sarah to her youngest daughter and replied in anger, "I told you that you are not to pester your sister with your whining. Sarah comes home to visit, and all you can do is cause trouble. Get back to bed and don't get out until you are in a better mood."

"Come, Mia. I will lie down beside you until you fall asleep," Sarah offered to comfort the distraught child.

"No, you will not. I forbid you to pamper the brat." Nadia stood glaring at Sarah.

Mia crawled under the bed sheets and covered her head. She lay sobbing until she was drenched in her own tears. In defiance of her mother, Sarah lay down beside the child to comfort her. Mia hated when anyone touched or tried to hold her. She fought to get out of her sister's grasp. There was no one she could trust. Would Sarah hurt her, too, like Koss, Kassie, and Nadia did?

Sarah held on tightly as she tried to comfort her. "Don't cry, little sister. I won't let them hurt you. I won't let them hurt you again."

Mia was overcome with exhaustion and fell asleep to Sarah's meaningless words. When she awoke, it was to her father's rage. Mia wondered why her father was shouting at Sarah.

"I will ask you one more time," he bellowed. "You will answer me!"

"Um-um," was the only reply Sarah gave through tightly sealed lips.

"Don't murmur; answer me!"

Mia shrank at her father's fierce rage.

"I can understand why Hilda and Kassie won't speak. They still live under this roof—under her power. They know they will be punished if they do. You will be leaving today, so she won't punish you. She never does. Tell me what you know! Tell me what goes on in this house."

"Um-um," Sarah repeated stubbornly.

"Don't murmur," her father exploded. "Before you leave, I want you to tell me what you know about what is happening to Mia." Her father's fists were tightly clenched. His face was filled with rage.

"Um-um," Sarah continued.

"What is wrong with you? Can't you speak? Stop murmuring!"

"Um-um," Sarah continued unyieldingly.

"Stop that! I want an answer." His enraged voice echoed throughout the house.

This should have been a happy time because Sarah was home visiting. Mia wanted to cry. She could not understand the reason her father was so angry at Sarah, and she feared he might strike her sister. She wondered why he was angry at her because she didn't want to talk to him. She wondered what the word "murmur" meant and why her father was angry because he said Sarah murmured.

Acknowledging defeat, her father stormed out of the house. The shock of the door slamming behind him rattled the windows and jolted the frustrated child. Mia felt she was the center of the problem even though she could not understand what the problem was or why her father scolded Sarah and not her.

Sarah was quiet for the rest of her stay. Mia sensed that her sister was unhappy and wanted to keep her distance from everyone. Mia was sad to see Sarah leave.

Before she left, she spoke quietly to Hilda; Baily's name was mentioned in their conversation. Mia overheard her say, "Find out and tell me. I have to know."

Sarah left the house without saying good-bye to anyone.

"Why was Father so angry at Sarah?" Mia mustered her courage to ask Hilda.

"Because she wouldn't talk to him," Hilda snapped in irritation.

"Why did he tell her not to murmur? What does 'murmur' mean?"

"Murmur is when someone mumbles and says 'um-um' or 'um-hum.'"

Mia looked at Hilda in confusion. "But 'um-um' means 'um-um,' and 'um-hum' means 'um-hum.' Why does it mean 'murmur'?"

"Ask Jacob; he will tell you what it means," Hilda replied, brushing her off.

Mia knew that Jacob went to school and was familiar with many things. She waited until Koss wasn't around before she approached Jacob.

"Well…" Jacob paused thoughtfully before he spoke. Mia looked up at him. He seemed to be studying the question before he answered her. "Murmuring is what mermaids do. They don't talk; they murmur."

"But, Jacob, what is a murmur-maid, and why don't they talk? Why do they murmur?"

"Because they live in water, and they can't open their mouths to talk; they just murmur."

"Why do they live in the water?"

"Because they are half fish and half person; that is why they are called mermaids."

The child looked at her brother in bewilderment. "But how can a person be a fish?"

"It's half a person and half a fish."

"Is that why Father doesn't want Sarah to murmur because he doesn't want her to turn into a fish and be a murmur-maid?"

"Yes."

"I don't want Sarah to be a murmur-maid because she might drown in the water. If Sarah lives in the water, could I go and see her?" The prospect worried her.

"You would only see her from afar because she would live in the ocean."

"What is an ocean, Jacob?"

"Its lots and lots of water; it's more water than there is in all the lakes put together."

When Mia returned to the house, she was deeply troubled. She didn't want Sarah to murmur; she didn't want her sister to turn into half a fish. How could she live with Sarah if she lived in the water?

"Are you going to murmur like Sarah did?" Hilda tried to hide her amusement at the child's bewilderment.

Mia shook her head.

"What will you do if Father asks you a question and you don't know the answer? Will you murmur?"

"No." Mia shook her head sadly.

"Why not?"

"Because I don't want to turn into a murmur-maid."

"What will you do?"

"I will go like this." The child shrugged her shoulders in reply.

Mia desired closeness with her family. She had no memories of being held or hugged by Nadia. She was made to feel worthless by Nadia's standards. Was it because she was the youngest, or was it because she was born a girl and not a boy?

She longed to know the grandparents she no longer had and wondered what it would be like to sit on their knees and talk with them. Her bond with Nikola and Rachel was the closest one she felt, akin to that with grandparents. However, over time, she developed distrust of people. If Koss came into the yard unexpectedly and caught her off guard, Mia froze in terror. Her screams of sheer panic cut through the yard until Hilda or Kassie came running. Grabbing the shaken child, they took her into the safety of the house. It was the only way they could deal with her fears.

She wanted a playmate of her own age and gender. There was Yuri, but he was younger than she was, and he didn't always like to play as girls played. Still, Mia found solace in the company of her younger brother. When her older brothers were sent into the orchard with their father, Mia felt less threatened. She was safe to share a few carefree, childish moments of innocence, playing make-believe games with Yuri. They stacked empty bottles they had collected and pretended to operate a store like Mr. Wilson's in Belcourt.

Periodically, with the coming of dusk, Mia would watch Nadia as she singled out Koss and called him to her side. With their backs turned to the others, they talked and held their arms around each other in a hug. They seemed to share a special secret. Then Jacob was called to stand on Nadia's other side. A sick feeling swept over Mia as she watched them. It was as if they were conspiring. Mia shrank back, wanting to disappear, not wanting to be in the room where the atmosphere of corruption hung so heavily. Sometimes she crept toward the door as she fought for a breath of air.

"Where are you going?" Hilda's whisper cut through the stuffiness of the room.

"I can't stay here. I have to go outside." Mia was hyperventilating. She felt smothered by the stale air where Nadia sat, conspiring with her sons. She needed the fresh air to fill her lungs and help her breathe.

"You can't go outside; it is getting dark. Mother says you have to stay in the house while she is talking to the boys," Hilda scolded.

"But I have to go outside. I won't go far," she begged. "I can't breathe in the house. I will only take a few steps out the door, and then I will come back."

Mia knew she couldn't escape Nadia's bizarre conspiracies—she had to live with them—nor could she understand why she suffered from attacks that made her fight for each breath of air. Sometimes she felt that she was on the verge of collapsing. Each breath felt like it would be her last. When it happened, Hilda allowed her to go outside into the evening air. Sometimes her sister took a few steps out the door with her to ensure she was safe. She would live with these hyperventilation attacks for years, but as a young child, Mia couldn't understand why she was plagued with them.

Often, her father had to run extensive errands to the mill. In the winter, he would hitch the team to the sled and not return until late at night. In the early summer or fall, he made the same trips. Mia hated the long periods when her father was absent. As Nadia's resentment of Hilda grew, complete bedlam seemed to take over when her father was not around.

One cold winter day when her father was away, Mia found herself wondering why a heavy wool blanket was strung as a curtain over the door leading into the bedroom. She couldn't understand what was going on behind the covered door. She heard the sounds of a struggle followed by shrieks and cries. Nadia was having another argument with Hilda. When Koss was called to help Nadia, Hilda's mortified cries and Nadia's angry shrieks echoed through the room. Yuri was asleep, and Jacob sat on the other end of the cot. Mia noticed Jacob's hands were knotted on his lap, and his head was lowered.

"I'm not going to go there if she calls me," he mumbled to Kassie.

"But if she calls you, you have to go," Kassie answered.

"I don't want to."

The noise from the room behind the blanket continued, reverberating throughout the house.

"Why is Hilda crying?" Mia looked at Kassie for an answer.

"Because she doesn't listen to Mother; she doesn't want to do what Mother tells her to do."

Mia knew Nadia's violent temper erupted in rage when the children didn't listen to her. Kassie was given strict orders to keep Mia on the cot, where she sat quietly beside her sister.

"I am going to tell Father what you are doing to me!" Hilda's cries cut through the high-pitched noise.

"What is Mother doing to Hilda?"

"Nothing," Kassie snapped at the child.

"Then why did Hilda say that, and why is she crying?"

"Shut up. You are not to ask questions," Kassie sputtered at the child.

"Is Mother going to kill her?" Mia's fearful question went unanswered.

Hilda's shrill voice rose hysterically. "Father said you are not supposed to do this to me. I will tell him when he comes home!"

"No, you will not," Nadia snarled. "If you breathe a word to him, next time I will deal with you more harshly."

Time passed, and the sounds of protests and shrieks continued, accompanied by loud thuds. Mia sat on the cot, listening fearfully to the sound. The early evening shadows had begun to descend through the crispness of the winter day. Nadia could be heard barking orders at Hilda.

"Get up and make yourself look presentable. The evening chores have to be done before dark. I have wasted enough time grappling with you, you bitch. Do you hear me? Get up!"

"I won't get up, and you can't make me. I hate you. Why didn't you kill me? I am going to lie here until Father comes home, and then I won't have to tell him what you did to me. He will see for himself," Hilda sobbed.

"No, you won't. I don't have time to argue with you. I am going to go out and attend to the chores with Koss and Jacob. I want you to put another dress on. When I come into the house, I want to see you in the kitchen preparing dinner with Kassie."

Mia watched as the heavy gray blanket was removed from the door. Nadia came out of the room, her eyes bulging with anger and her face red and sweaty. She pulled on her heavy coat and followed Koss out the door.

When they left the house, Mia craned her neck to see Hilda. Her sister was lying on the floor, sobbing. Her dress was ripped off. She watched her sister crawl into the closet as if to hide from the terror she was trapped in.

"I am going to stay here until Father comes home," Hilda wailed from the closet.

"Mother said she wants you to help me make dinner." Kassie sounded amused.

"You can go to hell! I'm not going to help. If we had rat poison, I'd put it in her food!"

"Well, it's your fault. You should know you can't fight her. Why do you try? She wouldn't beat you if you didn't stand up to her like you do," Kassie continued. "You know she gets angry when you don't do what she tells you."

"Shut up! What is wrong with this family? I'm not a slut like you are. I hate all of you; I wish you were all dead. Wait until Father gets back!"

"If you tell him anything, you know what Mother will do to you next time he is away."

"I will tell him! She can't do anything worse than she has already done," Hilda shrieked.

"Yes, she could kill you," Kassie said.

"I don't care! It would be a blessing." Hilda broke into sobs.

When Nadia came in from the outdoors, she whipped her coat off and marched into the bedroom.

"Where is she? I told her I wanted her in the kitchen when I got back. How dare she disobey me? Where did she go?"

"She crawled into the closet," Kassie informed her mother as she hid a snicker. "She said she will stay there until Father comes home."

"Did she put another dress on?"

"No, she didn't."

"Koss, come here and help me put her dress on," Nadia bellowed.

"No!" Hilda's shrill voice cut through the air. "Keep away from me. I don't want any one of you to touch me. If you do, I will kill myself!"

Another scuffle ensued, and Hilda's anguished screams reverberated throughout the house again. Mia couldn't stand to look at what was happening in the next room; she lay on the cot sobbing, covering her ears until it was over.

When Nadia came out of the bedroom, Mia closed her eyes and pretended she was asleep. She could hear muffled sobs coming from the bedroom.

Mia was not hungry as she took her place at the table. A long time seemed to pass before she heard the horses come into the yard.

"Go and help your father put the horses in the barn," Nadia ordered her sons. "I don't want you to tell him that Hilda is having a fit," she cautioned, "or he will wonder what happened. Maybe I can still tempt her out of the bedroom before he comes in."

Mia waited for her father to come into the house. Nadia's attempt to get Hilda out of the bedroom was futile. The door opened, and, with the blast of frigid air, her father entered the house. His face was frosted with icicles. Mia watched him struggle out of his old buffalo coat and lay it on the cot.

"Why is there an extra plate set on the table?" He looked at Nadia when he spoke. "Hasn't everyone had their dinner?"

Nadia busied herself while Kassie answered. "Hilda didn't want to eat."

"What is wrong with her?"

"I don't know. She was in the bedroom most of the day and refuses to come out. I think she is sick."

Mia watched her father go into the bedroom. At first, the voices coming from the other room were muted. Then, like a roar of thunder, her father exploded into the kitchen to confront Nadia.

"What have you done to Hilda?" His voice erupted like a volcano. "You mentally ill sicko! What have you done to her? I am going to go to the police. This has gone far enough. You should be locked up in the Kingston Penitentiary with all the other criminals and mentally ill, warped sickos. That is where you belong. You are disgusting!"

Mia had never seen so much anger in her father. For once, Nadia seemed unable to say anything to defend herself. Her father's anger continued.

"Are they going to put Mother in jail?" Mia asked.

"Do you want Mother to go to jail?" Kassie asked.

Mia thought for a moment. If they took Nadia away, there wouldn't be a mother in their home.

"Would Sarah come home to be our mother?" she asked.

"No, Sarah is our sister; she can't be our mother."

"Will Hilda take care of us?"

"Yes."

"Then I want Mother to go to jail. Hilda can take care of us. She is not as mean as Mother."

Time passed in the troubled house, where the matriarch pursued her fiendish sexual and physical abuse. Mia watched the torment her father endured. She would often see him sitting in his chair, absentmindedly twiddling his thumbs or sadly holding his hands over his drooped head in deep thought.

"Are they going to put Mother in jail?" Mia asked again.

"No, Father said he will take us and we will leave Mother."

"Where will he take us?" the child wondered.

"I don't know. We'd have to find a place to stay. Father will have to find us a place."

Mia listened to Hilda and Kassie as they discussed the plans to split up the family. They said Koss would stay with Mother.

"What about Jacob and Yuri?"

"Yuri will have to come with us."

Mia remembered the terrible beatings Nadia inflicted upon Jacob. Her brother always looked so sad. She started to sob. "I want Jacob to come with us."

"We will see what Father says."

"If we can't find a place to stay, will we have to live outside in the snow? It's so cold outside." Uncontrollable sobs wrenched the child's body. "Where will we live? Will we have to live under the pine trees?"

"Father will find a place for us," her sisters whispered.

Mia continued to watch her father sitting in his chair in deep thought. It was as if going to the police or leaving Nadia was too much for him to bear. If Nadia's secret was known, it would create too much of a scandal. Mia realized that her father, although physically big and strong, was too weak to bear such a scandal.

CHAPTER EIGHTEEN

There were other trips that Mia's father made when he was not expected home until late at night. The days were longer then, and it disappointed Mia when Nadia told them they had to go to bed right after dinner; it was not dark yet, and Mia and Yuri liked to play about the house after dinner.

"But I am not tired. Can Yuri and I play until it gets dark?" she begged Hilda..

"No. Mother said she is tired, and she wants to go to bed early."

"Father isn't at home, and I don't like to sleep alone. Who will sleep with me until he gets back?" Nadia asked.

Mia detested the thought of lying beside the woman. She shrank back, hoping Nadia wouldn't notice her.

" I will, I will!" came the voices of Koss, Kassie, and Jacob.

Then, just as suddenly, Jacob stopped. He seemed to have second thoughts.

"No, I don't want to," he murmured. "I want to sleep in my bed in the granary." He slithered out of the house while Koss and Kassie bickered over who would sleep with their mother.

"You can take turns sleeping with me." Nadia beamed at the twins. "First Kassie and then Koss."

Hilda lay down beside Yuri in another room. Mia was told to sleep on the cot, but try as she might, with the absence of dark, sleep would not come.

Kassie lay with Nadia. When Mia heard moans coming from her sister, she sat up, terrified. Fully awake, she wondered why it sounded like Kassie was moaning and wanted to cry.

Hilda was alerted by the child and came to her side.

"Hilda, I am afraid. What is Mother doing to Kassie? Why is she hurting her? It sounds like Kassie wants to cry."

"She is not hurting her; now go to sleep."

"I can't. It isn't dark outside, and I am afraid. Mother might hurt me." She tried to hide her fear. "Hilda, I am afraid, and I want you to sit with me."

"I can't. I have to sit with Yuri until he falls asleep."

As Hilda stood beside the cot with Mia, Kassie walked out of the room. Mia wondered why she looked as if she were in a trance.

"What did Mother do to Kassie? She looks like there is something wrong with her," Mia whispered to Hilda.

"Nothing is wrong with Kassie. Now go to sleep."

But Mia couldn't go to sleep. Koss came into the house and went into the bedroom to sleep with Nadia. With Hilda close by, and in the middle of Nadia's corruption, the child finally fell asleep.

<hr>

One morning after they had their breakfast, Mia stepped out the door to play with Yuri. She knew it would be safe because Koss and Jacob had gone to work in the orchard with their father, and they wouldn't be back until lunch time. The two youngsters bartered and exchanged the make-believe goods in their make-believe store. Hilda and Kassie were sent on an errand. Absorbed in play, the children left Nadia's calls unanswered.

"Mia! Yuri! Come here this instant!" When their mother's shriek reached them, all play came to a standstill.

"It's Mother. She sounds angry."

They stood and looked at each other, gathering courage before they scampered toward the house. Both came to a stop when they saw Nadia standing in front of the house waiting for them. They were afraid to go any closer.

Fuming and with sweat pouring down her crimson-red face, Nadia stood with her eyes blazing in anger. "Didn't you hear me calling you?" she shouted at them.

Yuri stood behind Mia. They did not answer.

"Where have I gone wrong to deserve such ungrateful children? You have to answer me the instant you hear me call you." Her rage turned to wailing and tears as they watched her beat wildly on her chest and stamp her feet. "You ungrateful children! You are going to be the death of me. Why can't you answer me when I call you?"

"We came when we heard you." Yuri looked at his mother as if he were a whipped puppy. Mia lowered her head, afraid to face Nadia's rage.

"How many times did you hear me calling you?"

"Just once," Yuri, the young toddler answered.

"And what about you?" She snarled at Mia. "You are older."

"I only heard you call us once," Mia answered.

"I called you three times!" She spat the words viciously at the terrified youngsters. "Three times! Why didn't you answer me at once?"

"Because we didn't hear you," Yuri murmured.

"If I told you once, I've told you a thousand times. If you are not going to listen to me, my heart will burst, and I will die." Nadia exploded in fury.

The children watched in horror as Nadia flew into a fit and dropped to the ground, lamenting wildly and kicking her feet. Then she stopped suddenly and went limp.

"Did she die?" Yuri looked at Mia wide eyed. "Did we make her die, Mia?"

"I don't know. I can't see any blood around her," Mia whispered.

They took in the scene before them. Nadia did say her heart would burst if they didn't listen to her. Mia remembered the dead dog on the road that Kassie showed her with the explanation that if she didn't listen, her mother would die just like the dog. Now Nadia lay as still as the dead dog.

"Do you remember the dog that died because he ran on the road? He had blood all around him because a car hit him. Kassie said the blood comes from the heart. If we made her heart burst, I think there would be blood around her too."

They stood petrified, watching for trickles of blood to flow out of her body and surround her. Even though there wasn't any, they thought they had made her die like she said they would.

"I don't want her to die." Yuri stepped closer to the woman's bulk lying on the ground.

Mia stayed back, hesitant to approach. If they had made Nadia die, she must be the one who was responsible because she was older than Yuri.

Kneeling beside the still form of his mother, Yuri sobbed. "We don't want you to die. We didn't hear you call us. We are sorry we made you die. We will listen to you, Mother. Wake up; don't die."

Guilt swept over Mia for what she believed was her fault. She feared death and the demons. The fear of being found out also terrified the child. She knew she would be severely punished for making Nadia die. No one must find out they were responsible for Nadia's death. Mia wanted to run and hide, but where? Maybe if they hid Nadia's body and someone else found her, that person might think that he or she was responsible for her death.

Mia tried to contain her fear as she stepped closer to the huge shape. "Yuri, help me pull her behind the house so no one sees her here. Then we can hide until someone comes home for lunch and finds her. They wouldn't know we made her die."

They tugged at Nadia but to no avail; they couldn't budge her large, sweaty bulk.

"Mia, maybe we can make her alive again if we open her eyes." She watched Yuri as he knelt beside his mother's body and tugged at her eyelids. "Come and help me, Mia. I can't hold both of her eyes open at the same time. I will open one eye, and you open the other."

Mia felt fear and repulsion at the thought of touching Nadia. Her red face still glistened with sweat. The child often wondered why Nadia's face turned red and glistened when she was angry. She finally came to the conclusion it could only be that Nadia's heated fit of anger melted the globs of fat that glistened as they rolled off her face.

She stepped closer and touched the woman's glistening, red face. She had to help Yuri hold her eyelids opened. Nadia's face felt sticky and slimy with sweat. Mia was repelled when she touched her sticky eyelid. When they opened Nadia's eyelid, it slipped and kept closing.

"Look, Mia," Yuri squealed excitedly. "I think she can see. Her eyes are opened now. She doesn't close them anymore."

Mia watched Nadia move. Overcome by fear of what they had done, she shrank back.

"Mia, we made her alive again. We made her die, and then we made her alive again."

Mia watched Yuri as he continued to kneel beside his mother. The thought of what they did haunted Mia.

"Yuri, we can't tell anyone that we made her die," Mia whispered to her brother later.

"But we made her alive again."

"But only bad people make people die. If anyone finds out what we did, the demon will hear them talk about us. I am afraid of the demon, Yuri." Mia tried to hide her alarm and spoke in a whisper as though she expected the horned monster to be close. "I think the demon didn't find out how bad we are 'cause we made her alive before death came to take her away. I am afraid, Yuri. It must be our secret; we must not tell anyone."

"Mia, what will the demon do if he finds out?" Yuri looked at his sister with uncertainty, waiting for her answer.

"He will come in the night and hurt us, or when we go to sleep he might make us die. Then he will take us to hell and burn us." Her eyes reflected the fear she felt as she whispered to her brother.

They stood in silence, enveloped in the terror of their deed. Yuri shuffled uneasily. He was younger, and Mia knew she must protect him. If he didn't think of opening Nadia's eyes and bringing her back to life, she would have been guilty of causing her death. She shivered as the thought unfolded within.

That evening, they were still consumed with fear. Yuri begged that Mia be allowed to sleep on the cot with him. As they lay on the cot, side by side with their arms around each other, she bravely whispered, "Go to sleep, Yuri. I will take care of you. I will stay awake and watch for the demon. I will not let him take you." They only had one another, and they had to protect their secret.

After Yuri fell asleep and rolled to his side of the cot, Mia awoke and looked at his innocent, chubby face. She felt alone. Later, when the lights were put out, her conscience and fear gripped her, and she couldn't sleep. Quietly stifling her tears, she listened for a creak or footstep that would alert her to the presence of the demon coming for them.

If Nadia was brought back to life by having her eyes opened, Mia wondered why other people were not brought back to life that way.

Time took its toll. She lay sleepless, bathed in guilt and fear—fear not only for herself but also for Yuri. She dozed off but awoke and anxiously touched her brother to reassure herself that the demon hadn't taken him while she slept.

As days passed, the children were consumed in silent thought. They did not reveal to anyone what was bothering them. Mia knew she must ask one of her sisters if a person could be brought back to life after he or she died. She longed for Sarah, who was kind and gentle and wouldn't punish her for not hearing Nadia calling to them. Hilda was mean; if she couldn't find out why they asked disturbing questions, she used punishment and scare tactics on them.

At times, the children whispered, disclosing their fears to each other. Otherwise, they sat in silent thought as they leaned their backs against the house and waited.

"I will ask Kassie if anyone can come back alive after they die," Mia whispered to Yuri.

"But we can't tell her we made Mother die, can we?" He looked at Mia with uncertainty; she was older, and the guilt would lie on her shoulders.

Mia shook her head sadly. "No, we can't."

"And you must not talk loud because the demon might hear you."

Mia nodded her head solemnly. They spoke quietly and waited for a chance to talk to Kassie. Finally, their sister made an appearance. She walked out of the house and stood beside the door.

"Look, Mia, there's Kassie. Should we go and talk to her now?"

"No, let's wait to see if Hilda comes out too. If she does, we can't ask Kassie. You know Hilda always pries and finds out about everything. She gets very angry and mean. She will punish us for making Mother die."

They waited until they were satisfied that Hilda wouldn't join Kassie outside the house.

"Should we go and ask her now?"

"No, not yet; maybe we should wait until she is farther from the door because if Hilda sees us talking to her, she will come out to see what we are talking about. Maybe we could call Kassie and get her away from the door. If we can get her to come closer, Hilda won't see us talking to her." Mia looked at Yuri "And remember, I will ask the questions. You can stand behind me and listen. But don't tell her what we did."

He nodded in agreement.

After calling out to Kassie, Mia slowly walked toward her, intentionally meeting her out of view of the house.

"Kassie," she looked up at her sister and spoke quietly. "If a cat dies and we open its eyes, would it come alive again?"

"No, it wouldn't. Not if it was dead. Why do you ask? Did you find a dead cat? You know, if you see something that is dead, you shouldn't touch it."

"What about a dog?" Mia ignored her sister's question as she continued. "Remember the dog that was dead on the road? Could we have made him alive again if we opened his eyes?"

"No, we couldn't do that either. Don't you remember all the blood around the dog? He was dead."

"Can somebody die without having blood all around them?"

"Yes."

"If somebody dies and doesn't have blood around them, would they come alive if we opened their eyes?"

"Why are you asking all these questions? Do you want me to call Hilda so she can answer your questions?"

"No, we don't want to ask Hilda."

The screen door slammed, and the children knew Hilda was coming out to find Kassie. Their time alone with Kassie had run out.

Yuri poked his head out and looked at Kassie. "Mother died because we didn't hear her calling. I told Mia to help me open her eyes, and we made her alive again." Yuri looked at Kassie expectantly.

"What are you talking about?" Hilda's voice cut in as she walked toward them.

Wanting to make an uneventful exit without facing Hilda, Mia responded nervously, "Yuri and I want to play now." She turned and scurried off with her younger brother.

"What is going on here? What were they talking about?" Hilda asked again as she approached them.

"Mother used her trick tactic on them that she uses on us when she doesn't get her way. She got angry and pretended she was dead. It frightened them."

"Well..." Hilda shrugged. "We can't do anything about it. She still fakes a death scene when she gets angry at me, but nothing frightens me anymore. Sometimes I feel like using a stick to club her like she clubs us. That would get her up in a hurry." Hilda smiled, and Mia heard her quietly laugh at her suggestion.

"You know where that would get you, don't you?"

Mia and Yuri didn't wait to hear the rest of their sisters' conversation.

"Mother didn't die?" Yuri looked up at Mia. "She just pretended we made her die?"

"Yes. Hilda and Kassie say she pretended," Mia answered.

After that, Mia's fear of her mother and the mistrust of her surroundings continued to grow.

CHAPTER NINETEEN

Mia liked the innocent company of her younger brother; with him, she could experience an uncomplicated childhood. Koss and Kassie were entering puberty. Mia heard her father's anger explode when he entered the house one day.

"What is going on in this family?" he demanded of Nadia. "Did you know that your daughter Kassie is pregnant?"

Nadia looked at her husband sharply and lashed back. "What is wrong with you? She can't be pregnant. She is too young; she doesn't even menstruate."

"She is pregnant," he spat angrily at her again.

"She can't be pregnant," Nadia shrieked in denial. "She is too young."

"Well, if she is not pregnant, why has she been sick?"

"Kassie has been sick with the flu." Nadia blinked her eyes nervously as she spoke.

"Is that why you've been keeping her home from school?"

"Yes, of course that's the reason," Nadia spewed back at her husband.

"Then why does she only have the flu in the morning? Why is she OK for the rest of the day?"

"She is not pregnant," Nadia screeched, angered by her husband's speculation.

"Then take a closer look at her; she is showing signs of pregnancy."

Mia watched her father as he angrily turned and walked out of the house. She hated tense situations and moved toward the door; she froze in her tracks when Nadia bellowed.

"Where are you going? Sit on the bed. You're not to leave this room."

"I want to go outside and play with Yuri." Mia looked at Hilda and added, "Can he come into the house and sit beside me then?"

"No, you have to listen to Mother. Now go sit on the bed."

Mia sat and listened as she watched Kassie being grilled, although she could not fully understand what they were talking about.

"I want you to stand sideways and bring your dress tightly against your stomach."

With reluctance and on the verge of tears, Kassie obeyed her mother. Mia was told to observe Kassie while she was being interrogated by Nadia. Kassie, with her string-bean figure, stood looking extremely uncomfortable. Hilda brought attention to the slight bulge on her stomach.

"You do look like you are putting on extra weight."

"I am not," Kassie lashed at her sister in denial.

"Why have you been wearing loose-fitting clothes?"

Kassie was silent and lowered her head against the barrage of questions.

"Why haven't you worn your blue skirt and blouse to school lately?"

"My blouse fits me, but I can't wear my skirt because it is too tight," she snapped defensively.

"Bring me the skirt." Nadia turned to Hilda. "I want Kassie to try it on."

"If I have to try the skirt on, I don't want the brat in the room. I want her to go outside," Kassie blared as she looked at Mia.

Mia did not like the tense situation she was caught in and turned toward the door.

"No. She stays in the house with us."

Mia could not understand the problem. Why wouldn't Nadia permit her to go outside and play with Yuri? She watched Kassie reluctantly step into the skirt. The buttons shrank pathetically from the button holes. Kassie couldn't even attempt to button them. Hilda looked at her sister and gasped.

"Do you know why you can't button your skirt?"

"No." Kassie winced as she answered.

Later, with Mia still standing in the room, Hilda disclosed some information to Nadia. "Kassie said she did menstruate but only once, and it was very slight. Nevertheless, she is definitely pregnant. She has been sick in the mornings, and she has put on a few inches around her stomach."

"Why didn't she tell anyone when she started to menstruate?" Nadia rasped. "She should have told me."

"Well, she told me, but she only spotted slightly. We didn't realize it was her menstrual cycle."

"Why didn't she tell anyone she was pregnant?" Nadia muttered.

"Because she didn't know she was. She knew her skirt didn't fit, but she didn't know why she was gaining weight."

"From now on, I want you girls to tell me when these things happen. We have to be on the lookout for such things. The sooner I know that you girls miss a cycle, the less risk there will be in getting rid of the problem," Nadia lectured sharply.

Mia was too young to realize what was happening to Kassie, the principle of the questioning, or the conversation she was overhearing.

"Who did you fool around with?" Hilda confronted her younger sister later.

Kassie stood sullenly and refused to answer Hilda's question.

"Mother wants to know who you have been lying around with. Who got you pregnant?"

"Why did you and Mother have to embarrass me like that? You didn't have to make me show my stomach to you," Kassie muttered, still angered by the display.

"Apparently, you have no problem showing the boys the private part of your body," Hilda snapped back.

"Why did the brat have to be here watching me too?"

"You are pregnant, and Mother wanted to see how far you were gone. She wanted Mia there because she said she isn't too young to learn about the facts of life."

"She is still a brat. She doesn't even go to school yet."

"Well, you go to school, and apparently you don't know all the facts of life either. You have to tell me who you fooled around with."

"Koss. But I know a brother can't get his sister pregnant, so it can't be him."

"Why are you so brainless?" Hilda was angered by her sister's answer. "Of course Koss could get you pregnant. I've told you that being a blood relative does not mean he can't get you pregnant. Blood doesn't have anything to do with getting pregnant. Why are you such a fool? Was there anyone else?"

"Yes." Kassie's answer was subdued.

"Who?"

"Willis Richardson…and others."

"By others, do you mean other boys at school?"

"Yes."

"Boys who are in your class?"

"Yes."

"Well, I can imagine. What about Alden? What about Igor? They are older. Did you sleep around with them lately?"

"No."

"Well, if it was Alden, Mother could have made him marry you. But if you didn't fool around with him, you know Mother is going to have to do something about it. You know those boys in school are all too young. You are not to tell anyone about this. Do you understand?"

Kassie did not look up and didn't answer her sister.

A few days later, when Mia came into the kitchen, Hilda was preparing lunch, and Nadia was crushing a concoction in a cup.

"What are we having for lunch?" she asked Hilda as she eyed the cup Nadia held in her hand. "Are we having fish?"

"No, we are not."

"Then what is Mother crushing in the cup?" Her father's favorite dish of fried fish with garlic sauce had grown on Mia. "What is Mother crushing in the cup? It is garlic for the sauce. We are having fish. Can I taste the sauce?"

"No, we aren't having fish," Hilda snapped angrily at the child.

When Nadia finished crushing the contents of the cup, Mia watched her reach up and put it on the top shelf of the cupboard. "There now, that's done. Make sure no one touches the cup or that it isn't put on the table by mistake," she cautioned.

"Mother said we should bring a rope into the house." Mia overheard Koss as he spoke to his younger brother. "She said we must get everything ready."

"Why does Mother want a rope in the house?" Mia asked Hilda after her brothers left. Looking at Hilda questioningly, she waited for an answer.

"Who said Mother wanted a rope in the house?"

"I heard Koss tell Jacob she wants them to bring a rope into the house."

"No. Koss must have said something else. He didn't say Mother wanted a rope in the house. She doesn't want a rope in the house. Understand?" Hilda gave the child a glaring look.

Mia wondered why Hilda snapped at her as if she touched a tender core. When Koss and Jacob returned, they motioned to Hilda.

"We left it outside."

Mia wanted to go outside to look beside the house.

"Stay in the house," Hilda commanded. "Lunch is just about ready."

When the lunch dishes were done, Hilda took Yuri and Mia and went outside. It was not a common practice for Hilda to do that. The hot sun beat down on them, making the children very uncomfortable. As time passed, they got restless.

"I'm thirsty." Mia looked up at her sister. "Can I have a drink of water?"

"It won't take long. We'll be back in the house in a little while. Then you can have a drink of water."

The scorching heat became unbearable as they continued to stand beside the house.

"Can we stand in the shade beside the trees?" Mia asked.

"No. We have to stand right here beside the door, close to the house." It was as if Hilda was standing guard.

"Why do we have to stand here?" Mia moaned.

"In case someone comes," Hilda snapped irritably.

"It would be cooler if we stood under the trees."

"We can't stand there. We have to wait right here in case someone comes."

"If anyone comes, we will still see them from the shade of the trees," Mia reasoned.

"I said no, so stop pestering me. We have to stand here in case Mr. Gabriel decides to pop in unexpectedly like he always does." Hilda looked perturbed.

"Can I have a drink of water? I'm so thirsty."

"No. I told you that you can't have a drink of water. We can't go into the house yet. It won't take long. We'll probably be going into the house very soon."

With the hot sun beating down on them, their throats felt parched. Yuri and Mia started to cry.

"Why don't you shut up?" Hilda lashed out. "Why are you crying?"

"Because we're thirsty," Mia moaned.

"Why didn't you have a drink of water before we left the house? If you are thirsty, go to the stock tank and have a drink there," Hilda suggested crossly.

Mia was tempted until she thought of the green slime that floated in the stock tank. She started to cry again. "But the water in the tank is not clean."

"All right," Hilda snapped. "Go into the house and have a drink of water and bring some for Yuri. I don't care; it would serve them right. I wish Mr. Gabriel would walk in and catch them at what they are doing."

Mia slipped into the house and picked up the dipper of water to quench her thirst. Kassie was lying on the bed looking lifeless. Mia could see her legs; her knees were bent, and the upper part of her body was covered with a comforter. Mia didn't see the rope that Koss and Jacob had brought into the house. For a moment, she stood in the room unnoticed.

Her mother was anxiously taken up with Kassie, and Koss was helping her. Jacob stood absorbed in what they were doing. Nadia suddenly looked up and noticed Mia standing by the pail, sipping water.

"What are you doing here?" she hissed. "Get out of here right now."

"I'm thirsty. I wanted a drink of water."

"Get out of here right now," Nadia angrily sputtered again. "You are not supposed to be in the house."

"Get out of here. Kassie is very sick, and if she dies, it will be your fault." Koss spewed the words at her in heated anger.

Mia instantly dropped the dipper back into the pail and ran out the door.

"What's wrong? Why didn't you bring some water for Yuri?" Hilda asked.

"Kassie looked like she died, but she didn't die. Koss said if she dies, it would be my fault because I went into the house for a drink of water." Mia tried to hold back her frightened sobs as she spoke. "What's wrong with Kassie? Is she going to die?" The tears flowed; she couldn't hold them back any longer.

"I don't know."

"Is Kassie going to die?" she questioned incessantly. "Is she going to die because I went to the house for a drink of water?"

"Maybe…I don't know. But if you don't be quiet, she might die."

Later, as Kassie lay still in the room, no one was allowed to see her.

The next day, Mia watched her father solemnly walk into the room where Kassie lay.

"Did Kassie die?" she whispered to Hilda. "Is that why Father went into the room?"

"No, but she is very sick."

"Can I see Kassie? I want to tell her I'm sorry I went into the house for a drink of water. I don't want her to die."

"You can see her when she is feeling better."

Mia brooded in silence, fearing her sister would die. Finally, the day came when she could go into the room to see Kassie.

"You can go and see Kassie if you want to," Hilda advised.

Mia stepped into the room where Kassie lay. Her waxen body looked lifeless; her vacant eyes were unaware of her surroundings. Mia looked at her sister in anguish.

"I am sorry that I went into the house to have a drink of water. I didn't want to make you die. I am glad you didn't die." She hurriedly left the room.

"What's wrong? Don't you want to see Kassie?"

"Something is wrong with Kassie. Her eyes are open, but she can't see. What is wrong with her? Why can't she see me? Is she going to die?"

"Kassie will be OK. She won't die."

"Why does her skin look different? Her arms are so skinny. Why can't she see if her eyes are open?"

"She is pale because she's not been in the sun. It is the sun that makes your skin rosy and healthy looking."

"Oh." Mia looked at her own sunburned arms. "Why do her arms look so skinny?"

"Because she has not eaten for a long time."

"For how long?"

"Three days."

"If I don't eat for three days, will I get skinny arms like Kassie?"

"Yes."

"If I don't eat for three days, would I be hungry?"

"Yes."

"Do Kassie's eyes look like that because she is hungry?"

"Yes, already," Hilda snapped at the child, irritated by the incessant questioning.

"If she is hungry, why doesn't she eat?"

"Because she's sick."

"Will she get better if she eats?"

"Yes." Hilda was agitated by the child's constant string of questions. "Do you feel better now that you've seen her?"

"Yes."

"Now you know she won't die, don't you?"

"Yes."

"Then go beside the house and play with Yuri," Hilda said. "You can see Kassie again tomorrow."

"OK."

The next day, when Mia went to see Kassie, she was wrapped in a blanket and propped up in the rocking chair, catching the ray of sun that shone through the window.

As Mia left the room, Hilda stopped her. "Do you know why Kassie is sick?"

The child looked at her sister and shrugged her shoulders. "No."

"You were in the room when she tried her skirt on."

The child nodded her head. "Uh-huh."

"Do you know why she couldn't button her skirt?"

"Because her stomach was too fat."

"Do you know why her stomach was fat?"

Mia shrugged her shoulders again, not knowing why she was being given the third degree. "Because she ate too much?"

Hilda looked at the child in exasperation. "Well, that lesson was a lost cause." Mia realized Hilda wasn't addressing anyone in particular.

Looking back at her youngest sister again, Hilda continued, "Remember, if you ever start getting fat like Kassie did, you have to tell me. Understand?"

The clothes Nadia sewed for Mia from bits of remnants weren't very roomy. She understood that Hilda was trying to get a point across. Mia mused for a moment. "OK, I won't eat so much."

A few weeks later, after Kassie recovered, she came home from school in tears. Her given name infuriated her. Often, Mia heard her tell Sarah and Hilda that she wanted to change her name. Once again, Kassie broached the subject of her name.

"Why did Mother call me Kassandra? I don't like my name, and I want to change it."

"Why don't you like your name this time?"

"Because the boys in school don't call me Kassie," she flared in agitation.

Hilda gave her sister an amused look. "What happened this time?"

Mia watched Kassie lower her head before she answered. "Everybody is calling me Assy again."

"You really are making a reputation for yourself. You must know why they call you that." Hilda snickered.

"Well, I am going to ask Mother if I can change my name."

"Like the saying goes, a leopard can't change its spots. If you change your name, are you also going to change your ways? You must realize you've already built a reputation among your schoolmates; they will remember you by your reputation."

"If I change my name, they will forget. I will use my second name instead of my first, and then the boys will stop teasing me. I'm going to change my name to Belle."

"You know that changing your name to Belle isn't going to make the boys stop teasing you," Hilda said with a snicker. "The boys will only call you Assy Belle."

Kassie's face paled as she turned on Hilda. "You are jealous because I have more boyfriends than you do, and I am prettier than you are."

"Why, you," Hilda sputtered as she wielded a sharp slap against her sister's face. "You are ugly. You are not prettier than me. The boys always stop and stare at me because I'm so beautiful. The boys don't even notice you. You're so ugly."

This infuriated Kassie. Mia stepped out of their way as a hair-pulling wrestling match ensued.

"They do notice me!"

"The only time they look at you is when you are tagging along behind me."

"Yes, they do notice me. I am more popular than you ever were. I have a prettier voice and prettier legs. The boys in school still laugh at you and call you names."

"Everyone knows I have the pretty voice and pretty legs. They tell me I do, and they don't laugh at me. Your legs look like matchsticks."

"Well, your legs wobble like jelly, and everyone still laughs at you at school."

"They don't laugh at me in school."

"Yes, they do. You don't hear what they say about you because you don't go to school anymore," Kassie shrieked.

"They don't laugh at me. If they did, you would have told me. I asked the Thompson girls, and they said no one laughs at me anymore."

"Yes, they do. They laugh because you were angry at the boys, and you broke the broom on them when you chased them out of the school."

"They don't call me Broom Hilda anymore. If they did, you would have told me."

"Honest to God, they still call you Broom Hilda. Even the teacher still laughs and talks about having to come into the school to get things back to order."

Hilda simmered in heated rage. "You are lying because you are angry at me for being more beautiful than you are and for having a boyfriend. Why do you think they call you Assy?"

"Well, they don't call me a witch; they call you a witch. You always walk around with a frown. You will always be Broom Hilda. I am going to tell Koss to hide the broom from you so you don't fly to school on it."

"You are not supposed to say that." Hilda shrieked and lunged at her sister again. "You Assy Belle. You are a whore!"

Mia detested violence. She silently sat out of their way and ignored these frequent hair-pulling, feline squabbles.

CHAPTER TWENTY

The cool days of spring extended into summer, and with the hot weather came the drought. Like a stifling shroud, it reached out, sizzled, and scorched everything in its way. Hopelessness accompanied the aridity that extended through the land. A blanket of dust settled over the countryside. Orchards and gardens lay withering in the stagnant heat. The parched earth cracked and thirsted for rain. As if forsaken, the land wasted as it waited for a refreshing breeze to stir the air and bring the much-needed rain.

Mia existed but knew no peace. Each bleak day continued to bring gloom and a barrage of unknown fear. Nadia's temperament matched the wave of stagnant heat; the child felt asphyxiated by the heat and by her surroundings.

To control Nadia's dysfunctional deviousness, her husband sealed the windows of the bedroom. He didn't want anyone entering or leaving the room by those means. Screens could no longer be used in the windows. Sleeping in the bedroom was stifling.

Mia didn't like to sleep with Kassie; she would disrupt the child's sleep, causing her to wake up and cry.

"Why are you crying?" Hilda fretted in exasperation from her bed across the room.

"Kassie hurts me." Distraught and half asleep, Mia cried.

Hilda would angrily accost Kassie about her depraved action. Hilda made room on her bed for Mia, but a stinging pinch would frequently waken her from her sleep. Hilda complained about the child's restlessness during the night.

"I can't sleep with the brat anymore. She moans and squirms continually throughout the night. I don't want her on my bed anymore. It is bad enough that I have to put up with the heat." Her complaints carried on into the night.

Mia's father didn't think it was wise to have Mia out of Hilda's care while she slept. However, because of her sister's complaints, he told Mia to share the kitchen cot with Yuri; she would sleep at one end of the cot while Yuri slept on the other. It would be cooler that way.

Their parents' bedroom was just off the kitchen. With the screened doors in the kitchen, Mia found sleeping in the coolness of that room more comfortable than the bedroom. Her father's snoring comforted Mia, who was lulled into a secure sleep knowing he was nearby. Occasionally, though, the noise of an intruder would cause her father to call out and disturb her sleep.

"Who is in the house?"

Without a word and with only the telltale creaking of the screen door, the intruder was gone. Her father's question went unanswered. The next morning, he confronted her brothers at the breakfast table.

"Which one of you walked into the house last night, and why didn't you answer me when you were spoken to?" Her father clenched his fist as he spoke to his sons. Mia knew he was angry. "The next time one of you enters the house in the dark, I want you to answer me when I speak to you."

Koss didn't take his gaze off the floor as his father spoke. The corners of his thick, ugly lips were turned down in a mournful sulk. It was the look he used when he wanted to gain Nadia's sympathy.

"Maybe somebody walking down the road came in to get a drink of water," Nadia said to her husband.

"If anyone walked in off the road, they would have knocked on the door."

Knowing her lame excuse was in vain, Nadia just glared back. "Well, maybe the boys get thirsty when they sleep in the shack. You know they have to come into the house for a drink of water," she said reproachfully. "Or are you going to tell them to drink from the stock tank?"

Mia's father ignored Nadia's sarcasm. "If they come into the house for a drink of water, they could speak when they are spoken to."

"Perhaps they don't want to wake the whole household like you do when you bellow in the night," she taunted him.

"Well, I didn't hear anyone pick the dipper up to have a drink of water." He held his stern gaze on her. When he spoke to Nadia, his jaw muscle twitched.

"Maybe you scare them off before they are able to have a drink of water," Nadia snapped back with her manipulative argument.

"Why should they be scared off by being asked what they are doing in the house in the middle of the night?"

Mia watched her father put down his fork; a few morsels of food remained on his plate. He got up from the breakfast table and walked out of the house in resignation. Nadia's attitude made their father's questions pointless. It was a wasted effort. Koss looked smugly at his mother.

"Next time you come into the house at night, I want you to rattle the dipper in the water pail loud enough to wake everyone in the house. Then he will not have all these questions to ask us." Nadia's beady eyes bulged as she briefed her sons.

Koss smirked sickly and nodded. Mia noticed Kassie smile. The child didn't understand her father's concern or the danger that surrounded her.

The sharp thud of the dipper stirred Mia's sleep that night as someone deliberately dropped the scoop into the water pail.

Her father's jarring voice followed. "Who is in the house?"

"It's only me. I came in for a drink of water." Mia recognized Jacob's voice in the dark.

"Can't you lower the dipper into the pail quietly?" Her father sounded irritated.

The following morning was uneventful. As they gathered around the table, Koss gave Nadia a knowing snicker when his father was not watching as if they had a hidden secret.

Walking into the kitchen during the night became a common practice for Mia's brothers, especially Koss. If he walked in quietly and didn't awaken his father, it worked to his advantage. If his father was awake and asked why he was in the house, he rudely answered that he came in for a drink of water. Koss, in his deviousness, was testing his father and pushing his luck.

Mia was again finding herself outside in the night. When her father checked on her and found her missing from the cot, he would go outside to look for her. She would be found crying, drifting in and out of darkness. She was molested and left to lie in the dirt, unable to move or crawl back into the protection of the house. Her father would pick her up and carry her in.

It was as if nothing could stop Nadia's madness. She protected her eldest son, who she trained to walk in her footsteps. Her family legacy must carry on.

One morning, it was Kassie who found Mia lying and moaning in the dirt, holding her stomach. She went back into the house to get Hilda. It was as if they had to protect Nadia and their family from the horror of what was happening in their household. Finding the child outside in the night was covered up with excuses because they knew the repercussions it would bring if the abuse was exposed. The truth had to be suppressed within Nadia's house; it could not get carried beyond the door, and neighbors must not know.

"Why are you lying out here?" Hilda asked her.

"I can't get into the house. My stomach hurts very bad." Mia lay writhing in pain and tears.

"Well, if you had to go to the privy, why didn't you use the back door? The back way is closer than the front door." Hilda knew what was happening. She knew the truth, so why was she denying it?

"But I didn't have to go to the privy."

"Surely you must have had to go there if your stomach is sore," Hilda snapped at her.

"I can't move." The child moaned as she fought back tears. "It hurts too much when I move."

"We should get her into the house before Father wakes up and finds her outside again," Hilda told Kassie.

"I don't think I want to chance putting her back on the cot. It will wake Father up. Let's carry her through the living room door and lay her down in our bedroom." Knowing what really happened, Kassie spoke cautiously.

"We must not let Father know we found her outside again."

When Mia's father woke, he noticed she was not sleeping on the cot. She heard him ask about her whereabouts before they left the house to attend to morning chores.

"Mia came to sleep in our bedroom during the night," Hilda answered promptly.

Mia stayed in bed for most of the day.

"You must not go outside during the night," Hilda warned.

"But I don't go outside in the night. I'm afraid of the dark, and I don't remember going outside. I don't know how I get there."

"Don't you remember getting out of bed in the night and walking out the door?"

Mia sadly shook her head.

"Tell me everything you do remember after you go to bed," her sister pried.

"I remember being tired and falling asleep. Sometimes when I am sleeping, I dream that I am not in bed. I feel someone is carrying me."

"What else do you remember?" Hilda continued.

"I don't remember. Sometimes I hear Koss talking to me in my sleep, but I am tired, and I just want to keep on sleeping. He sounds angry. When I wake up, I am outside, and Koss is hurting me and doing bad things to me. He tells me I should keep sleeping because I am only having a nightmare. But I cry because even if I am having a nightmare, he's still hurting me. Then Koss gets very angry with me and beats me with his fists. He tells me he will beat me much harder if I tell Father or wake anybody up. Then he says I should go into the house and go back to sleep."

Hilda listened to the child, and when she spoke, it was with apprehension. "I want you to listen to me, and I want you to listen really well."

Mia looked at her sister gravely.

"You should never go outside at night with Koss."

"But I don't know that I am outside when I am sleeping, and I don't know that Koss is there. If I'm sleeping, I don't know anything. If I am sleeping, I don't know if it's a nightmare. When he hurts me and hits me, then I really wake up. He says it is not him; he says it is a nightmare."

"Nightmares don't talk. Remember, when you hear Koss, it isn't a nightmare. You should wake up and wake Yuri up. Don't let Koss ever take you outside."

Mia looked at her older sister, somewhat disheartened by the lame attempt to protect her. How could she protect herself from the inevitable? The small child could not protect herself from Koss when she was awake. How could she protect herself when she was asleep?

"When you feel someone carry you outside, wake up, and wake up Yuri. Don't let Koss take you outside; if he does, call out to Yuri and ask him to go with you. If Yuri is with you, Koss won't hurt you. You must remember that when you hear someone talking, you aren't having a nightmare. Nightmares don't hurt you or talk. Nightmares only scare you."

"Can I call out to you or to Father? Can you wake up and help me?" She looked up at her sister, expecting more.

"No, you can't do that. If you wake Father, Mother will be angry with you, and Father will be angry with Mother and Koss. Then everyone will be angry at you for waking them up. You can't even call out to me because you will wake everybody else. You mustn't wake anyone while they are sleeping except Yuri because he is sleeping on the cot beside you. Do you understand?"

Mia nodded her head; she didn't want everyone to be angry with her. At such a young age, she did not realize that her older sister was shoving the responsibility of protecting her from her pedophile brother onto the shoulders of her youngest brother, who was no more than a baby. Mia went to bed with Hilda's warning instilled in her mind.

The manipulation in Nadia's house continued. Mia was tired and fretful; she wandered around the house like a zombie. Knowing that danger lurked in the night, she feared sleep.

The child's fretfulness angered Nadia. She spitefully ordered her to have a nap before noon and after. It kept her out of everyone's way during the day. Mia was exhausted, and she welcomed the daily rest but only if she was sure that Koss was not in the yard.

She begged Hilda to watch for Koss and protect her from him in case he came into the yard unexpectedly.

The horrible nightmares about Koss, the fear of the shadows and darkness, and demonic terror closed in on Mia. The disturbances constantly interrupted her sleep, haunting her night after night. Her screams of terror continued to disrupt the entire household. This only brought on more frenzied anger from Nadia.

The children born to this barbaric woman had the unfortunate luck of being placed in life with a nightmarish mother who was determined that her offspring would forever live in the shadow of her legacy.

No Thank You
The legacy you leave us has caused us so much pain.
You said you couldn't love us but brought us down with shame.
You did not hold us on your knee or teach us a love from within,
But took us to your bedroom for your ungodly sin.
The wedge you leave between us—the terror, hate, and lust
Are teaching of the evil, not a mother's loving trust.
The legacy you leave us, the pedophile fame
You leave upon your children, linked to a mother's name.

Made in the USA
Columbia, SC
13 June 2017